SP I R I TS

Spirits of St. Louis II:
[RETURN OF THE GATEWAY CITY GHOSTS]

Spirits of St. Louis II: Return of the Gateway City Ghosts

First Edition

ISBN: 1-891442-18-X
Library of Congress Control Number: 2002108087

  Acknowledgments: Peter Sotiriou, creative director; Lisa Pepper, editorial assistant.

VIRGINIA PUBLISHING CO.

To Sara,
sweetest Bird

CONTENTS

CONTENTS

[SEARCHING FOR ANSWERS]

Is your garden-variety ghost really the spirit of old Uncle Fester, returned for a little unfinished business or just a friendly visit? Is it a film-like impression, stamped on the atmosphere decades ago and destined to replay again and again like last night's leftovers? Or is it some incredible concoction of the mind, conjured up over a chunk of earth that leaks electromagnetic energy like a sieve?

The answer is any of these, depending on the authority consulted and the specific phenomenon under consideration. Those who investigate the paranormal run the gamut from intuitives, who pick up much of their information through what they call psychic vibrations, to scientific investigators, who rely on math, statistics, psychology and controlled conditions. In between are those who combine a little of both methods, or shun both methods, or have come up with their own ingenious solutions, such as "spirit guides."

Local authorities on the paranormal include the Haunt Hunters, Gordon Hoener and Philip Goodwilling; intuitives Antoinette Eason, Shirley Blaine, and the late Bevy Jaegers; and the high-tech ghost-hunting organization Para-Vision. All are featured in the first *Spirits* book, *Spirits of St. Louis: A Ghostly Guide to the Mound City's Unearthly Activities.*

There are many more, and this chapter includes just a few: Joseph Immethun, founder of the St. Louis group G.H.O.S.T.S.; E. Rick Dixon II, a veteran spirit photographer from North County; Troy Taylor, author of numerous books on ghosts and founder of the American Ghost Society; and James Houran, an instructor of clinical psychiatry at the Southern Illinois University School of Medicine, who is considered in scientific circles one of the world's foremost experts on paranormal phenomena.

Many readers will not agree with everything that is said on the following pages, but each of these experts is sincere and has intriguing insights to offer. Two of them, Immethun and Dixon, investigate phenomena strictly as a hobby and are nonprofit in nature; the other two, Taylor and Houran, are Decatur, Illinois, natives who have made professions out of the study of paranormal phenomena. Taylor lives in Alton, while Houran is a Springfield resident.

Joseph Immethun: Interest and Common Sense

A merchandiser-distributor for Coca-Cola, Joseph Immethun has been interested in the paranormal and the unknown since he was a small child. He is a native of the city of St. Louis and now lives near St. Louis Hills. In 1998, he founded the paranormal research team Ghost Hunters Of St. Louis Transcendental Society (G.H.O.S.T.S.).

"We've had a lot of investigations since '98," Immethun said. "We've had a lot of personal homes people have asked us to investigate, and we've got video of hundreds of orbs, mists, ectoplasms…as for an explanation, we're still working on that. A lot of people call us from their homes, and [the cause is] either pipes or electrical fields.

"A lot of electrical problems within people's houses, I think, have a lot to do with it," he added. "Ghosts, if you want to call them that, manifest themselves off the electrical systems within people's homes and are able to energize off that. People with high electromagnetic fields around their houses, I think, are the most haunted."

The group has four core members and belongs to Taylor's American Ghost Society and Chicago investigator Dale Kaczmarek's Ghost Research Society. Immethun is the first to admit he doesn't have all the answers and would like to see all the investigative groups work together to reveal the true nature of ghostly phenomena.

"I feel like the more people that come together—there's all these little spotty research groups; we all have the same goal in mind—it's going to take everybody working together, one big, massive group together to figure this out," he said.

In the meantime, the group offers free investigations of homes and businesses. For more information, visit ghosts.veryweird.com.

"We're interested in seeing how people live with ghosts or interact with them," he said. "We give them a tape and a full report and all that."

Dixon: "A Great Ride"

Many people believe in the paranormal in Albuquerque, New Mexico, where E. Rick Dixon II and his wife, Mercedes, grew up.

"There's a strong heritage of belief in black magic and black and white witchcraft and the paranormal on my wife's side, although my wife has pretty well tried to ignore it," he noted. "The Indian tribes have a belief in ghosts, and actually most of them don't speak of the dead, but it's very well developed among the Navajo and the Apache. I spent a lot of time in my youth with the Navajo—they were some of my best friends. It's quite fascinating there."

Today the Dixons live in North County, and Rick is a research technician in the sleep disorders unit at Alton Memorial Hospital. The couple has three grown children: Russ, Kimberly, and Selina.

"I've had, ever since I can remember, a belief in a connection of the paranormal, not myself as much as with family and friends," he said. "My daughters, they've always been sensitive. They talk about ghosts being in their grandparents' house and in our house. It was just accepted; it was what they felt."

About eight years ago, a fellow staffer at Alton Memorial talked Dixon into going on one of Antoinette's Haunted History Tours, hosted by psychic Antoinette Eason.

"I had a great time, took my camera with me, didn't expect to find anything or see anything," he recalled. "I had two quite dramatic photos the first time, and then it was almost to the point of obsession. The first one I took was at the McPike Mansion, what's become known as 'Paul in the doorway.' Night shot, no one was in front of the house, the tour group was back on the trolley, and I shot off about six frames real quick, black and white film, of the front of the house. When developed, here's more or less this large figure filling the doorway."

Dixon's photographs have been featured on the Fox Family Channel's *World's Scariest Places* and *Real Scary Stories*. A history buff, he began doing historical research and taking photos as an assistant to Eason and Right Brain Activities a few years ago.

"I don't make any money off of all this stuff—it's all out of my pocket," he said. "I joined Right Brain Activities because of the fun of it and also because it gave me a greater opportunity to divulge in my hobby. Now I've made my own contacts and I do a lot on my own on the side of doing investigations."

His granddaughter, thirteen-year-old Elyce, is much like the little boy in the movie *The Sixth Sense* and accompanies him on shoots.

"I took her on many of the investigations I ended up going on," Dixon said. "She'll crawl around the McPike Mansion in the dark with me, no hesitation, no fear, because for her it's normal. Very normal, very intelligent [girl]. She talked to Paul [Laichinger, a former resident of the McPike Mansion who is believed to haunt it] there; she's familiar with all the resident ghosts, same at the Lemp Mansion. She said there's an evil one on the third floor, which most people sense."

On the side, Dixon researches historical data for authors, magazines, and other outlets. He enjoys southwestern topics, particularly, as well as trains, and is now working on two books.

"I've got some great photos—it's been a great ride, fun," he said. "It's interesting to study. For instance, it's not like all ghosts or spirits live on the same plane or the same time period. They can be in a different period by an hour or a day or something. Spirits can be on a different plane or time where they're not even aware of each other. I've heard that over and over, and I've found that, doing research."

What Dixon doesn't like is the growing competition and back-biting in this popular field.

"What's really irritating to me is there's overall such a competitiveness, especially among investigators more than the psychic people," he said. "There's very little communication between them, which is a shame. Even the ones that don't have a commercial business, like Right Brain or Troy's Ghosts of the Prairie. They're competing for the money. It's too bad there isn't more cooperation: 'Here's the work I've done—it's fun; it's not for profit.'

"I've got a bunch of e-mail recently that's really disheartening," he added. "It goes on and on about how my pictures are phony and I should stay out of the business and stuff. On one hand, you want to ignore it. On the other, it's kind of irritating: why is there this competition?

"No one has any answers—even those who express the opinion that ghosts come back and talk to them."

Troy Taylor: Historic Approach

He proudly admits he's "psychic as a fence post."

"For me, the psychic thing is something I completely avoid altogether," noted Alton investigator Troy Taylor. "Unless somebody can stand and tell me exactly, some exact evidence, there's no way I can possibly know and look it up and find that it's true. To me, that's just another story about Great-Aunt Tillie who showed up at the top of the stairs."

And he's not high-tech or stringently scientific.

"As far as the scientific evidence goes, too, while it's interesting, I'm not sure what it accomplishes as of yet," he added. "We're probably never going to be able to scientifically prove there are ghosts: that's why the stuff with all the instruments is hard to do. Because science demands that something, to prove its existence, be repeated over and over again under strict conditions. You can't do that with ghosts. You expose ghosts to science and, usually, they disappear."

Taylor said he looks for historical evidence of ghosts.

"In other words, I've got a family who lived in a house for ten years, and they moved out," he said. "And the next year, another family moves into the house, and they have the exact same experiences, and yet they don't know the people who lived there before. To me, that's really good evidence of ghosts. What I'm looking for…is a story I can confirm.

"Let's say somebody sees a ghost in their house, and you can find that fifty years ago, such-and-such lived in the house, and here's a photograph of him," Taylor added. "Well, you show it to the people who saw the ghost, and here he is—that's once again pretty good evidence that there's something there that we can't explain."

The unexplained has become the stock in trade for Taylor, who has authored numerous books on ghosts, founded the American Ghost Society, hosts the History & Hauntings Tours of Alton, publishes "Ghosts of the Prairie" Magazine and an Internet Web page, and owns Riverboat Molly's Books, in Alton, and Whitechapel Productions Press.

"I don't know what's going on out there," he noted, "but there's some neat stuff, and it's spooky. I like it because there is no real answer. I do think that a lot of [stories], whether they were embellished or not, were not stories that people just pulled out of the air. I think something weird happened, and they've turned into great lore."

For instance, cities all over the country have a "vanishing hitchhiker" tale which, in most cases, is probably just a tale, he said. In St. Louis, Calvary Cemetery has such a story (see *Spirits of St. Louis: A Ghostly Guide to the Mound City's Unearthly Activities*).

"The perfect example of that is Resurrection Mary, from Chicago: to me, that's my favorite ghost story," he said. "It's spawned so many of the other vanishing hitchhiker stories. She's different, though, because the quality of the witnesses is far superior…It isn't just 'some guy.' It's somebody who actually has a name.

"There was a guy named Jerry Palus who in the early '40s met a girl at a dance, went to take her home, they got to the gates of Resurrection Cemetery, she turns and looks at him and says, 'I've got to get out here.' He asks, 'Why?' She said, 'Where I'm going, you can't follow,' gets out of the car and vanishes.

"That guy tells that story for the next forty-five years," Taylor added. "And he never changed the story, never got rich, never got famous, but he always swore that this really happened. How do you shake something like that? He had no reason to lie."

Taylor also takes issue with the assumption that ghosts linger on this plane because they underwent a traumatic death or couldn't cross over to the next life.

"Everybody always assumes, because we have a need to make everything scary, that if there's a ghost they're here because they committed suicide or died suddenly or had this awful, traumatic murder, or they got stuck behind," he said. "All that could happen, but who's to say some of the ghosts aren't here because they want to be? Maybe they wanted to stay behind and watch over their husbands or their wives or their kids—who knows? I don't think that those types of hauntings are extremely common, but probably they do occur. Probably much more common would be the recorded imprints of things that have kind of stayed behind."

Despite his psychic shortcomings, Taylor has had several experiences he can't explain and believes he met his first ghost while researching ghost stories at a theatre in Springfield, Illinois, several years ago.

The theatre was supposed to be haunted by the ghost of an actor there in the 1950s, Joe Neville.

"I started to walk around the theatre beforehand, walked into one of the dressing rooms in the basement…and the only way to say it is that I was overwhelmed by the smell of Noxzema," he recalled. "I mean a gagging-strong stench. I left the room—it smelled awful—and never thought another thing about it.

"I sat down with all the people who knew him or had experiences to hear their stories," Taylor said. "The last person I interviewed was the theatre manager, Rebecca Sykes."

Taylor asked Rebecca how anyone knew for sure these strange events were caused by Neville.

"She said, 'Whenever anything weird happens or anybody encounters the ghost, there's kind of a telltale sign that goes with it, and that's how we know it's Joe.'"

The telltale sign, of course, was the smell of Noxzema.

"I said, 'Wait a minute. This is a theatre. I thought you guys had Noxzema here,'" Taylor recalled. "She said, 'We used to. When Joe was alive, he had a psoriasis on his legs, and he would slather on a layer of Noxzema, so everywhere he went he would walk around in a cloud of it. Even a couple years after he died, when people were having these weird things happen, they would get this terrible smell of Noxzema.'

"They banned Noxzema in 1965 from the theatre. So, do I think I met Joe Neville? Yeah, I think I did. I'm pretty convinced," he said. "As far as I'm concerned, that was my first encounter with a real ghost."

James Houran: A Golden Book Began His Career

Parapsychologist James Houran is quick to blame his mother for his unusual occupation.

"Like any other psychology thing, I blame my mother for that," he explained with a chuckle, "because she actually bought me my first book on the subject. It was called *The Golden Book of The Mysterious*. I still have it. One of the chapters in this book was on ghosts, and in it was an image of a ghost walking in a cemetery that just stuck with me—it stuck with me to this day. That's what motivated me to study parapsychology, and that's why I wanted to pursue it in college."

Pursue it he did. The Springfield, Illinois, resident was honored with the Eileen J. Garrett Research Scholarship in Parapsychology in 1992, and he went on to receive approximately $70,000 in grants and scholarships in support of his research on apparitions, haunts, and poltergeists. This research has resulted in more than seventy articles in scientific journals worldwide. In April 2001 he co-conducted the world's largest and most systematic haunt investigation in Edinburgh, Scotland (see Chapter 18, Down in the Vaults).

Along the way, he became a professional magician, which has helped him immensely in his research.

"Between the age of ten and eleven I developed asthma," he recalled. "I had to go to Champaign-Urbana to a place called Carl Clinic for medical treatments. It was an uncomfortable thing, but after every time I went to the doctor, my mom would cheer me up by taking me to a magic shop in Champaign.

"I know from my experience with magic...what people explain to other people about what happened is quite often not what actually happened.

I'm sure they're telling the truth the way they see it, but I'm sure there's some distortion along the way."

From his research, Houran has concluded that people do have genuinely strange experiences that science cannot always explain. However, there's a pattern there, he said.

"I know that it's an interaction between people and their environments," he said. "I can't just take anybody and put them just anywhere and they'll have an experience: I need a particular type of personality type, and I need a certain type of environment. And that's when I'll start getting these experiences. It's such a reliable thing that I can induce experiences. I can cause hauntings to happen in places where there were no reports before. And the interesting thing is, the patterns that I get with people on what they experience, and the timing on how they experience it and those types of patterns, very nicely parallels what parapsychologists have been documenting from what we call 'spontaneous cases' for years.

"I'm trying to see if there's anything left of these experiences, once you take the psychology and science out of it," he added. "Is there anything left of the ghost experience? Is there anything left of hauntings? So far, I haven't found anything compelling, but I'm still looking. I feel so strongly, though, about still keeping a parapsychological focus, that that's why I put a unique book together."

Houran and fellow researcher Rense Lange co-edited *Hauntings and Poltergeists: Multidisciplinary Perspectives*, (2001, McFarland & Company, Jefferson, NC). It is the first academic book that provides a holistic analysis of haunts and poltergeists by the world's leading authorities.

"We have people that are believers, like William Roll [the father of poltergeist research], who believes that poltergeists and some haunts really are paranormal. And we have people like Joe Nickell [from PSICOP], who believes it's all just fraud or misinterpretation," he said.

"We've also found out—and this is something new to this book—that the timing of events is predictable," he added. "We know mathematically when the next experience is going to happen. So if I have a haunt or poltergeist case, and I know the times of your, say, previous five experiences, I can tell you when you're going to have your sixth and your seventh and your eighth experience."

People who observe ghosts and other phenomena tend to have distinct personality characteristics, Houran said. They're also reacting to something special in their environment, and one of those special things could be electromagnetic fields, he said.

"Self-styled ghosthunters go to sites with tri-field meters and related equipment, and they say, 'Yes, here's the ghost,'" he noted. "They think that people experience the ghost that way, that ghosts are electromagnetic fields. The scientific research says it's the other way around. Electromagnetic fields are not the ghosts. It's our brains interacting with those fields, and those are causing changes in our brains.

"At times, such as near fault lines and areas where electromagnetic fields are more active, energy is released up through the earth's crust, and we call that tectonic strain," Houran said. "If a person is in the area of where that tectonic strain is, that can actually cause different chemical changes in the brain that actually induce in people the equivalent of epileptic seizures. They can be low levels, and they can be high levels. So you can get very subtle phenomena like, 'I smell things. I see strange lights,' to very intense feelings like they are leaving their bodies, people are touching them, intense feelings of fear or emotion, a wide spectrum. You can also get the same effect if you live near high power lines.

"We now know that the temporal lobe is involved and that certain neurotransmitters like melatonin and serotonin are involved. The person who's been a large advocate of this research is Michael Persinger, who has a chapter in our book. He's an internationally renowned neurologist and parapsychologist at Laurentian University in Ontario, Canada.

"Actually, you'll find that a lot of haunted houses tend to be located near fault lines or high power lines, or you'll see a lot of haunting reports happen when there are natural increases in geomagnetic activity."

Houran, thirty-three, admits that he probably won't see such phenomena either explained or attributed to the paranormal in his lifetime.

"It may be the case that all haunts and poltergeists may be reduced to normal variables—conventional factors in the environment you wouldn't think of or combinations of those," he said. "But as parapsychologists, as open-minded, objective researchers, if we can control for all the major artifacts, all the major sources of error, and people still report things, we have to consider: is there something else? But only at that point. We will not jump to the conclusion it's a ghost, it's life after death, it's ESP, until we can rule out everything else. And to rule out everything else is actually a tremendous task: no one's been able to do it yet. What we know today will probably be greatly modified five years from now. So we can never completely rule out the normal because we're always still discovering what is normal."

From what researchers now know, psychology and the senses seem to play a huge role in the shaping of ghosts and poltergeists.

"So, again, as an objective researcher, you've got to ask yourself, 'Man! With all this going on…so far, we don't have to turn to the paranormal to begin explaining and making sense of this,'" Houran said. "Does this mean that there are no ghosts? No. Does this mean there is no life after death? Of course not. We have no way of knowing that. But we do know this: psychology plays a *tremendous* role in this. People's sensory systems play a *tremendous* role in this.

"This is actually what modern parapsychology is like," he added. "It is math. It is statistics. It is science. It's not sitting in a 'haunted' cemetery with a digital camera and a tri-field meter—it's light years beyond that. We test scientific theories and we try, again, to be at the right place at the right time to try to control for natural events that might look paranormal to the untrained person—lights always flicker, my TV always goes out sometimes, and my car keys disappear inexplicably on occasion—but we tend to overlook those things. Unless, of course, you're in a haunted house. Then strange, freak events tend to take on a new meaning."

That's not to say, however, that Houran hasn't had experiences of his own that he is at a loss to explain. In 1991, he conducted the first formal scientific investigation of the Country House Restaurant, in Clarendon Hills, Illinois, which was profiled on the History Channel's "Haunted History: Chicago."

"The building had two levels: the bottom part was the restaurant/lounge; there was a top part that was business offices," he said. "I was able to go upstairs, and we were listening because we thought we heard some footsteps on the staircase. The person I was working with was at the bottom of the stairs; I was at the top. And all of a sudden I hear someone say to me, I mean right next to me, 'Hey, you!' I thought it was one of the employees asking—maybe they didn't know I had permission to be up in the office area. It was a stern voice, male, very clear. I turned—there was no one there. I thought maybe they were around the corner. There was no one on the second floor. There was just no one there."

Another time, Houran and his colleagues investigated a house in Elgin, Illinois, near Chicago.

"We were tape-recording a conversation, setting up an experiment, and we were done for the night," he recalled. "We were playing back the tape while we were packing up. You hear us on this tape, talking, and all of a sudden you hear this woman scream. People have different opinions of what the woman's saying, but it sounds like it says, 'Help me,' and she's saying something to somebody. I think she's saying, 'Hey, Amanda, help, help.' Other people say, 'Yeah, it's "Amanda," but...' or 'Yeah, I hear the "help, help,"' but this woman's screaming it. Screaming it over our voices. We heard this after the fact. The effect paralleled the well-known electric voice phenomena, which is a phenomena that I also have doubts about.

"But anyway, we hear this noise. 'My God, what is this?' Well, we went back upstairs where this happened—we were the only ones in the place; we were all in that room. We also had an 8-mm camera, down the hall filming in another room, that was running. We played that tape back. The voice is on that tape, too. It's lower, because it was ten feet away from the room, but we hear the same woman on that tape. It picked up in both places; no one heard a damn thing. So we're like, 'Someone had to hear this, right?' No one heard it. So we try to reconstruct what happened, and we had a female who was with us, and she gauged how loud she'd have to scream and we would not have missed it. It was absolutely eerie."

Houran smiled. "I don't have an explanation for those sorts of things," he said. "So there's still a part of me that says, 'I hope there's something more to this.' But I have to go where the evidence leads me, and so far this is where it is."

[Grave Matters]

Many experts in the paranormal believe ghosts shy away from graveyards and cemeteries.

They argue, and reasonably so, that spirits tend to haunt the places they enjoyed most in life. Nonetheless, our local cemeteries have no shortage of strange tales blowing around.

And one of those tales concerns a place that used to be a cemetery and is now used for police purposes. That's not unusual, because as the population spread west from downtown through the city, formerly out-of-the-way burial grounds were moved elsewhere as the land was needed for new homes and businesses. In many instances, the bodies themselves weren't moved, only the tombstones.

Central Patrol Division: Ghostly Groundhog or Cholera Victim?

No one disputes that the St. Louis Police Department's Central Patrol Division, 919 North Jefferson Avenue, is built over an old cemetery used around the time of the 1849 cholera epidemic. What's up for grabs is whether it's haunted.

John Rice, a First District patrolman and resident of St. Louis' Near South Side, said the cemetery was closed after the cholera epidemic, but not all of the bodies were moved. According to a newspaper account, officials concluded it was a Catholic cemetery because of a rosary found in a baby's coffin.

"The area around the station was pretty much a wasteland for a long time," Rice said. "By wasteland, I mean a pretty bad neighborhood with a lot of vacant buildings. When they moved most of the cemeteries out of the city limits, the people with the money took the remains of their families, and the people that didn't have that much money just moved the head-stones and left the graves. It wasn't marked on anyone's map as a cemetery."

Rice said he hasn't heard any strange stories about the station, but if there are it could be due to a satirical piece he penned for the February 1990 issue of the *Gendarme*, the official publication of the St. Louis Police Officers' Association (SLPOA).

"The haunted part I'm kind of responsible for," Rice said. "There's a picture of the station under construction and a large, crude drawing of a groundhog. We called it "Baer Pit," because Robert Baer was then the president of the Board of Police Commissioners."

Rice's copy reads:

An officer detailed to guard the Baer Pit, Area 2 Superstation, reported an interesting conversation to the Gendarme. The officer claimed he spoke to a six-foot-tall groundhog early on Feb. 2. The groundhog apparently lives on the site, which combines an old cemetery with toxic waste. The groundhog told the officer he saw his shadow, which means there will be six more months of construction delay. It remains unclear whether the large groundhog is a mutant caused by exposure to carcinogens in the area, or hallucination of the officer caused by toxic fumes. An obvious question arises from this debacle: if the department knew there was enough toxic waste on the site to warrant professional decontamination, why were the officers detailed to the site with no Hazmat protection?

"They had Hazmat people out there because [they found] several fifty-five-gallon drums containing unknown chemicals," he explained. "So rather to be safe than sorry, they called in a Hazmat team, which wore full protection while the police just stood around in their uniforms."

Hazardous materials and large groundhogs aside, the new station could be very creepy at three or four in the morning, noted St. Louis Police Sgt. James R. Wurm, who retired last year from the department. Wurm worked in Central Patrol for about a year while the building was under construction and encountered some unusual situations.

"It was my responsibility to check the doors and make sure everything was secured and, when they were building, make sure nothing was getting stolen from the area," Wurm said. "I was working eleven at night till seven in the morning. This would be like three, four in the morning.

"I remember one night I was going in there, and I checked the door, opened the door and walked in, checked around to make sure everything was secured...went out the one door, and just as I opened that door another door slammed. So I went back to try to find out where that door was at, and when I came back, I swung around the door I was going to come out, and it was locked. So I couldn't come back in.

"I'm thinking, 'Now wait a minute.' It was open when I went out. I would imagine some of the officers might have had that same experience. It's a funny feeling. I was startled and a little frightened because you never know—was it a burglar that's over there, what is it, or who's in there? You think if a door slams somebody's going out because you've startled them, so I checked real fast, and that wasn't the case.

"These doors aren't supposed to be closing, aren't supposed to be locking on me while I'm making my rounds here. It was just a weird situation."

Oak Grove Cemetery: Happy Haunting Grounds?

Be careful while driving along North Hanley Road near the intersection of St. Charles Rock Road and Page Avenue—you just might pick up an extra passenger.

According to a local ghost Web site, the spirit of an extremely well-dressed man in a suit and hat is said to appear inside the cars that are making their way past the cemetery. Before he disappears again, it is said, the ghost often engages in some lively chitchat with the driver. The Web site's address is http://missourighosts.net/.

Is this vivacious ghost none other than Henry Kiel, the esteemed St. Louis mayor who is known as the "father of the Municipal Opera"? Always a dapper gentleman, former Mayor Kiel died in 1942 and is buried in none other than Oak Grove Cemetery, according to a fascinating Web site called Political Graveyard. The site notes the achievements of politicians across the country and their burial sites. The address is http://politicalgraveyard.com/geo/MO/SL.html.

South Side Cemeteries: A Rocky Reception

Joe Immethun, founder of the paranormal investigative group G.H.O.S.T.S., calls it Rock Cemetery. Located on Gravois Avenue not far from Loughborough Avenue, it has become one of Immethun's favorite haunts for its strange phenomena.

"About 90 percent of the time we get something there—often an EVP," Immethun said. "EVP is called Electronic Voice Phenomena, and that's where you would be recording on an audio cassette, and you can't hear it at the time, but when you play it back you can hear voices."

Shadowy figures also have been observed there, he said. But the most extraordinary experience he's had was a rock shower about a year ago.

"I was walking down the road, I was kind of separated from the group, and I kept hearing these noises, like little pings on the ground," Immethun said. "So I would look up—I was thinking a squirrel was throwing acorns or something, but I wasn't around any trees at the point where the rocks were falling. Normally, if you would throw a rock it would bounce or skip, you know? These wouldn't. These would fall straight down from the sky and just land right at your feet, straight down and stop. It was probably about ten o'clock at night, and it only lasted three minutes, and probably ten, fifteen rocks fell. One other time, another member had that experience while we were together at a different place in the cemetery."

This cemetery also is the final resting place of a man on whom a miracle was worked more than a century ago, Ignatius Strecker.

In the *St. Louis Guidebook*, published in 1964, contributing writer Edna Carroll noted that Strecker was incurably ill and sought the assistance of Peter Claver in 1864 in services at St. Joseph's Church, Eleventh and Biddle Streets.

"[Strecker] was subsequently cured and lived till 1880 when he died of typhoid fever," Carroll wrote. "A modest stone marks his grave."

That miracle was one of two officially accepted in Rome during the St. Peter Claver canonization process, Carroll said.

Immethun and his colleagues have snapped numerous photographs at cemeteries. They have captured what they believe is a photo of a real apparition at a cemetery on Bates Street.

"I took a picture of the mausoleum, and you can see the real distinct figure of a person within the mausoleum, in the glass, so it's pretty neat," he said.

Did Dr. Smith Return for His Treasure?

Della Lang, the Jefferson County historian, dug deep into area lore for this intriguing tale:

"One of the granddaughters of James Byrne, the miller at Byrnes Mill, was riding her horse on the Byrne property many years ago," Lang wrote in her book *Witchcraft, Wickedness, And Other Wacky Happenings In Jefferson County History*. "When she crested the top of the hill, her horse suddenly became skittish. As she was struggling to get the animal under control, she glanced in the direction of a small cemetery that had been on the property for more than a hundred years. She noticed an old man sitting on one of the tombstones."

The woman finally was able to calm the horse and continued toward the cemetery to talk to the man. When she arrived, however, he was gone and was nowhere to be found.

"Was this the ghost of Dr. George A. Smith, the Southern sympathizer who died on the property and was buried there in 1863?" Lang asked. "According to folklore, Dr. Smith buried a fortune in gold in the family cemetery during the Civil War, but he died before he had a chance to retrieve it. Had the doctor returned to guard the gold that he had buried during the war?"

Over the years, a number of vandals have literally destroyed the cemetery looking for the treasure and found nothing, Lang said. She continued her research on the topic after her book was published and turned up even more juicy lore.

"When he died, he did have some gold," Lang confirmed. "Gold bars, I guess they were—they didn't actually say. Anyway, his second wife—the Smith family didn't much care for her. His family was from England, and they came over here and stirred up a big thing about this gold. They said that she stole the gold.

"Anyway, as I looked through the court records and everything, I found that she did actually have the gold, which I think she was probably entitled to because he was her husband. But for some reason, they didn't think so. She finally did turn the gold over to the court. Now, whether there was more gold...obviously there wasn't, because people would have found it by now, they've dug that cemetery up so badly. But the gold, I think, was a story that came out of the story that she had taken the gold and hid it for a while, and she finally had to turn it over to the court because they insisted upon it. You know how these stories get started."

Little Girl Lost: Lucy Haskell

Her grandfather was Lucas Pfeiffenberger, Alton's famed architect, one-time fire chief, and four-term mayor. And through his generosity and whimsy, little Lucy Haskell received a beautiful playhouse as a birthday present in 1880. An exact, miniature replica of the Haskell family home, which has since been demolished, Lucy's playhouse still stands in Alton and is listed on the National Register of Historic Places, noted Troy Taylor, author and founder of the American Ghost Society.

Unfortunately, Lucy wasn't able to enjoy the playhouse for long. At the age of nine, she died of black diphtheria and was buried in Alton City

Cemetery in the Haskell family plot, Taylor said.

Interestingly enough, Lucy's spirit is said to haunt the cemetery near the Haskell plot, not the charming playhouse built just for her, Taylor said. Her spirit is often seen by children, but never by adults.

Who Was Set in Stone at Wilson Price Hunt Home?

The Normandy area and some twenty-one different municipalities in North County take in a large and colorful chunk of St. Louis' heritage.

Land now covered by shopping centers and subdivisions was once part of huge estates: those of Jean Baptiste Charles Lucas, governor of the Louisiana Purchase; the Francis family, which included David Rowland, president of the Louisiana Purchase Exposition; and explorer William Clark, whose estate is now the Northwoods community, noted Eleanore Waldt, co-chair of the Normandy Area Historical Association.

"One of the Lucas boys, Charles Lucas, was killed in a duel by Thomas Hart Benton on Bloody Island, and his [old] estate is right across the street from me," Waldt said. "St. Charles Rock Road was the start of the Santa Fe Trail; I live a couple of blocks from where it started.

"We had the very first black convent west of the Mississippi; we have the oldest golf course in continuous operation in the Normandy area, Glen Echo; we have the German St. Vincent Orphan Home—the cholera epidemic and then World War I came along, and no one wanted those 'German-speaking nuns' in the city, so we still have St. Vincent's Orphans Home," Waldt noted. "We also had the first psychiatric [treatment center] where people were not treated like they were in snake pits—they are now the Castle Apartments. Right across the street from me, there's six or seven convents on land that Anne Lucas Hunt, the daughter of Jean Baptiste Charles, inherited from her father and dead brother and gave to the convents—at one time, it was known as 'Little Rome.' And now the university [University of Missouri - St. Louis] is slowly buying all those convents."

One area landmark is the Colonial Revival-style Wilson Price Hunt home, built in 1906 at 7717 Natural Bridge Road on land Wilson Hunt inherited from his grandmother, Anne Lucas Hunt. Now privately owned, the white frame home formerly served as the headquarters of the Normandy Area Historical Association, which occupied and cared for the mansion with the consent of a local funeral home that owned it.

"I used to take little Boy Scout troops, Girl Scout troops, and other groups on tours of the house and show them the daughter, Anne's, rosebud room," Waldt noted. "Her whole room was done in tile embossed with rosebuds, and her linens were all embroidered with rosebuds. The canopy on her bed was done in rosebuds.

"Until she died several years ago at the age of ninety-three, she [Anne Hunt, Wilson Hunt's daughter] would call me, and she'd say, 'Did you have a tour?' 'Yes, I had a tour.' 'Did you tell them about the room with the rosebuds?'"

And for years everyone wondered about the mysterious secret that was sealed inside an old tombstone laying in the backyard over an old cistern, Waldt noted.

"Because it was all inscribed in German, the story used to fly around here that somebody was buried in the backyard," she said. "With rain and everything, the lettering had been pretty much washed away. So everybody believed that, ohmygod, there must be somebody buried back there.

"So one day a college student asked if I would take him through the house. He saw it, and I think he did a rubbing of it. And he got someone to try to figure out what it said in English."

Soon after, a local television program about the house detailed the home's history with the Hunts and its subsequent use as a convent. The producers also interviewed a member of the Crawford A. King family, which owned the home during the late 1950s and early '60s. The King family also owned a monument firm, and the family member was asked about the mysterious gravestone.

"She laughed and she said, 'No, it was just a monument that hadn't been used and had ended up in the backyard,'" Waldt said.

[THE STUFF OF LEGENDS]

Glitzy Hollywood, California, isn't the only town with bizarre legends. Proper old St. Louis, Missouri, and vicinity have several, as well, enmeshed in our patchworked heritage.

Such strange anomalies as the Gooseville Bear, Zombie Road, Fifollet, Loup-Garou or werewolf, Kaskaskia Curse, and the legendary Monkey Boy are imprinted, for better or worse, on the cultural history of our beloved Mound City.

The Gooseville Bear

Gooseville is the informal name of a small area of farmland and roadside businesses in Madison County, Illinois, about three miles east of Bethalto at the intersection of Illinois Route 140 and Indian Creek. History has it that the community received its name in the 1850s when farm geese followed grain wagons to gobble up the wheat and corn remnants, according to an article by Charles Burgess in the *St. Louis Post-Dispatch*.

Reports of a giant bear in the vicinity of marshy Indian Creek were made more than fifty years ago, and "huge animal prints" were discovered in the late 1940s and in the mid-1960s.

Most observers thought the tracks belonged to a bear. A few identified them as panther prints.

"But nobody that I know of ever really saw it," said Arvel Fowler, director of the Bethalto Historical Museum. "It's the nearest thing to a ghost story that we have in the Bethalto area."

Were the tracks the work of pranksters or natural soil formations, as some Madison County authorities have concluded? One thing is for sure, Burgess noted: no sign of the Gooseville Bear has turned up since the mid-1960s.

Zombie Road

Would-be ghost-hunters looking for zombies around Zombie Road will probably turn up disappointed. In fact, just finding the place can be an ordeal, noted Joe Immethun, founder of the Ghost Hunters of St. Louis Transcendental Society (G.H.O.S.T.S.).

"Every person you ask, they say it's in a different place," Immethun said. "The Zombie Road that we know, that we've been going to, it's called Wallerford. If you go down Manchester and Old State, you make a left on Old State, go down to Ridge, and it's right off of Ridge. It's a dirt road in Ellisville. We looked up the records, and the only thing we could find out about it was [it served as a] horse and carriage bypass through Ellisville and has been in the area for over eighty years. The area near the road is under construction, due to a growing subdivision."

Legends abound, but the main story entails a man who was walking along the railroad tracks late one evening, unaware that a train was approaching. As he reached a bend in the tracks, he was caught between two railroad ties, struck by the train and killed, and his ghost is said to haunt the area.

"We went all the way down to the railroad tracks, and...it's like a mini-train for kiddie rides," Immethun noted. "It would be pretty impossible to be hit by that."

Another legend concerns a small clapboard house at the end of the road, where an old woman is said to haunt the area, screaming and shouting at passersby. That story also is pretty far-fetched, Immethun said.

But the G.H.O.S.T.S. crew has had some disconcerting experiences of its own while investigating the road, which is about two miles long.

"We just walked the road because it's pretty impassable with a vehicle," Immethun said. "We were down about halfway, and the road's in between two real tall hills and forest, and all of a sudden we heard something falling down the hill and breaking trees. It was a real large object, sounded like a train coming off the hill or something. So we booked it out of there, and I came back the next day. At the same area, all the trees were uprooted—real big trees. Something big came down that hill. I'm not sure what it was.

"You go down there sometimes and it's fine—it feels like there's no problem there, but when you go back other times it seems like a force is pushing you out, you don't want to be there," he added. "I've seen a lot of people—I don't know if they're witches or what they do—they go down there and beat on drums and have fires, and it's kind of strange. You kind of have to watch out for that."

Nicole, a north St. Louis resident who asked that her last name not be used, also recalled encountering some creepy feelings when she visited the area with friends in 1987.

"I just felt that sour feeling again in the pit of my stomach, and I just felt that we shouldn't be there—that something just gross, something bad happened on the earth. Something inside me said, 'You're not supposed to be here.'

"About the point we were going to turn around and leave, there was a shack, a garage-sized shack, this rundown little house," she added. "Our headlights apparently interrupted some kids that were in there doing who knows what. But there were things on the wall, like pentagrams or stuff like that. I don't know if they were in there practicing black magic, or what. It would certainly contribute to the negative feeling of the earth."

French Folk Legends: Fifollet and Loup-Garou

For decades, the hardy French settlers of Washington County and vicinity lived as an isolated, yet welcoming, community with their own Missouri-French dialect and many colorful customs and beliefs.

With them came the legend of the fifollet, or will-o'-the-wisp, brought over from France by way of Canada. Also known as the Jack-o'-Lantern, the will-o'-the-wisp is a light that hovers over streams and marshy spots, or among the trees on solid ground, Ward Allison Dorrance noted in his doctoral dissertation, "The Survival of the French in the Old District of Sainte Genevieve."

The hapless observer is lured toward water, where he drowns, and remedies such as prayer or a Saint Christopher medal fail to help.

"But if a man keep sufficient presence of mind to thrust the blade of his pocket knife into a tree trunk, the light is obliged to play about that spot," Dorrance observed.

The settlers also brought the story of the loup-garou, or werewolf, which is common from the Balkans throughout Europe and into certain countries in Asia and Africa, noted Joel Bartow in an article in the *Missouri Folklore Society Journal*.

"Werewolf tales were most common in remote areas where the wolf, a silent and often invisible monster that carried off children and dug up fresh graves, was a deadly enemy feared for its ravenous attacks on villages," Bartow wrote. "It is not hard to see why it became a creature of evil."

The garden-variety werewolf, according to legend, has no tail, retains its human eyes and voice, and is branded with the mark of the Devil. The hairy creature is said to hunger for raw flesh, using huge teeth and claws to tear its victims apart and drink their blood. Supposedly it has a special affinity for tender infants.

"In France, those destined to be werewolves were transformed at the full moon," Bartow wrote. "The urge to run wild came upon them at night. They left the house by jumping out a window and plunged into the nearest fountain, coming out covered with fur. When they returned from their run, they again plunged into the fountain and returned to human form."

A cross is considered to be the most effective weapon against the loup-garou.

"It was believed that the Devil accompanied the werewolf on its run, and would scourge the wolf if it came near a cross," noted Bartow.

Another old legend is that of the Chasse-galerie, which was brought to Canada from Saintonge and Anjou, France, and describes a rushing sound heard over the rooftops at night, produced by devils that had come to carry men off.

"In Canada it is said to be hunters who, in order to have rapid transport through the air, have bargained with the devil," Dorrance wrote. "The Missourians have an explanation more immediate. They will tell you that in the early days of the colony a certain man, having started to Mass, was unable to resist the temptation to hunt on Sunday, and disappeared in the forest with his dogs. Found dead beneath a tree, he was condemned by God to hunt eternally in the sky, leaping cloud-chasms, skimming the plains of light and heat without repose. He can be heard once every seven years—no oftener, because the forest of heaven is vast."

Ampakaya's Revenge: The Kaskaskia Curse

The first capital of the Illinois Territory, Kaskaskia was founded as a Roman Catholic mission in 1703 and was built around a large parklike square on the Illinois mainland. Log houses with pointed roofs of thatch or bark sat in contrast to the quarried stone homes of the wealthy residents.

But periodic floods hastened Kaskaskia's decline, and near the end of the nineteenth century the Mighty Mississippi broke through the low peninsula that separated the town from the Kaskaskia River, changed its course, and eventually destroyed the town. Homes were twisted on their foundations, and some of the dead floated away from their cemeteries. Approximately 3,800 boxes—some containing whole families—were relocated to the Garrison Hill Cemetery north of town, according to the *Federal Writers' Project Guide to 1930s Illinois*.

Today, much of the old village of Kaskaskia—now known as Kaskaskia Island—lies west of the Mississippi River and can only be reached from Missouri, although a small portion remains in Randolph County, Illinois. The original village truly has become a feeding place for fishes.

Is the Curse of Kaskaskia at work? Many of the old villagers believed this, according to Jean Kueker, a charter member of the Randolph County Genealogical Society.

The legend centers around a young Indian man named Ampakaya, who had fallen in love with a Frenchman's daughter named Marie Bernard. In those days, it was common for a French man to marry an Indian woman, but for a French woman to marry an Indian man was very rare, Kueker noted. So the two ran off.

Marie's father caught up with them, bound Ampakaya to a log, and sent him to his death in the river. But Ampakaya had the last word:

"...May the filthy spot on which your altars stand be destroyed, may your crops be failures, your homes be dilapidated," he shouted. "May your dead be disturbed in their graves and your land become a feeding place for fishes!"

Marie, according to the legend, was put in a convent, where she died.

The Monkey Boy of Lemp Mansion

One of St. Louis' most popular legends centers around the Lemp Mansion, former home and office of the nineteenth-century brewing dynasty and now a restaurant and bed-and-breakfast. It has been rumored that the Lemps had a mentally retarded child whom they locked in the attic, and countless observers have sworn to the presence of what they call the "monkey boy."

"The attic, that's probably the worst place to be," said paranormal investigator Joe Immethun. "Just the feelings you get, real sad and depressed, especially up in the attic where they kept the monkey boy. That was the Lemps' retarded child that they locked in the attic. If you look at the records, they did, but they keep it real guarded because back then you didn't want people to know that your children were odd or anything like that. They tried to hide him away...and schoolchildren would walk by and see him up in the attic windows."

Many years ago, Randy Bibb, of Belleville, said he felt the presence of the monkey boy.

"There was one room [at Lemp] that I walked into, and I felt an intense feeling of—back then we used the term mongoloid, that was before we started saying Down's Syndrome," he said. "[Later] there was talk of a monkey boy on the third floor, and I thought, 'Oh my God, I picked that one up twenty years ago.'"

The monkey boy is never mentioned in *Lemp: The Haunting History*, the definitive biography of the family by Stephen Walker. Despite all the stories, Walker has failed to turn up a shred of evidence revealing the existence of such a child.

"No one's ever convinced me it's anything but an urban legend," Walker noted. "I never came across anything. Everything the Lemps did was front page news...Every rumor and innuendo was on the front page. I can't believe something like this would have escaped everybody else's notice. I would think that would be ripe for a scandal page or something. I'm sure Mr. Lemp had a lot of enemies, just like any other big businessman."

Flushing Out the Evidence

The attic aside, Immethun and members of G.H.O.S.T.S. have had some creepy experiences in the old Lemp Mansion. The first involves the period-perfect women's bathroom, with glass-enclosed shower and a privacy stall around a single toilet.

"I don't know if you know the story, but a lot of the women complain that someone keeps looking over the stall when they're in the bathroom," Immethun said. "And they come out, and no one had gone in there. So they think it's William Lemp.

"We were there with Dale Kaczmarek's group [Kaczmarek is a Chicago-based paranormal investigator and founder of the Ghost Research Society], and they were being kind of funny and joked about one of their members going down and sitting in the bathroom.

"We dared one of their investigators to go down and sit on the toilet in the women's bathroom. And he did, and we had all these cameras set up, these closed-circuit TVs, and he was sitting down there a couple minutes, and then all of a sudden you could see him jump up and run out of the room, running frame by frame, up to our room.

"He said that while he was down there, the toilet started flushing, and he heard somebody speaking. He didn't know what they were saying—he just took off. That was the only time I was a little freaked out."

"Nice Try, Dogbreath"

Another time a workman came face to face with a ghostly dog believed to be the pet of Charles Lemp. Lemp, the final member of his illustrious family to live at the mansion, fatally shot his dog and then himself in the home in 1949.

"One of my friends, Joe Gibbons, was working there as a carpetlayer some years ago," Immethun said. "He was working on the main staircase and was kneeling down, taking up carpet, and all of a sudden he heard what sounded like dog nails coming up the stairs. He stopped, looked around, went back to work, and all of a sudden he felt a breath, and he could hear the dog tags—he could feel the breath on his face. And then he took off."

"[The dog] did die on that staircase. Charles shot the dog in the basement and went up to his room to shoot himself. And the dog tried to follow Charles, but he didn't make it all the way."

The story of Charles' shooting of the dog has been corroborated, Walker said.

"It's kind of a morbid, grisly story—I've heard it from several reliable sources," he said. "His dog was kind of vicious and loyal to Charles, and the thought was that when they came to retrieve the body upon his suicide, the dog may attack the police or whoever came in. So he thought it would be better if the dog wasn't there."

[Creep-O-Rama]

Presented for your approval: three deliciously creepy tales from the dark and fuzzy outer roads of St. Louis history. If these stories don't send chills up your spine, check your pulse—you may be a ghost yourself.

The Blue Pool

A stone's throw from the Great River Road, a short distance north of Alton, is a bluff-bordered pool of water that always gave the illusion of being bottomless.

"The pool itself was extremely blue and very clear, back years ago," noted Troy Taylor, author and host of the History & Hauntings Tours of Alton. "Tales have been told that people have dropped everything from automobiles to railroad cars into this pool and that they were never able to find them...They couldn't find a bottom. Divers supposedly went down, and not only did they not find a bottom, they didn't even find the railroad cars that had been dropped in there."

As the years went by, the pool was used as a local swimming pool of sorts, but accidents began to happen, Taylor said.

"What a lot of people didn't know was, as they jumped from the top of the bluff over the pool and into the water, not far below the surface was a rock ledge," he said. "And a lot of people hit that ledge and died. Stories went on to say that during the Prohibition era, gangsters who had some bad dealings with people around St. Louis would come to the Blue Pool, weight down their victims, and throw them into the pool, thinking the bodies would never be found.

"As time went on and people began to use the place as a kind of party spot, a place to go out and neck with your girlfriend, they began to tell stories about hearing screams of people around the rocks, echoing off the rocks and around the river. They claimed that they saw ghosts on the top of the rocks and the edge of the water, and people said that these ghosts and the screams were either the victims of the gangsters from the '20s or the people who had the accidents there at Blue Pool. And the story is that place is still haunted."

Over the years, Taylor has heard plenty of ghost stories, each of which he takes with a generous grain of salt. But an experience of his own at the Blue Pool left him chilled, to say the least.

"A year or so ago, we had gone out there for one of the tours," he said. "Sonny Irvin, who does the tours with me, and I were out there, and we'd gotten the group together, and we'd told all the ghost stories about Blue Pool.

"It was an early October evening, noticeably warm for October, and we got everybody headed back toward the trolley. Sonny and I were bringing up the rear, about thirty or thirty-five feet behind everyone else. As we were walking along talking, all of a sudden we got this—the only way I can describe it is to say it was like a wave, a cold wave of air, just ice-cold—it went right between us and kind of passed us, and then it was gone.

"And I looked at Sonny, and he looked at me, and he said, 'Did you feel that?' I said, 'Yeah,' and he said, 'What was it?' I said, 'I don't know,' And so we sped up back to the trolley. We still kind of scratch our heads over that one. He and I are certainly not the first ones to swallow anything that comes along, to look for ghosts where we don't think there are any, but this was pretty weird!

"I don't have an explanation for that one," Taylor said.

Lemp Brewery: Home to Manufacturer of Artificial Haunts (And a Few Natural Ones)

He's a thirty-year-old whiz kid and true entrepreneur, the talented creator of everything from a sixteen-foot Great White shark that thrashes around to curved funhouse mirrors, theme park novelties, set pieces, and haunted house props.

Meet Mark McDonough, a Des Peres native who now lives in south St. Louis and operates his business, Creative Visions, out of office space in the old Lemp Brewery complex.

"There are twenty-six buildings in this complex, three more across the street where they used to keep the horses," he said. "This place has about a million square feet of space."

A graduate of Chaminade Prep and St. Louis University, McDonough has a background in theater and worked as a disc jockey before founding Creative Visions in 1992. In 1995, his shop in Maplewood burned down, and he moved to the third floor of the Lemp Brewery.

There, he and several part-timers craft everything from the rubber molds to the circuit boards that control the robotics, sound effects, lighting, painting, and more. Assorted heads, hands, tails, and other human and reptilian body parts line shelves and dangle off tables.

"We start out with piles of goo, raw materials, and whatever, and build it up into a lizard, a dinosaur, a shark," he explained.

The creations include a Death Row inmate who sits in an electric chair and shakes and screams when a switch is thrown; a huge lizard that lurches forward, tries to bite, and breathes smoke; and a large and realistic swordfish that flips back and forth and makes squeaking noises—"It's like a Billy Bass, only a $2,000 Billy Bass."

McDonough is not sure what the space he leases was used for originally.

"It appears to have been used to store some kind of liquid, but it wasn't the fermentation room," he said. "You can see filled patches on the floor where the tanks had been anchored down."

An Impressive History

For years Adam Lemp, founder of Lemp's Western Brewery, had hauled his beer by wagon from Second Street downtown to the brewery's lagering cave on Cherokee Street, noted Stephen P. Walker in his book *Lemp: The Haunting History*. After he took over the brewery in 1862, son William J. Lemp Sr. purchased additional property in the area of the caves and relocated Western Brewery directly over his father's cave.

"Lemp's lagering facilities consisted of three levels of cellars, which included a marvelous series of natural caves and artificial caverns three stories in depth, the floor of the lowest cellar being 50 feet underground," Walker wrote. "The upper cellars were used for the storage of beer in fermentation. In the lower one...some 50,000 barrels of beer [were] stored in huge casks of from 30 to 60 barrels, arranged in rows sometimes two tiers high. The artificial cellars connected to the vast natural cave...The subterranean region was kept at a year-round temperature of 35 to 40 degrees by means of flues which conveyed cold air from Lemp's extensive ice houses.

"By 1892 the plant covered three city blocks and was putting out some 300,000 barrels of beer annually, with total sales surpassing $3 million,"

Walker wrote. By 1895, he noted, Lemp had become the eighth-largest American brewer.

When it came to beer, William Lemp showed amazing savvy. His was the first brewery to use mechanical refrigeration and to establish a national, and eventually worldwide, strategy for marketing beer, Walker said. The buildings of the Lemp Brewery were designed by renowned local architects and were truly state of the art.

"The [architectural] partners utilized the Italianate/Renaissance Revival style, characterized by semi-circular arches for window and door openings, pilaster strips, and corbelled brick cornices," Walker wrote. "This design precedent was set in the plant's earliest structures and was maintained throughout the nearly forty-year building history of the brewery."

Today, the complex is home to businesses ranging from artist studios and theater groups to computer programmers and systems engineers and boasts a 40 percent occupancy rate. And the caves and subterranean tunnels remain spookily dark and vacant, accessible by a noisy freight elevator.

McDonough jokingly compares it to Dracula's Castle.

"You see very few bugs," he said. "And I've never seen a rat or a mouse. It's one thing no one complains about here, is rodents. There aren't any. And you expect to find them in a place like this."

After dark, even the locals won't come around, he added.

"It's kind of like a built-in theft prevention system," McDonough said. "Sometimes the kids during the day will ride their bikes through, but if you ask any of the older people, they don't particularly want to be in here. When the sun goes down, this place is like a ghost town—no pun intended."

Ghost Town Come to Life?

"You get a good breeze blowing, papers flying around, everything's creepy," McDonough said.

"A friend of mine was in charge of security for the haunted house that used to be here. They had walkie-talkies and whatnot. After they closed for the evening, somebody said, 'There's a little girl wandering around down here.' He said, 'I'll go find her.'

He had been there long enough that he could walk through the haunted house without his flashlight, which you have to do in case there's customers—you don't want to kill the illusion. He was walking through, and he got where he needed to be and clicked on his flashlight. As he did, he was walking, and there was a little girl right about here," McDonough said, motioning within arm's distance. "Well, his momentum carried him—he didn't react quick enough—he walked right through her. That threw him for a loop.

"I also know that, in 1993, the guy that opened the haunted house was taking some reference pictures of the haunted house for insurance and got them developed, and one of the pictures had a strange, cloudlike thing in it. First he thought it was bad film or something. You look carefully, and you can see a person. He managed to take a picture of a ghost."

McDonough has had several experiences of his own at the brewery. When moving in, for instance, he left a number of light boxes scattered around because the room where they were to go wasn't ready.

"So they were just laying there," he said. "The next day, they were all set up, nice and neat. I was the only one who had keys at that point—not even the landlord had keys, because I had just changed the lock and hadn't given anybody keys."

Once while working on a Saturday afternoon, he heard what sounded like chamber music with lots of instruments.

"First I thought it was a radio—it was kind of classical music with singing, like an orchestra," he said. "Thought about it, and I thought, 'You know, it's all guys here. Guys don't listen to this kind of music.' After an hour of hearing it on and off, I started trying to figure out where it's coming from. I noticed I could really hear it through here [a spiral staircase accessible through the office]. I thought, 'Oh, there must be somebody renting out the second floor, rehearsing,' because a couple of the theatre groups have storage for props and things on the fourth floor above us.

"So I came over to the door, and I heard people walking up the stairwell. I didn't want to look like the guy that's all nosy, so I just kind of stopped for a minute. Then I thought, 'You know what, I pay rent in this place, I want to see who it is.' Pulled the pin, opened the door—nothing. The noise stopped. Just stopped, gone. I walked down to the second floor, and there was nothing there. The only place they could have been would have been the second floor. I checked the rest of the building just to make sure."

That stairwell also caused a couple of McDonough's employees to re-think their job status.

"In 1997 one of my artists, Gina, left at five or six o'clock, going home, and came back up white as a ghost," he said. "She said, 'There's something in the stairwell.' 'Something?' 'I don't know—this big, black shadow thing following me.' It wasn't a dimensional thing; it was like a shadow. It freaked her out. We had to bring her up and down on the [freight] elevator for the rest of the time she was working here.

"My office manager, a couple of years ago, had a similar experience," he added. "She's one of these level-headed people. She had an experience with something in the stairwell—not some*one* but some*thing*. You could just see it out of the corner of your eye. It was a black shadow, the best way I could explain it. And she said it gave her this horrible feeling of dread. These people were separated by two years, probably."

People around the brewery also have reported a dog barking in the caverns, which some have said is a three-legged dog, McDonough said.

"I was working here one evening, and I had gotten past the willies," he recalled. "There was nothing that could freak me out at this point—the building settling, all the things people were calling ghosts were actually just old building noises. I was working, and I heard something. I looked out, there was nothing there, went back to work. A half hour later, I heard something else.

"Suddenly this burst of wind came by—I thought it was a burst of wind. In retrospect, there wasn't any wind," he said. "You know how they talk about the hair on the back of your neck sticking up? That happened. This cold wind went by me or through me. It was like walking into a magnetic field or something, the best way I can explain it. It was kind of like being zapped with a low-level juice or electricity—it made your muscles contract, and all your hair just went up—it was unlike anything I've ever felt. But obviously it wasn't [electrical]. There was no power, nothing around me that could possibly have done it.

"That convinced me to leave for the day," McDonough said. "It was probably eight or nine o'clock at night."

Smallpox Island

Today it's known as the Lincoln-Shields Recreational Area, at the foot of the approach to the new Clark Bridge on the west side of the Mississippi River at Alton, Illinois. But during the Civil War, it was known as Smallpox Island. The bodies of many who died there remain today—and so do their spirits, some believe.

E. Rick Dixon II, a research technician at Alton Memorial Hospital who specializes in spirit photography, has spent much time researching and photographing this strange landmark. Dixon, who lives in North County, assists Antoinette's Haunted History Tours as a historian and photographer. A division of Right Brain Activities, Antoinette's is hosted by psychic Antoinette Eason and her daughter, Alixandria, as well as business partner Marlene Lewis.

"That's my favorite place," Dixon said of the landmark. "It was originally known as Sunflower Island and also as McPike Island, because Henry McPike was said to have tried to buy it—it's questionable whether he actually bought it."

During a smallpox outbreak at Alton's Confederate prison, officials needed a place to house—and bury—victims of the dreaded disease.

"It's a debilitating, fatal disease," Dixon said. "You have the most horrendous abdominal, intestinal cramping, diarrhea, you name it. You literally waste away within a week to two weeks. You dehydrate, [you have] high fever, you die. At the time, it was a common cause of death."

Officials built a long, crude wooden building on the fourteen-acre Sunflower Island to house sick prisoners and staff. In 1863, guards began rowing the sick prisoners across the river to the island, according to historian Don Huber in a *Post-Dispatch* article by Tim O'Neil.

It is not known how many people were taken to or died on the island, although Dixon estimates between 1,000 and 2,000 people died there.

"As they died [on the island], they just dug up trenches around the side of what they called the hospital, which was just a makeshift building of pallets on the floor," he said. "No heating, no air conditioning. And they started digging trenches around it to start dumping the bodies in. Most were dumped in without any identification. There were no coffins."

The caretakers also contracted this malicious disease and spread it to their families. Before long, it had spread to the civilian population.

"The epidemic spread beyond the prison to the town of Alton, and very quickly, from what I understand," Antoinette Eason said. "By the time that Smallpox Island had a makeshift hospital set up on it, people were contracting it so fast that they were sending everybody over there, trying to isolate them. The awful thing about smallpox is that you can walk around infecting people for two weeks before you know you have it. So there are men, women, children, soldiers buried over there."

Over the years, the once-round island changed in shape, and during periodic flooding bones would wash down the river. In 1935, workers for the Army Corps of Engineers hit a mass grave while excavating for the old Lock and Dam 26.

"They actually scraped up skeletal remains," Dixon said. "When they were working on the original lock and dam, dredging up the land to the west of there, they actually came across bones embedded in tree limbs, where the tree had actually grown up through the slip trenches and had captured bones in the structure of the tree."

The old hospital was located approximately at the towhead, or the side piece of the old lock and dam, Dixon said.

"That's all that's remaining," he said. "The reason why they didn't blow that up to get rid of that remaining concrete structure [when the new lock and dam was built in 1998] is because the engineer and the ones who did the investigation found that that was the approximate location of the hospital. This is all documented in old records. If they'd blown that up, there's a good chance there would have been a lot of remaining bones of bodies, a burial ground, so they made the decision not to remove that remaining concrete structure. They went to the west from there, upriver a little ways.

"The actual Sunflower Island, that more or less was the eastern edge of the island; the island actually went to the west more. You can see remainings of it, though, when the water level's down."

Much spirit activity remains under the portion of the old dam that still stands, Eason said.

"In that same general area, we would see, not apparitions, but misty forms moving around, things like that," she said. "And for some reason, there was one area that was always warm—I walked through it one night when it was very cold, walked through this warm spot. So we started every night looking for the warm spot, and it was always in the same general area. The only thing I could come up with was that it was some kind of a good-hearted spirit trying to warm us up," she chuckled.

"You could walk out past the dam structure on that promontory toward the water and actually feel the difference psychically, I guess," Eason said. "You could tell where the bodies were not buried. As soon as you took that one step out onto the area that had been added, you felt different. It was amazing how many people commented on that."

It was Antoinette's Haunted History Tours, several years ago, that first introduced tourgoers—and many Alton residents—to Smallpox Island. Eason always told each group what a shame it was that all the people buried there had been forgotten. One night, a woman in the group said that her father worked for the Army Corps of Engineers and that she would talk to him.

A monument to the smallpox victims was erected by the Army Corps of Engineers in April 2002, honoring 233 soldiers and 16 civilians known to have been buried on the island. Not long ago, Antoinette, Alix, and a couple others went over to see it.

"I'm just so glad they finally got something," Eason confided to her friends. Almost immediately, stunned, she felt the firm but friendly clasp of a woman's arms around her shoulder and a disembodied voice said, "Thank you." Of course, there was nobody there.

Nobody visible, that is.

5

[Of Angels and Indian Princesses]

Some people think angels are a figment of some greeting-card creator's imagination. They shake their heads in disgust at the mere mention of Indian princesses, and they refuse even to entertain the idea of a magical rock garden.

Of course, they've never read this chapter.

Angels Served at Arlington Bed and Breakfast Inn

The stately old Arlington Hotel, 207 East Main Street in DeSoto, is perhaps the only bed-and-breakfast inn around that has guardian angels on the premises.

"I'd have to say that the spirits we have are probably ghosts of angelic means rather than of anything else," said Rich Jenkins, who owns the inn with his wife, Brenda.

With fourteen guest rooms, each furnished with antiques and bathrooms, the historic inn features a restaurant with Brenda Jenkins' downhome southern cooking, as well as a heated pool and hot tub. The hotel regularly sponsors special mystery dinners, Christian marriage encounter events, and holiday gatherings such as a non-alcoholic New Year's bash.

And a few ghosts: holy, of course. Rich Jenkins, a Baptist, regularly blesses the house in a two-and-a-half-hour, casting-out ritual with blessed oil.

In fact, the Holy Spirit may have made a special appearance on the third floor of the Arlington not long ago, after a sleepless guest, a Roman Catholic nurse, rose from her bed to pray at 3:00 in the morning and witnessed instead what she believed was a revelation.

"She came down the next morning [to breakfast] and said that there was such a tremendous experience and she was 'so glad I came here,' and that she had spoken to the Holy Spirit that morning," Jenkins noted. "She was to go check out a particular neighbor, and that it would be determined what she was to do for the rest of her life."

Also staying on the third floor was a couple from DeSoto. The wife, originally from India, had adopted Christian beliefs, Jenkins said.

"About thirty minutes [after the nurse], the Indian lady came downstairs to have her breakfast," Jenkins said. "She said, 'I can't believe this, but about 3:00 this morning there was the most tremendous amount of energy on the third floor, and it was just such a warming, peaceful feeling that came upon that floor. I don't know what happened there, but I believe the Holy Spirit was on the third floor that night.'

"Neither one of them knew each other or had any conversation together about this prior to telling me," he said. "So something happened up there."

Something's always been happening at the Arlington. Built about 1860 to accommodate people passing through town on the railroad, it originally was painted green and known as the DeSoto House, with about forty small rooms.

"The city of DeSoto at that time was a booming frontier city—it was the largest city in Jefferson County," Jenkins noted. "A lot of the dignitaries and people lived here. In the 1870s Mr. Arlington bought the building and changed the name. It was an elite place to come, and Mr. Arlington had coats available for those that did not have a coat, for the men. It was a pretty fancy place."

In 1875, Confederate president Jefferson Davis is believed to have stayed at the Arlington, devouring a breakfast of biscuits and red-eye gravy and the works. Other guests over the years have included Charlie Chaplin during vaudeville days, Eleanor Roosevelt in the 1950s, and, more recently, Peter Graves from *Mission Impossible*, the Kingsmen gospel group, and Congressman Richard Gephardt.

"Through the years the Arlington has been about everything," Jenkins said. "It's been a place for weekly residents, it's been a railroad hotel, it could even have been a funeral home at one time, which is kind of interesting. It could possibly have been a field hospital at the end of the Civil War."

But tougher times were to come for the Arlington. In recent decades it developed a reputation as an eyesore, as well as a hangout for spirits from the Civil War and the railroad.

"The old-timers talk about, in the 1920s and '30s, the Arlington at that time was not a place for young people to come because of the transient people coming through and the vagrants on the railroad—there was a lot of stabbings and things in this area," Jenkins said. "There's just tons of stories about this place."

The Arlington was saved by the wrecking ball in 1994 by Dennis and Judy Welsh, who renovated it using old photographs and historical data.

"When we came in, we just kind of put our own little personality into the place," Jenkins said. "When you walk in, it's like walking back in time a hundred years. It just feels like Grandma's house and smells that way, especially on a Saturday morning when I'm frying bacon."

Other "guardians" have left their touches as well. A couple of years ago, an area woman who described herself as a ghost hunter visited the building, took pictures, and claimed that she felt a number of spirits who for some reason were held back from going on to the next life.

"But they weren't bad people—there were no demons or poltergeists or anything," Jenkins recalled with a chuckle. "I said, 'Of course not, because we've cast all those out. Whatever spirits you probably feel here are angels.'"

An odd event occurred two Christmases ago, Jenkins said.

"I had a granddaughter that was a year old at that time," he said. "She was in the living room where we were all unwrapping presents on Christmas Eve, and she lifted her little arms up into the air like she was wanting someone to pick her up, but there was no one there—she had her back to all of us.

"So we snapped a picture. Then her little arms came down and one stayed up in the air with her little finger stuck up like she was pointing to the sky, and she walked out of the room with her arm up in the air, as if someone were holding her hand. When we got the pictures back, sure enough there was an orb there (see Chapter 8, Strange Snapshots) where she was standing, and other orbs, white orbs, throughout the room. I feel they're just angels that are watching over us. I believe that there's a heaven and a hell, and that when you die, you go either to heaven or to hell. I also believe that there's a spiritual warfare going on up there between good and evil, God and Satan, and I also believe there are guardian angels that come to be with us, that watch over us and protect us."

Morse Mill's Indian Princess

In 1950 the hundred-year-old farmhouse in Morse Mill, Missouri, was literally falling down, had no bathrooms and no plumbing or electricity.

Then an amazing transformation took place. Dr. Cecil Smith, a retired physician, and his wife, Helen, decided to move back from Pasadena, California, to Helen's hometown of St. Louis. They bought the ailing farmhouse, renovated it extensively, and created a welcoming new home for their children.

"We moved there in 1951 and Mom sold the house in 1972, and I was there starting in the eighth grade and all through high school, and then I left for college and the army and that," recalled their son, Cecil J. Smith, now a retired newspaper editor who lives in Salem, Indiana, with his wife, Martha. "It was a great house. I couldn't have been in a happier place to grow up. They were a retired couple and they had a lot of fun there. They were good to us kids, so it has a lot of good memories. The property was different than what it is now—it's been subdivided. At that time it was all one farm."

In this Cinderella-turned-princess of a home resided another princess— an Indian, Smith said. He discussed her in a column he wrote for the *Salem Leader*:

I first heard about her from my mother. Whether she learned about the princess from a reliable source, or if the princess was just local folklore, or if the princess evolved from my mother's imagination, I'll never know.

My mother always claimed the Indian princess had died somewhere on the land occupied by our 60-acre farm. Mom didn't know where the princess was from or what she was princess of, but she was, nonetheless, a princess, and her final resting place, mom said, was in the vicinity of our house.

No one ever saw the princess, who became a scapegoat for a variety of offenses, Smith said.

"Didn't turn the lights off before you went to bed," my dad might say.

"I'm sure I did, dad," tossing in my ultimate defense. "The princess must have turned them back on."

If mom misplaced her glasses, or a book, or anything, she quickly asked the princess to bring the lost item back. Naturally the item would turn up after a short while and mom would talk about what a nice ghost we had that liked to play tricks on us.

Try as he might, the young Smith never did find a likely resting place for the Indian princess, although he said about 200 yards from the house there was a picturesque spring bubbling out of a hillside.

"I do know that on the property there is a stone structure that looks like a bridge abutment but there's no place for a bridge—I've often wondered what that was," he said.

No matter. It was a warm, happy house, Smith recalled, and in later years it was the scene of some festive political gatherings, due to the involvement of Smith's aunt, Margaret Fitzsimmons, in Jefferson County politics.

"There were some very nice receptions there, I recall," he said. "[Former Missouri governor] Warren Hearnes—there was a reception there for him and others. It was just neat having people there, and attendants parking cars, tables out on the front lawn, and things like that. It was nice."

Some later residents didn't treat the home so well, however, and may have been into black magic, said Rich Jenkins. Jenkins owned the house in the mid 1990s with his wife, Brenda, and their six children. They sold the house a few years ago to buy the Arlington Hotel.

"None of us were ever hurt or anything like that, but there were things that happened there prior to us coming that were pretty evil," Jenkins recalled. "We found on the floor the satanic star, marked with a black magic marker in the floor. We found things like that and moon signs and different zodiac type things around—one room was painted totally black.

"We changed all that when we got there, and of course we brought a lot of love and everything into the home," he added. "Some people in the neighborhood said that the house had been built on an Indian mound, but it was 125 years old—I don't know if that was true or not. It was just kind of an eerie place. Some weird things could be felt in that house.

"That home, something was terribly wrong, but at the time I lived there I didn't know anything about blessing the home and casting out the evil spirits," Jenkins said. "It was a really neat old house, had a beautiful old banister going up to the second floor, a formal dining room, and a fireplace in the kitchen that you could serve through the dining room as well as the kitchen."

Things would turn up missing, never to be found. And all too often, Jenkins would feel a faint sense of fear in the house, and the hair on the back of his neck would stand on end.

"I felt very uncomfortable in that house, and I've lived in a lot of old homes in my lifetime," he said. "You could feel cold-air drafts at certain times. My children were so afraid of that house that—and they were in high school—when they got home from school they would sit in their car and wait until one of us got home. They wouldn't go inside by themselves, and we lived there."

The home's current residents have reported no strange activities, Jenkins said.

"Maybe whatever was there left or something—I don't know," he said.

Dr. Teiber's Magical Rock Garden

It was a special garden, designed to ward off evil spirits, and Ron Elz—a.k.a. radio personality, author, and bon vivant Johnny Rabbitt—remembers it fondly.

Tended by caretaker Heinz Preidecker, the whimsical rock garden was located in the yard of Dr. Fred W. Teiber's office, at the northwest corner of Compton and Washington Avenues.

"It had been there way before I was a kid—probably since the teens or twenties, and it may have been there long before that," Elz recalled. "There are rock formations—little arches, little buildings, and paths—and it was more rocks than garden. Dr. Teiber felt there were spirits in the garden. I wouldn't call it haunted. It was a spirit garden."

A medical doctor, Dr. Teiber lived on a fancy street in Ladue, Elz noted. Preidecker lived on the second floor of the house. Remnants of the garden may still be seen today.

"There are a lot of things that have to do with evil spirits," Elz said. "You go on the Hill, and you'll see lots of houses with fences in front. The reason for these fences—and you can see these are not very effective fences, usually not very big—was to keep evil spirits out.

"And I think that was the key in this, to drive away evil spirits. And these came from old European superstitions, whether they were German or Italian or wherever they might have been from. And if people believe that they work, what the heck? Why not? They talked years ago about the 'evil eye' and all this kind of stuff. People still believe in spirits and spiritualism and so on, so why not?"

Jerseyville, Illinois, is one of those charming cities that the ravages of time forgot, but Wal-Mart didn't.

While it has all the modern amenities and fast-food joints one could ask for, Jerseyville has managed to save many of its beautiful Victorian homes, shops, and landmarks. Its centerpiece is a downtown business district that's straight out of a Disney movie. Attractions include an old-fashioned Victorian Festival each year at the Fulkerson Farm (see Chapter 11, Civil War Chills), a seemingly unending supply of friendly and hospitable residents and helpful police officers, and a picturesque balance of town and country that's practically unheard of these days.

Located about a twenty-minute drive north of Alton on Highways 67 and 267, Jerseyville also may be, per capita, the most haunted borough around. Alton has earned its reputation for ghosts, to be sure, but at a scant 7,500 residents, Jerseyville may well surpass it. Read on for stories of three haunted homes in the area, and decide for yourself.

Centuries of History

First discovered by Father Marquette and Louis Jolliet in 1673, the land that takes in Jersey County was formerly the home of the Kickapoo, Menomini, Potawatomi, and Illini Indians. It is located just northeast of the confluence of the Illinois and Mississippi Rivers, and Jerseyville is the county seat.

The New London Company first granted the site for Jerseyville in 1602, and the first permanent settler was James Faulkner in 1827. Faulkner built first a log cabin, and then a frame house known as the Old Red House, which is now part of the Cheney Mansion (see Chapter 7, Victorian Visions, Part II: Jerseyville Landmarks).

The settlement was originally known as Hickory Grove until 1834, when a post office was established and a doctor from New Jersey, Dr. Lott, suggested the name Jerseyville. It was here that the first bank in Jersey County was established, a tin box with money collected by local residents and buried under a large rock in an unidentified yard.

"Next door" to Jerseyville is tiny Otterville, which was chartered as a town in 1867 and is one of the last remaining "towns" in Illinois.

Shadows and Spirituals at Otterville House

The simple two-story frame house in Otterville was already eighty or so years old when Debbie Hotz and her family moved there in 1956. Hotz, now a Jerseyville police dispatcher, was five years old; her sister, Susie Schulte, was six months old.

At one time the house had belonged to a doctor, and was located catty-corner to a local cemetery. When Hotz's family bought it, the windows had been nailed shut by previous owners. And there was something very creepy about the house, particularly around the upstairs closet at the top of the stairs, Hotz recalled. The closet also provided the home's access to the attic.

"Upstairs when I came out of my bedroom one time, I was going down the hall, facing the closet, and there was a hook-and-eye closure on it, and the hook just came out of the eye, for no reason at all," Hotz said. "It just looked like somebody lifted it up; it wasn't real fast; it just came out of there. The hook was on a circular thing, so it swung back and forth."

The family would hear footsteps coming down the stairs; doors in the house rattling, and one that closed on its own; scritching noises, as though somebody were scribbling on the wall with a pencil; and, occasionally at night, African-American spirituals being sung.

The strange activity didn't bother tiny Susie much; in fact, once when asked by her mother who she was talking to, Susie replied she was "playing cards with the angels." As she grew older, that all changed.

"One night I was lying in bed [upstairs], and I had the light on because I was afraid to be up there by myself, and I saw a silhouette of what I believed to be a woman with a scarf on, with her head covered, and it just moved around the wall," Schulte recalled.

Strange shadows were prevalent in that house, Hotz said.

"When the light would go off, it would look like someone sitting or standing in the corner," she said. "Whenever we'd turn on the lights, there wouldn't be [anyone there], and we'd move stuff around, but whatever the shadow effect was, it would still be there when the lights went out.

"There was a light from the hall that was kept on at night, and it would cast a square light over my bed, and one night, all of a sudden, it was there—a silhouette of what looked like a man's face, almost like a clown face. We turned on the lights, and we moved everything in the room, and we moved everything in the room behind it, and we turned the lights out, but the light still cast the silhouette.

"But then we noticed in the daytime, too, that the silhouette would still be there on the wall, and eventually it just faded away after about a week or so. We moved everything."

The girls' mother also was frightened out of the house one day.

"Something sat down beside her on the sofa," Schulte said. "She could see the indentation and feel it."

The family lived in the home 15 years. A murder occurred there many years later, when a man killed his cousin out in the garage in 1996, Debbie Hotz said.

And to this day no one is sure who—or what—was causing the strange phenomena. But Hotz has never forgotten a strange dream she had at the home shortly after she moved in.

"I remember walking to where the fence was, and everything was real light, real foggy, and there was a figure there, and it was like somebody standing there with sheets, and I was trying to pull them up, pull them up, and see who it was, but all it was was a ghost," she shuddered. "I just kept pulling up and pulling up, and I never could see a face, and then I remember turning around and running back to the house. I never have forgotten, and I don't think I could have been more than five or six years old when I had that dream. It was just weird.

"It just occurred to me, too, when we were little, I think maybe the fear came then from not being able to identify the spirit in form like now," she added. "At that time, I couldn't identify what I was feeling, just that something was there. Like I said, nobody was ever harmed."

Strange Lights, Girl in White in Jerseyville

Back in the nineteenth century, the big white house on the outskirts of Jerseyville was known as the Massey House and was part of a large dairy farm. Today it is one of several houses on quiet Dogwood Lane, just a few blocks from the bustle of the city.

Two reclusive men and their sister lived there in recent years, and the house was truly a "fixer-upper" when Jerseyville natives Dennis and Donna Fry purchased the home in 1987.

The brothers were heavy drinkers and smokers and eventually died, Dennis Fry said. The sister remained until she—and the house—were in a truly sorry state, and she wound up in a nursing home.

"She had an old pump sink here, and the water just ran out on the ground," Donna said. "She would try to wash off her plates in a sink—it was a mess—never took a shower or a bath, just greased herself. All the light switches about this far around [about six inches] were just slick. And she had a black snake living with her. They came to pick her up, and there's this black snake lying alongside her on the couch."

Dennis and Donna bought the home with contents included, but the place was unlockable, and the contents, which included a large piano, were missing when they moved in.

"The furniture that was in this place when we bought it you would not believe," Dennis said. "It was fancy, it was expensive. Everything was eagle claw. The couches were fancy, but she had slept on the couch, and it was just as slick as that wall was. We came up here two days after [the purchase], and everything was gone."

After much work, the Frys replaced the rickety wiring, restored collapsing plaster, adapted the layout to the twentieth century, and stripped layers of paint off the richly varnished woodwork. They raised three children—Carrie, Jennifer, and Jacob—in the home and operated a grain farm on the property.

"When we redid this house, we found all kinds of treasures in the walls," Donna said. "Between the ceiling and the [second] floor it's like this much, and we were tearing all the plaster out, and we got to looking through there, and there were these old-fashioned little button-shoes, a couple of little school slates, a real old baseball bat, handwritten bills for horseshoeing, old coins and an old button box, newspapers.... We found letters of some relatives in Missouri. They were coming up, and it was taking them a day to get here. It was like living in the old days, reading those old letters."

Donna frequently hears footsteps in the home when nobody else is there, and she and her daughter, Carrie Baiers, have seen a perfectly round, orange light near the floor that begins to wiggle and shoots up and disappears.

"We had my brother housesit one time when we were gone," Donna said. "And he was in the living room and he said, 'I'll never housesit again.' He saw this large frame of a man that was kind of gray, but you could see through it, and he said it just went real fast through the living room and into our bedroom. He said it felt kind of cold. He got up and went in and looked around, but there was nothing. He said it was a huge thing."

But it was a little girl in white who awakened Vernon Baiers, Carrie's husband, from his rest on the couch in the living room one night. The family was leaving on a trip to Arkansas at 4:00 the next morning, and Baiers was spending the night.

"I think it was on the second or third step, and at the time, Jenny [the Frys' daughter] was about the same height," Baiers recalled. "I rolled over, and I said, 'What the hell you doing, Jenny?' As I got to noticing, it was a long, off-white, like a nightgown thing, had little ruffles around the bottom, and the sleeves were kind of poufy, and she had long, dark hair about midway down her back.

"I realized it wasn't Jenny—she had no face, no hands, no feet," Baiers said and shuddered. "Her face was just kind of dark, and I looked at her dress, and there were no hands. I didn't know if I should run in [the bedroom] with those guys. Then I kind of did that thing where you cover up your head, and when I pulled the covers back down, she was gone."

Donna did more research on the home's history and found that a little girl named Katie Massey had lived in the house. Katie was born in 1870 and died in 1878.

"Jake had friends spending the night, and they were talking about something they didn't want me to hear about," Donna recalled. "Two fourteen-year-olds probably looking at a magazine or whatever. But they thought I'd come upstairs, because they'd heard something and their door shut, and Jake came down and said, 'Were you upstairs?' And I said, 'No. We were watching TV.' He said, 'Somebody came up and shut that door.'"

Donna laughed. "I said, 'Well, maybe you shouldn't have been doing what you were doing.'"

Carrie Baiers was a fourth-grader when she moved into the home.

"I used to have dreams all the time, and I'd wake up screaming, and I'd sit up in bed, and I didn't have any of those until we moved here—I'd just sit up in bed, and I'd be sweating," Carrie Baiers said. "I never had that till I moved here, and I've never had it since I've moved out."

The house was rumored to have lots of money buried around because the reclusive brothers didn't believe in banks. But after an exhaustive search through the many whiskey bottles and Prince Albert tobacco cans that had been left behind, the Frys came up with a quarter, a dime, and a couple pennies.

"They're real old ones, though," Dennis said with a smile.

Murder in Otterville

Jerseyville Police Officer Roger Kirby's boyhood home is a real conversation starter.

Kirby's family lived in the Otterville home twice: for about four years in the mid-1960s and again beginning in 1983. The house was located off the beaten path, near a hollow with a great legend of its own. And in the 1970s, some drug dealers occupied the home and during their stay tortured and murdered one of their own.

Little wonder, then, that some strange things have been reported in the 1917-vintage home, mostly in the basement. Roger's parents, Wayne and Shirley Kirby, still live in the home.

"I'm not afraid of that," Wayne Kirby said. "As long as it's in the basement, I don't fancy anyone can get in."

Originally from Arkansas, the Kirby family moved to St. Louis after Wayne got a job with McDonnell-Douglas and originally lived in Soulard on Geyer Avenue. On August 1, 1963, they moved to the Otterville home.

"There used to be an old house back up the hollow there," Roger said. "The people's name was Wall, and they had two boys that weren't mentally right and kind of ran the woods as woodspeople. They would show up at nighttime in some of the surrounding houses and steal things—chickens and stuff—[people would] find the heads of chickens and stuff thrown around, and they'd always say it was these boys.

"The people with the white coats came and took them away, but it was always said after that sometimes during the night you could hear them hollering—it would echo out across the bottoms," he added. "The people that lived there before my parents lived up here would see footprints out around the house, in the dust, and they always said it had to be the Wall boys. But nobody ever saw the Wall boys there."

"It wasn't carpeted on the steps," Wayne added. "They'd go up there and they'd see barefooted tracks in the dust, dust on the steps."

That story, however, pales in comparison to what happened at the former Kirby house in the mid-1970s. Enraged drug dealers forced an accomplice into the kitchen where they tied him in a chair, cut his feet off, then dragged him across the creek and up the hill to a shallow grave, where they shot him. His skeleton was found in April 1975 by a man and his son who were out hunting mushrooms.

"The guys that were living here were heroin dealers, and this guy had taken $1,200 worth of heroin to sell and then didn't bring the money back," Roger recalled. "And they were after him: 'Hey, man, get the money back, get the money back.' And finally that day they went and got him, brought him back here, and I guess he didn't have the money."

"The investigation started with a psychic [called in by the Jersey County sheriff's office to assist], and she talked about a railroad, but the only place I know is, there used to be a road that would go through that field there, and these guys got stuck, and they went to the sawmill and got slabs and laid them across like this to drive on. I assume she was seeing that.

"She said, 'You haven't found his feet—his feet's not where he was.'" That was true, Roger said, although the information was never published. The murderer of the man was never caught, he added.

Shirley Kirby remembers the crime well, because her daughter Tina was off on her bike at the time, and she couldn't find her.

"I drove down this way to see if I could find her, and there were people laying on cars, people laying on the road, they were everywhere," Shirley said. "Hippies. Cars all the way up and down the road. It scared me because she was little, and I couldn't find her. I went back to town, and it turned out she went another way instead of this way."

When the Kirbys purchased the house again in 1983, it was a shell.

"It didn't have windows, the doors had all been kicked in, and they took all the plaster lath down from the walls," Wayne said. "Somebody was going to redo it, and I don't know if they ran out of money or not."

The Kirbys also heard stories, but they didn't take them seriously.

"A previous resident had seen a lady in white standing at the top of the stairs," Shirley said. "But she drank a lot, and I just figured that was—"

"What she drank!" finished Roger.

The noises in the basement sound as though someone is down there tearing things up, dragging heavy objects and throwing things.

"One night I came home from church. [Wayne] was sitting there, and he was nervous," Shirley said. "I would have been, too, if I had heard all that."

But what really startled him was when someone tried to talk to him in the middle of the night.

"I got up to go to the bathroom one night, and Shirley, she was asleep," Wayne said. "I thought she was awake because when I went into the bathroom, somebody called my name. 'Wayne,' they whispered. I thought she'd heard something, so I came back over and said, 'What?' But she wasn't awake.

"I did hear that. It was a woman's voice. It did unnerve me when I got back to the bed and asked Shirley."

Wayne has heard voices on a couple of occasions, and the home's access to the attic is from the couple's bedroom.

"You feel uneasy, like there's something there, like there's a presence there that you can't see," Shirley said. "There was stuff in the attic when we moved in. Old trains—"

"There's still stuff in the attic," Wayne said. "It's ours now. A long time ago, most people died at home—they didn't go to hospitals. I assume they had more experience with this stuff then."

Whatever it is, it's never tried to do any harm, he said.

Shirley agreed. "If there's a spirit here, it's peaceful," she said.

[Victorian Visions, Part II]
Jerseyville Landmarks

A century-old chain of landmarks awaits history buffs along State Street, the main drag of Jerseyville, Illinois (Highway 267).

There's the beautiful Shephard Mansion, now home to a delightful restaurant known as 518 South; the old Cheney Mansion, now a museum and home of the Jersey County Historical Society; and Hazel Dell, the home of Confederate Col. William H. Fulkerson. Not far from State in downtown Jerseyville is the magnificent Jersey County Courthouse, built in 1893.

At least three—the Cheney Mansion, 518 South, and Hazel Dell—have had some strange occurrences in recent years. Look for Hazel Dell in Chapter 11, Civil War Chills.

The Cheney Mansion: Home of the Little Red House, Miss Dorothy

Built in 1827, the "Little Red House" was Jerseyville's first frame structure. The two-story building served as a stagecoach station, a Pony Express stop, the town's first tavern, the first school, and the first bank in Jerseyville. It was here, too, that the town's name was changed from Hickory Grove to Jerseyville. A slave cell in the basement was a stop on the Underground Railroad, connected via underground tunnel to a log home that once sat across the street.

The Little Red House still stands. One just has to search carefully for it. In 1843, it became the home of Dr. Edward A. D'Arcy, whose daughter, Catherine, would marry Prentiss Dana Cheney. And it was Cheney who built the modern-day Cheney Mansion around the Little Red House, enclosing it forever, noted S. Gene Prosser, past president of the Jersey County Historical Society.

A retired insurance agent and Jerseyville native, Prosser led a long and successful crusade on behalf of the historical society to buy and restore the home and many of its ornate treasures. The property now includes a large museum in back of the home, and the formerly rundown mansion has received about $325,000 in improvements, with about $100,000 left to go on its restoration. The grounds also serve as the site for Jerseyville's Apple Festival on the last weekend in September. For more information, call (618) 498-4613.

"The first P.D. was quite a businessman," Prosser said. "He became a broker and a banker in New York, traveled in society, and all that other good stuff. When D'Arcy died, Catherine inherited 3,600 of D'Arcy's 5,600 acres of beautiful black ground up in Christian County. That's when they started the present-day house and wrapped it right around the old red house. Two sons...both died in infancy."

Finally, when Cheney was forty-six and Catherine, forty-two, a son, Alexander, was born and grew up to become a doctor with a practice based at the mansion. An alcoholic and ne'er-do-well, Alexander and his wife, Sarah, both were pretty well up in years when their son, Prentiss Dana II, was born in 1916.

P.D. was a character, to say the least, Prosser recalled.

"Not more than two weeks before his death [in 1969], I sat on a piano bench with him up at the Elks one night," Prosser said. "P.D. told me, 'Gene, you know, this town's gonna miss me when I'm gone, because I've worked hard to be the town eccentric.' And truer words were never spoken.

"P.D. was educated to the hilt. He was chauffered by a black chauffeur in a big limousine just a few blocks to grade school, and little old P.D. sat in the back and waved his hand at his friends...He went to Washington University, got a degree for doctorship, never sat for the exams, never became formally recognized as a doctor, never worked a day in his life. He went through three wives, was on drugs and alcohol.

"He could play any musical instrument in the world, all of them. Big, beautiful baby grand piano in the south parlor of the Cheney house—under it was every instrument going, including drums and a little E-flight clarinet which he loved to play in the parades because it was high and shrill and made him show up. He also played the Sousaphone, and it really looked unique. He was a little guy, and here he'd be coming with this big brass bass, carrying it—quite a showman."

Cheney once was elected to the Jerseyville City Council, where he earned the title "honorable." Although few people used it, Cheney hung on to it vociferously.

"My brother was a precinct committeeman one time; he could have been addressed as 'honorable,' but he never put any force to it," Prosser said. "P.D. did, and when he ran for re-election, he got two votes. [After the defeat] he made his little speech: 'I ran for public office, and I got two votes, and I know one of them was mine. When I stand up and turn around here, I want you all to take a look at the mistletoe pinned to my coattail,' as he turned around and walked out of the meeting."

He laughed. "That's the kind of guy he was. So he became known as the Honorable Doctor Prentiss Dana Cheney. Wherever he'd go, he walked like the little king."

P.D. never had any money with him, although he was an avid collector and traveled extensively.

"He'd just tell them who he was: 'I'll take this—send the bill to my attorney,'" Prosser said. "When he'd buy all this stuff, the attorney would just add it to the mortgage against the good land up in Christian County, a section of land, 640 acres. When it'd get mortgaged to the hilt, couldn't carry any more, he'd [sell it]. When he finally died, he had 320 acres left, and very little else.

"But he had this big house full of all that land could produce all those years—probably in the neighborhood of $3 million or better," Prosser said. "P.D. died, I believe, at the age of 56, looked like he was 86. Snow-white hair, little old malnourished guy, just abused himself to the hilt. He left the house and everything in it to his wife. His third wife, Edith, was older, and she was just a little old barmaid from down in Grafton."

What happened to the estate after P.D. died is another story that's almost as riveting—Prosser can supply the details. Suffice it to say that P.D.'s two sons by his first wife, who had moved to St. Louis after the divorce, received nothing.

Both P.D.'s eccentricities and the ghost connection stem from his childhood years. He was raised almost solely by his mother, Sarah; his lifelong nursemaid, Miss Dorothy Hofsaes; and an old maid aunt, Miss Dorothy Barry.

"I have a picture of he and Edith and Miss Dorothy in 1961 at a big hotel in Florida, so she died sometime after that," Prosser said.

And Miss Dorothy, it seems, has developed an otherworldly fondness for the old place.

"We had some young men working there at night, and one of those boys got the socks scared off him," Prosser chuckled. "He was coming up the back stairs, which was the servants' quarters, and I think quite possibly Miss Dorothy's bedroom may have been at the top of the stairs."

The workers were Harlan Simpson and a friend, Neil Bushnell. Simpson was wiring outlets in the garage one evening, and Bushnell was laying a new closet floor upstairs.

"I was coming up the service staircase, going upstairs, and I kept hearing someone go up the stairs behind me," Bushnell said. "I thought it was Harlan, so I was talking to him, didn't think anything of it, and he never answered back. So I turned around and looked and saw this woman, kind of a medium-build gal with a long dress, hair all up in a bun, had glasses on, and she was kind of picking up her dress as she was walking up the stairs. She looked like she was there, but she wasn't, you know? You could almost kind of see through her just a little bit. She was a younger woman, maybe in her mid-30s. She just kind of looked at me, didn't make a face or anything, and kept on walking. It was so much of a shock, you didn't have time to be scared. So I just kept on going.

"The weird thing was, Harlan had just hooked up the service buzzers, and we kept playing with that back and forth, and I'd just rang that buzzer right before I went up the stairs," Bushnell added. "So I don't know if the buzzer had something to do with it."

When Bushnell told him about the experience the next day, Simpson decided to test him a little.

"Being a skeptic, I can torture people," Simpson said. "So I got the photo album—I had a damned good idea who it might be, if anybody—and I showed Neil pictures of Miss Dorothy, pictures of the mother, and random photos of people. He gets to that picture of Dorothy and he goes, 'It was her—100 percent.'

"I'm like, 'How do you know?' And he says, 'You just don't see someone that close and mistake them.' And I'm like, 'You could see her?' He said, 'Hell, yes, I could see her. She was standing right behind me.'"

Simpson said he believes Miss Dorothy might have had good reason to be so attached to the family.

"I did a lot of research into the family records, and I do believe Miss Dorothy was P.D. Cheney's mother," Simpson said. "His mother—the real one—had tried to have children, and none of them lived. All of a sudden she had this P.D., and she had a nurse for about a month, and this first nurse leaves real quick. Then Miss Dorothy comes in, gets treated like family, raises P.D., they look identical in all the pictures...She stayed in the home. And a hired nurse from Chicago does not live with you forever."

Other strange occurrences have happened in the house. The woman who did the home's wallpaper work would hear footsteps, windows shutting, and doors slamming after she arrived alone at the house early in the morning, especially on rainy days. She also had "help," with extra rolls of wallpaper repeatedly brought to her cutting board while she was away hanging cut pieces.

"Now that cracks me up," Prosser grinned. "I mean, I can see the spirits, but how do they get the power to pick up four rolls of paper and put them on the table?"

Simpson and a friend once had the water faucet shut off on them—as they watched the knob turn—while cleaning up after a job. And Simpson and Bushnell have heard conversations going on when no one was in the house.

"When I was doing the lights in the basement, I kept hearing people talking upstairs, like women holding a conversation," Simpson said. "I thought that was odd, but I just turned up the radio and ignored it. Some nights I worked up there till twelve, one in the morning—there was nobody in the house."

"There have been other times we've been working in the house, and especially around mealtime you can hear the dining room chairs moving, like somebody's pulling out the chairs getting ready to sit down, people moving about, but you go upstairs and there's nobody there," Bushnell added. "The contractors kept a radio on. The stations would just change, move right down the dial indicator."

But so far, P.D. Cheney himself has never shown up.

"That's sad because, man, believe me, some of the antics that he pulled, some of the things he did in life and in that house would have made a lovely ghost story," Prosser noted with a smile. "I suspect that when the divine powers decided to take him, they probably shipped him straight to hell."

Prosser chuckled. "Don't think he had a crack at a higher life."

518 South Restaurant and Lounge: Shades of the Past

Along with fine food, the three-story home that houses 518 South serves up hearty helpings of warmth and charm reflected in its brass chandeliers, ruby red glass, period wallpaper, and ornate woodwork.

That is, if you don't stay too late. Otherwise, the former residents might become a little *too* charming, as Lois Andrews learned late one night in

1985.

"I was vacuuming, and just minding my own business—I was never afraid in there—and something came up, just reached out and touched me on my left shoulder," recalled Andrews, a former waitress at the restaurant. "I rolled around, and there was nothing there, but I knew something was there. I got busy and I got my vacuuming done, and that's the only time I was really afraid. Something did touch me—it was a definite presence that was a woman, because I could smell her perfume, this light odor. Small hands.

"I finished my sweeping, and I didn't do a very good job when I finished up that last corner," Andrews noted with a smile. "I was out of there. I had heard stories that people had seen things, or thought they did, and I thought, 'Well, some of this is a little blatant. After that night, there was no doubt in my mind."

Located at 518 South State Street, the mansion was built in 1857 by William A. Shephard, an English immigrant and cobbler who founded what is now the State Bank of Jerseyville, according to a local newspaper article compiled by Andrews' son, James Scheffel, while a student at Jerseyville High School.

Shephard was appointed president of the Jacksonville, Alton and St. Louis Railroad and became a state senator. He and his wife had nine children, one of whom served as mayor of Jerseyville for four terms and as a congressman for four terms.

Only one of the Shephard daughters ever married, and all four sisters died in the house. Mary Elizabeth, who had assumed the role of matriarch, died December 8, 1927, and her sister, Ann Marie, died just three days later. Both were laid out in the front parlors of the house, and they received a double funeral at St. Francis Xavier Church, according to documents.

Local legend has it that Ann Marie couldn't stand to be without her sister and, distraught, jumped out the third-floor window on the home's north side to her death. However, no documentation has been found that supports this legend.

"I know two of the sisters died very close together, and one of them was laid out in one room, and one was laid out in another room, in the front of the house," said Susie Schulte of Jerseyville, who used to work at the restaurant. "I never did like the granny room [where one of the sisters was laid out], and that's where I always had to work when I worked up front. That's where the candles would relight after we'd put them out at ten

SP|R|TS

o'clock."

In 1928 the home became a boarding house, and from 1951 to 1958 it was a nursing home. From 1958 to 1980 it served as a shelter care center, and it was scheduled for the wrecking ball when five area couples—Barry and Virginia Ritter, Henry and Mary Ann Husmann, Ed and Pat Bonacorsi, Tom and Lou Edwards, and Joe and Beverly Susnig—formed the 518 South Corporation to save the house and open Jerseyville's only fine dining restaurant.

"They found windows and fireplaces boarded over, panelling covering ornate woodwork, years' worth of tarnish on brass chandeliers, and a lot of dust on everything else," Scheffel wrote.

After much work, they opened the restaurant on September 15, 1980, with many of its original features intact: the brass chandeliers converted from gas, blue tile imported from England in the dining room, glass panels above the doors and windows, original woodwork that is grained to look like walnut, three fireplaces, and the walnut staircase.

The current owners are the Ritters, Mary Ann Husmann, and Ken and Karen Blackorby. Husmann and Virginia Ritter manage the restaurant's day-to-day operations.

"There is a sense of grandeur about the house," Scheffel wrote. "Stepping through its doors is like taking a step back in time. The house also has a presence about it that is almost palpable. Some say it is the house itself, but others say it is the spirits of those who have died there."

Susie Schulte would go along with that. One night she felt a breeze blow past and the scent of perfume, and another time she turned to see a white figure moving down the hall.

"It was just like a ghost in the stories," Schulte chuckled, "dressed all in white with a flowing gown or cape or something on that drags behind her, and there she was, just walking up toward the front of the building. She's been seen going up the steps, and I've seen her, and another lady that I know has seen her sitting at the corner table in the tile room. They thought there was a customer; she sent the bus kid in there, and there wasn't anybody there.

"She's pretty active," Schulte added. "I remember one night I was so sick, but I was working and I ran upstairs, and the doors do this slamming thing, and I'm like, 'JUST LEAVE ME ALONE!!! GO AWAY! I DON'T EVEN HAVE TIME FOR YOU!' And she did."

Husmann's late husband, Henry, also had a strange encounter some years back. He and an employee had locked up the restaurant and were walking to their cars when they noticed a light on. The employee said he thought he had turned off all the lights but went back in and switched off the offending light.

Again they walked to their cars, and again they noticed the light was on. Again the employee turned out the light, and this time Husmann watched the window as it went black. Heading to their cars again, they noticed the light was on a third time.

"Mr. Husmann told the employee to leave it," Scheffel wrote. "When he came to open in the morning, the light was out."

Henry Husmann was never really upset by the experience, Mary Ann Husmann recalled.

"He was a really laid-back type person," she said.

Another time, Andrews wore an expensive pair of earrings to work and lost one of them.

"I paid way too much for them, and I shouldn't have worn them to work anyway...and when I got home that night, one of my earrings was missing," she said. "I had not been in the bar; I was waiting tables. I knew that I had just been in a certain area."

Schulte picked up the story.

"She was waitressing, and I was bartending," Schulte said. "The only people who had the key to the liquor room—which was locked, in the basement—was the bartender, and that was me, so I was the only one that had been in that room that night. When [Lois] got home she called me and said she had lost an earring, would I look around? I didn't find anything. And the next day a beer salesman was in the liquor room and found this earring, brought it out and set it on the washing machine. Found it in the liquor room. She hadn't been there."

But the story doesn't end there.

"Several months later, I was telling this story about the missing earring," Andrews said. "As I walked from the bar into the hall...the same earring in my left ear—it has a post, one of those plug-in things that hang on real good—I felt it pull out and drop on the floor right in front of me. The very same earring. It was pulled out—I felt it."

One night, Andrews and Schulte were playing with a Ouija board in the restaurant after it closed, and they received a message, supposedly from a little boy killed outside the 518 back in horse-and-wagon days. The name of the little boy, the board spelled out, was H-A-R-O-L-D.

Andrews and her son wanted to know more, so they began combing through county records and gradually pieced together the story.

"I believe his name was Harold Clore, and he was killed in a horse-and-wagon accident right out from the 518," Andrews said. "He was injured, and they brought him into the 518 to get him out of the weather and whatever until somebody could get there to help him. He did eventually die, from what I understand. There was indeed an accident outside the mansion; we didn't know anything about this until this all started."

8 [Strange Snapshots]

From little white balls of light to bright neon-like ribbons and smoky wisps emanating from tombstones, local photographers have caught some strange scenes on film. Whether these images are truly supernatural, or just the goofs of amateurs, depends on the source consulted.

The Elusive Orb

Chances are you've seen them in photographs: little white or translucent balls of light that seem to be floating in air, emerging from behind objects or lurking in some ghostly looking hideaway. They're known in paranormal circles as orbs.

Depending on who you ask, they're either discarnate entities, dust or water particles, or a little of both.

"It's very controversial," admitted Joe Immethun, the founder of the St. Louis ghost investigation group G.H.O.S.T.S. "Yes, it could be due to a lens flare or light reflecting off the lens, making a round, transparent image. But we have many tapes with the same image on video, where they would move.

"What we think is that [an orb] would be a ghost in its natural state, in its traveling state, if these orbs are actually what we think they are," he said. "It would be like stages—the ghost would be an orb, and then it would be an ectoplasm, which is a foggy mist, and then it would turn into an apparition. The main thing is electromagnetics—they use electromagnetic fields to manifest themselves in different ways. The more energy they have around them to use, the more energy they can use to manifest themselves."

Spirit photographer E. Rick Dixon II said he's taken very few orb photographs.

"There seems to be a certain speed of film, around 200 to 400, in which you get more pictures of orbs," he said. "If [you] use a higher speed of film, they turn out differently.

"All humans are energy," Dixon added. "And by the laws of physics, energy is never lost. And when we die, that energy isn't gone. It's there. Most of us think that ghosts and spirits, different forms of other life, are that residual energy."

Spirits don't always manifest in human form, because it takes much more energy to do that, so they usually travel as orbs, Dixon said.

"Apparently, in some cases they can present themselves as more than just this microscopic, concentrated ball of energy that shows up as an orb of any size," he said. "You'll see, especially as video cameras have improved over the years and videotaping in low light, a lot of people have taken videos of these microscopic orbs floating or shooting around that are not dust.

"More and more people were shooting these videos of these specks of light—everything from a speck to maybe a couple inches across on the video itself—having some sort of purposeful movement, maybe is the best way to put it. You can see them moving around solid objects or through solid objects or especially around people. They're interacting with humans, live persons."

Here, There, Everywhere

James Houran, an expert on the paranormal from Springfield, Illinois, disagrees. Published research by Houran and colleague Rense Lange indicates orbs are often produced under rainy or humid conditions and can be found at non-haunted as well as haunted locations. Houran calls them artifacts or photographic anomalies.

Houran would refer doubters to the March 2001 issue of *Fortean Times*, which includes an extensive article on orbs. Author Phillip Carr cites, among other causes, today's handy little pocket-sized digital cameras with all sorts of bells and whistles.

"The small size of these cameras has caused special problems for their designers," Carr wrote. "The camera's flash has to be positioned very close to the lens, in many cases less than twenty-five millimeters away, causing the often-experienced 'red eye' effect.

"Though the air around us appears most of the time to be clear and empty, it is in fact an invisible floating junkyard, with minute particles of dust, hairs, feathers, airborne seeds, cobwebs, spots of moisture, and tiny flying insects," he added. "If any of these are caught by the flashlight of a compact camera at the moment of exposure within a few millimeters of the front of the lens, they will be intensely illuminated, extremely out of focus, and rendered as balls of light...or 'orbs.' My own experiments confirmed this. Raindrops and dust in front of the lens produced some convincing examples. Also, because these particles are so close to the lens, they will not be seen emerging from behind anything else. It may sometimes appear they are doing so, but their 'transparency' will be the reason for this."

In some cases the "orbs" will be moving, Houran added, but that doesn't mean they're supernatural.

"For example, you can get light refraction effects, where reflections off, for example, your glasses can cause streaks on walls, things on tape," he said. "You can get dust particles that are close to the camera's lens that are reflecting light, that are moving. There are effects called autokinetic phenomena—in other words, if I have a stationary point of light and you just stare at it, pretty soon you're going to see it jumping around. That's because our eyes are never standing still—our eyeballs are constantly moving. When you start focusing on a single point of light in a dark room, pretty soon it's going to start buzzing around. You can get kind of the same effect with cameras, videocams, when people hold them. I don't know of any good, documented effect with someone who had a tripod camera."

The Bachelor's Grove Study

In 1996, Houran and Lange undertook a systematic study of Bachelor's Grove Cemetery, outside Chicago, at various times of day with a variety of film media and careful monitoring of electromagnetic activity in the area. They used only professional photographers to shoot the film.

"Bachelor's Grove reportedly has an impressive history of many people capturing strange things on photographs—everything from defined images, translucent women sitting on headstones, to orbs, light streaks, and this or that. We basically sectioned off Bachelor's Grove into quadrants, and we took a large series of photographs, starting from daytime to nighttime, randomly.

"We found nothing. No photographs came out that had anything strange on them," he said. "And I should say this: we had people standing in a line, so these photographs, with each different film, were taken in sequence. I take Polaroid, one, two; you take digital, one, two; you take black-and-white, one, two; so they were taken at essentially the same time."

The type of image received depends on the type of film being used, Houran said.

"We had a study where we actually look at effects people cite as photographic evidence for ghosts and what kind of film do they get it on? And we noticed that, if you look at very vague UFO photos, photos supposedly of the Virgin Mary, ghost photos, these types of things, they all can be classified reliably into one of five or six categories: shadows/shadow forms; amorphous forms—these are like blobs, maybe a firm shape, maybe a little translucent, but just a blob; density spots—not the orbs, but bright lights that are filled in, look like they have substance to them; fogging—this is where you see a blanket of mist; a defined image—maybe you literally see an apparition such as a translucent woman right there on the photo or light streaks that look like lightning or parabolas of light.

"We looked at those different categories against what type of film media they were using: Polaroid film, color film, infrared film, black-and-white, motion picture [like 8-mm], or videotape," he added. "When we looked at this statistically, we found that the type of image you get depends on the type of film you're using. So unless ghosts and these other things just happen to choose the kind of camera they think will look best to them, what this is telling you is that...we know that we reliably get orbs with digital cameras. I'm reliably going to get fogging and this type thing with Polaroid."

That's not to say that some of the photographs can't be explained, but they are uncommon, Houran said.

"You'll see some people who show you film and say, 'There's translucent figures of people and stuff,'" he said. "We know a lot of those are frauds. We also know a lot of those are double-exposures, that people don't realize that they're double-exposures. That's why we use professional photographers who know what they're doing, who know to keep the lens strap back, who know about different film and the processing of the film, who know you should use certain film in certain temperatures—you don't load infrared film in full daylight, you need to have complete darkness, and you keep the film refrigerated.

"Even if we can't explain it—blobs on tape, streaks on film—that's not what people report when they see ghosts," Houran added. "That makes you wonder: are these two separate things? All that shows is, we have something strange here that needs an explanation. I know some people send photographs to these Kodak processing centers, and they get these letters back saying, 'Yep, it's unexplained.' And they'll say, 'See, that's evidence for ghosts.' No, that's evidence for 'We don't know what it is.' If you say you have a cough, I don't know medically what's wrong with you. But I don't say there's a witch that's caused a spell on you. This just tells us there's a lot for us left to learn, and we don't want to jump to conclusions of it being paranormal."

Some Strange Subjects

Houran himself has a photograph he can't explain. In 1991 he conducted the first formal scientific investigation of the Country House Restaurant in Clarendon Hills, near Chicago. Houran spent the night there with a group of people.

"One of the things we did was take infrared photographs," he recalled. "The professor I worked with was sitting at a table, and we had a parabolic microphone, and it was picking up some high frequencies that were beyond the range of human hearing. We didn't hear anything, but the microphone did. It was going wild. There was nothing next to him. We took an infrared photograph, and we get this huge magnetic distortion on the infrared film. The frequency—whatever this interference was—just went away. We took another photograph, and there was nothing there. So what is it? I don't know."

He also cited an instance in which a parapsychologist set up a video camera in a well-controlled, tied-off area in a supposedly haunted location in New Jersey.

"When they played the videotape back, there was this huge distortion in the tape," he said. "And this is on fresh tape, and then it goes away. Was this a manufacturer error on the tape? Was it something that was just a fluke with the tape of the processing? We'll never know, but that's the only one I know that was captured under really good, professional conditions."

Dixon, who opts for color film with negatives over digital film, also has captured some unusual photographs. Every so often he has been accused of fraud, which he vehemently denies. Dixon's photography hobby is not a money-making venture, and he often supplies photographs to others free of charge.

"My best photograph is a family in Alton Cemetery—it still shocks me," said Dixon. "I've had paranormal investigators to my face tell me it's phony. I don't care—I've got that negative—I know it's not phony. I didn't see anything there when I took it. This is what turned out later. I researched, and the figures match the ages of that family, the Floss family, when they died, not all at the same time. I think for some reason they showed themselves to me."

Attic Antics in Manchester

Ken Aston isn't looking to photograph ghosts. In fact, he doesn't even believe in them. Restoration was his goal when he bought the home built for his great-grandparents Louis and Louisa Dependahl at 211 Henry Road, in Manchester, recently.

The frame farmhouse was built in 1910 by Henry Seibel & Sons Building Contractors, which was owned by Ken's other great-grandfather, Adam Seibel. The Dependahl home would overlook the largest working farm in the city of Manchester at the turn of the century, with 350 acres.

Now a year later, Aston, a real estate investment broker, is rethinking his views.

"It's weird," he said of his experiences. "I don't know how to explain the stories, and I don't know how to explain the photograph."

A previous resident of the Dependahl house had told of her family's strange experiences there in *Spirits of St. Louis: A Ghostly Guide to the Mound City's Unearthly Activities*. Aston was unaware of those experiences in 2001, when he purchased the handsome old farmhouse and led a successful battle against a plan by the county to straighten Henry Road, which would have required the home's demolition. Aston and his neighbors also are seeking National Register status for the home, a nearby schoolhouse, the shop known as 210 Henry, and even Henry Road, platted in 1855.

Aston would stop by the home after workers from the construction firm Melber & Sons General Contractors had left for the day. Invariably he would find the windows in the third-floor attic had swung open. He frequently complained to owner Mike Melber, who in turn admonished his workers. Melber's workers swore they locked the windows and noted strange noises coming from the attic.

In June 2002, Aston took additional photographs to document the on-going restoration and came up with something strange in the darkened attic.

"They had to cut a section out to run ductwork through the old ceiling," he explained. "I forgot to put on the flash, which I turned on immediately after I took the first picture."

About a week later, he got back the photos from the developer. All are standard renovation shots except for the one without the flash. In the center of that photo are a series of brilliant, double-edged ribbons of light, bordered by a dense fog in the lower right-hand corner.

Intrigued, he went back upstairs. "I tried to reproduce the photo," he said. "All I got was black."

Since then, he has heard strange stories about the home from the former owner, Ann Ingoldsby, and Melber's workers. Debbie Aston, Ken's sister-in-law, had a creepy encounter with the house at a recent Dependahl family reunion.

"We had gotten there first," said Debbie, a case manager with the U.S. Court of Appeals, who lives in Creve Coeur. "I went in and walked around on the second floor. I felt I had walked three miles; my heart just started racing."

The staircase that leads to the attic is in a back bedroom on the second floor, she noted.

"My husband and my kids were on the steps behind me," she said. "I got up to the top where I could see into the attic, and I turned around and said, 'Oh, no, no, no.' My kids were not going up there.

"I'm convinced there's something there," she added. "It's just too weird. I didn't even know he had taken that picture of the attic when I walked up into the attic. It's like 9,000 degrees outside, and this house couldn't have been more than 70 degrees."

Since then, Ken has learned from his mother, Carol Dependahl Aston, that Louis Dependahl—who is believed by former residents to haunt the house—made the attic off-limits to the children and would get very angry when they broke the rules. At the time, the only way to access it was through his and his wife, Louisa's, room.

"It was forbidden territory; it was off-limits," Aston said. "Maybe he's still in the attic keeping people out or something."

No Camera, But One Very Strange Light

He didn't photograph it, but retired insurance broker Bill Wunderlich had a strange experience with a spot of light just the same. It came as a part of his job back in 1961, after a couple with a small business in south St. Louis asked him to go over their insurance with them.

"So I get in my car, and I go down on Humphrey Avenue to one of the flats down there—they were working out of their home—and we sat around, and I went over the insurance they were probably going to need and how their business worked," recalled Wunderlich, of Chesterfield, "when all of a sudden—why I said this I do not know—I looked at the

SP|R|TS

man, and I said, 'Is this place haunted?' And he said, 'My God, how did you know?' I just felt that it was haunted.

"So they told me that they have a ghost living in their house and that it appeared as a light, like a reflection off of a car, for example, but it would appear on days when it was very cloudy. It would appear at night, when there was no way it could be a reflection. The light would go through the walls from room to room. And I looked up at the wall, and there was this light, and it was sort of bouncing around the side of the room and disappeared. I said, 'Was that it?' and he said, 'Yes.'"

Wunderlich was flabbergasted. When he returned to the office, his father was gone, most likely out to lunch at his favorite eatery, the Crest House, downtown.

"So I went over there, and he was sitting there having lunch, and I sat down and said, 'I just had the damnedest experience,'" Wunderlich said. "I told him the story I just told you. He said, 'Oh, yeah, that was Tillie Gockenspiel' (I don't remember the name). I said, 'What do you mean?'

"Now, you almost have to know my father. He didn't believe in anything that you couldn't touch, taste, or smell," Wunderlich added. "He didn't believe in ghosts. But he didn't so much as miss a beat when I told him about this ghost. He said, 'I used to go out with her. She committed suicide—they lived on Humphrey at that address. Her father was a grocer in south St. Louis and kept horses, and the daughter was just in love with the horses and really enjoyed having them. And the father said, "I'm going to move back into the city, and we'll have to leave your horses here." So she committed suicide, hanged herself in the garage.'

"Very amazing. Absolutely blew my mind."

[ON THE ROAD]

As one automobile manufacturer used to say, "Getting there is half the fun."

We Americans, it seems, have a special affinity for our vehicles, as well as for the highways and byways that take us where we want to go. And the next time you're out and about, pay special attention to what's happening around you, because ghosts tend to like a little adventure once in a while, too.

One Last Car Ride for Grandma Cora

Betty Crossno's Grandma Cora lived in a big frame house on Genevieve, in the Walnut Park neighborhood where several generations of the family lived for a time. Cora had fallen and broken her hip when she was in her early fifties and had grown heavy from lack of movement. She died in February 1954.

"After she died, friends of my mom moved in there," recalled Crossno, of Kirkwood. "Matt and his wife [or] girlfriend—we never knew if they were married or not—were living at my grandmother's house. Matt hadn't known my mother or my father before they were married, and he had never seen my grandmother.

"So he came home one afternoon and went in the front door, and there was this heavyset lady with gray hair standing in the middle of the living room. And Matt said, 'What are you doing in my house?' She said, 'This is not your house. I live here.' He said, 'No, ma'am, this is my house, and I live here.'"

Crossno smiled. "Right away she turned on him and said, 'Robert, I want you to take me for a ride in the car.' Every Sunday after my uncle had bought a car, he would have to take her for a ride. And he would take her out, put her in the back seat, with his girlfriend or whoever he was with in the front seat with him, and they would take her for a Sunday drive. Another thing—my grandmother was the only one who called my uncle Robert, because everyone called him Babe—that was his nickname.

"Anyway, Grandma said, 'Take me for a drive, Robert.' And he said, 'Okay'—he was going to take her to the police station," Crossno said. "He thought maybe she was someone with Alzheimer's or just a crazy lady. And he swears that he took her by the arm and took her out to his car, and she insisted on getting into the back seat. And when he went around the block, because it was a one-way street, and started up the other block, she was not there anymore.

"Mom said it had to be her—he described her—and how could anyone disappear out of a car when they were there with him? He said he took her by the arm because she could hardly walk. She was a heavyset woman, must have weighed 400 pounds because she filled a whole chair. When he told my mom what had happened, he was scared."

Believe It or Don't

This one comes from one of the numerous ghost Web sites on the Internet, Haunted Places (http://theshadowlands.net/place), a partnership between several sites: The Shadowlands Ghosts & Hauntings, Obiwan's UFO-Free Paranormal Page, and GhostHound.com.

And it's pretty farfetched but amusing: Upper Blackwell Road in Bonne Terre is said to be haunted, and those bold enough to drive it at night may be flagged down by a ghostly couple.

There's also a bridge called the Black Tram, and people who drive across it and flash their car's headlights three times will be chased away by a ghost car.

Haunted Hoofbeats on Wellman Lane

Bruce Carlson, author of *Ghosts of the Mississippi River from Keokuk to St. Louis*, unearthed this strange story while passing through town in the late 1980s.

"A real live cowboy along the river is the last thing I expected to find in my research for this book," Carlson recalled. "At least, I guess I found the ghost of one."

Carlson visited with a woman whose father was a farmer between Florissant and St. Louis. She shared with him the strange story, which happened on their St. Louis County farm in the fall of 1922. It was written on some now-yellowed paper by her mother, Mrs. Wellman.

"It seems that the lane to the Wellman house was a loop that swung off the nearby county road," Carlson wrote. "This loop came by the house and then led back to the county gravel. Its length didn't exceed 200 yards.

"During the evening of a late September day in 1922, the family was in the kitchen. They heard the distinct sound of a galloping horse turn off into the lane. This was not an unusual thing since horses were still used by some of the local farmers at the time, and many rode them for recreational or utilitarian purposes. By the time Mr. Wellman got to the front door, the horse and rider had traveled the length of their lane and was once again on the gravel, still galloping at full tilt."

The Wellmans chalked it up to neighbor boys having fun, but it happened several more times and began to become a frequent late-night event. In the meantime, Wellman was near the door when the rider came by one night and, despite the darkness, noticed that the clothing, saddle, and rigging "were all of a style common to much farther west."

"Be the man a farmboy or a cowboy, whichever, he didn't stop," Carlson wrote. "He rushed past Mr. Wellman, almost knocking him down."

Angered by the man's trespassing, Wellman decided to wait up for the rider each evening and put a stop to it. After about four nights, he was just about ready to give up when he heard the hoofbeats again.

"Mr. Wellman had planned to only yell to the man to stop him," Carlson wrote. "His anger got the best of him, though. He grabbed the nearest thing he could and took a swing at the rider. This turned out to be a stout garden rake leaning on the porch railing. The teeth of that rake caught on the rigging, and it was jerked out of his hands. He connected well enough, however, to tear something loose. That fact was momentarily lost to Mr. Wellman, for the horse and rider went straight up in the air and disappeared. Now an errant rider who disturbed a perfectly law-abiding farmer was one thing, but one who could disappear right up in the air was something else."

When a very shaken Wellman went into the house to try to explain the crazy episode to his wife, he was comforted by the fact that she had seen the whole event from the window. The next morning, Wellman checked the lane where he had accosted the rider.

"There were those hoofprints leading to the front of the house and then disappeared just where he had seen the pair rise up in the air," he wrote. "And off to the side lay his rake. Entangled in its tines was an old-fashioned spur. It was heavily inlaid with silver and of a style that was later to be determined to have been from a period long before 1922 and from either the southwestern part of the U.S. or from Mexico."

Carlson still hasn't figured that one out.

"Who was the cowboy, and why was he here near Saint Louis?" he asked. "If he was real, how did he disappear up in the air? If he wasn't, why was he wearing a very real spur? No one knows."

Did Wild Horses Drag Him Away?

The Manchester area has its share of creepy road legends, including the origins of Wild Horse Creek Road.

Back when she was a senior at Maryville College in 1964, Lucie Clara Huger compiled an assortment of fascinating legends from area residents. Those legends are reprinted in *St. Albans: History and Folklore of a Missouri River Town,* written by Lucie's mother, Lucie Furstenberg Huger.

Dr. William Small told the legend to the younger Lucie:

"In the early, early days of Wild Horse Creek, here before it was called Wild Horse Creek, there were some settlers living around the town of Centaur," Huger wrote. "And Johann Kuschwanz was a sort of eccentric old bachelor who lived there. And people were always having trouble with a white horse that he had, a great big white horse. He'd roam around and get in the gardens and paw up their vegetables, and so forth. And they were always after him to keep the horse bottled up, and he never would do it."

Then, one night, there was a fierce electrical storm.

"The lightning crashed, and the winds blew, and the rain came down, and there was a clattering of hoofs. And those who were up that late looked up in the flash of the lightning, and they saw Johann Kuschwanz seated backwards on his horse, facing the rear, clattering off down the creek. And that is the last that they ever saw of him. The horse and he all disappeared, and that's why they call it Wild Horse Creek."

Juanita McKee, a lifelong Manchester resident and member of the Old Trails Historical Society, recalled another "spooky" experience on Wild Horse Creek Road.

"My mother grew up in Gumbo," McKee said. "I always loved this story because it's Wild Horse Creek.

"She was on a wagon, and the horses got spooked, and she didn't have the reins," she said. "Well, they took off down Wild Horse Creek Road. She came to a bridge, wrapped her skirt around her, and dove off. One of her brothers started walking down after her—it was very dark. It was about four o'clock in the morning. They were going to market."

McKee also recalled a legend concerning an old bridge along Manchester Road. She heard the story from her grandmother, Catherine Seibert.

"Many years ago, when Manchester Road was not much more than a dirt road, there was a little bridge near Dietrich Road," McKee said. "If you had a horse and wagon, or whatever, just riding a horse, if you got to that bridge at exactly midnight, the horse would rear up, and he couldn't cross the bridge until I don't know how long after. And then it was okay."

Final Resting Place: Hopp Hollow Road

A creepy variation on the vanishing hitchhiker theme is the story of Alton's Hopp Hollow Road. Troy Taylor, author of a number of books about ghosts, has driven the road regularly as host of the History & Hauntings Tours of Alton.

"Hopp Hollow Road was the old dirt road that used to go from down near the old prison up to the Rozier Street burial ground," Taylor said. "The Rozier Street burial ground is where Confederate soldiers who died at the prison before the [smallpox] epidemic, and a few after it began, were buried.

"The story was that their bodies were taken on a wagon up Hopp Hollow Road, and they were buried up there. Some of the Union soldiers who were in charge of the burial detail sometimes didn't feel like going all the way up and digging an unmarked grave in this field, so occasionally they would take one of the bodies off and dump it either in a ditch or in the bushes or in the trees off Hopp Hollow Road, just leave the bodies to rot out there."

These neglected Confederate soldiers are said to haunt Hopp Hollow Road. Observers have reported apparitions walking along the roadway or standing at the edge of the woods, Taylor said.

"This old guy told me, back in the '40s and '50s, if you were driving up Hopp Hollow Road one night and you happened to see somebody standing by the side of the road trying to flag you down, that you should never stop," he said. "It might be one of those Confederate ghosts now, trying to get a ride up the road to the Rozier Street burial ground.

"This old-timer, so to speak, literally told me this story, so I always tell it on the tours."

Whether the product of an overactive imagination or a legend come to life, one of Taylor's tours took a bone-chilling turn while driving along the wooded road not long ago.

"As we take the trolley down through Hopp Hollow now—it's not the original road, but it's down through that area—it's always dark, trees overhanging," he said. "Sonny [the driver] always turns off the lights of the trolley; we always drive real slow through there. I always tell the story in a real low voice, because people always have to listen harder if you talk quiet. As I'm going along telling this story, talking about the people hitching a ride, one night we're on the tour, and all of a sudden these two women begin *screaming*, which of course scared everyone on the trolley. They said that they saw someone standing up there on the side of the road.

"I didn't see anything. Whether they did, I have no idea. But I'll tell you what, it scared everybody to death, and it made a story for every future tour."

Is Jean Lafitte at Hopp Hollow?

There's also a legend that the famous French pirate, Jean Lafitte, also haunts the area because his treasure is buried somewhere along Hopp Hollow Road.

"The story is that Benjamin Godfrey [the founder of Alton] became friends with Jean Lafitte, who was, of course, the scourge of the Caribbean around New Orleans back in the early 1800s, fought in the battle of New Orleans under Andrew Jackson," Taylor said. "After Lafitte retired, so to speak, from piracy, he moved north and ended up in St. Louis and Alton, where he had this friend and went into business.

"He brought with him some of his treasure, and some of that treasure was buried out along Hopp Hollow Road. Pirate lore always says that when the pirates die, and their treasure has been undiscovered, their ghosts will remain behind and guard over it."

Taylor, however, doesn't buy the story.

"It's not my favorite, because I don't believe it at all," Taylor said. "Here's why: I've always had a lifelong interest in pirates, and I've read a lot, and I don't think Lafitte ever came up this far. I think he ended up over in Galveston, and that was the end of it.

"The other problem is, when we do our tours, most people don't know who Jean Lafitte is, anyway."

[Haunting Hospitality]

Somewhere between the here and the hereafter, perhaps there is some sort of etherspace superhighway—with billboards, of course.

If so, the signs must read: "Century-Old Theatre, Distinguished Productions—Ghost Wanted—Next Right," or "Grand Historic Hotel—Stop In for a Swim."

Like the rest of us, the phenomena we call ghosts seem to be attracted to the entertainment and hospitality industries like moths to a light bulb, and that only makes sense. After all, everyone loves the thrill of a great performance and the amenities that an away-from-home stay can provide. Especially if you're not sure where your home is anymore.

The Chase: Who Is the Red-Haired Lady in White?

If you read the original *Spirits of St. Louis*, you were told that the legend of the red-haired ghost in the Chase Park Plaza Hotel is not true. Since then, we've learned there really are ghosts. Ron Elz, a.k.a. local radio personality and trivia expert Johnny Rabbitt, said he denied the ghost legend then because the former owners of the hotel didn't like discussing the subject.

Since then the management has changed, the lavishly renovated Inn at the Chase Park Plaza has reopened, and it seems there are two ghost stories, not just one.

The first, of course, is the story about the fabulous red-haired lady in the white dress.

"She has been reported to have been seen walking around on the third floor, and the story goes that she threw herself to her death on her wedding night sometime in the 1930s," noted Jeanne Venn, concierge and night manager at the Chase.

In fact, one employee once was so startled by her, he fell and broke his leg, Venn said.

"It's been a long time since she's been reported to be seen, not since the hotel opened again," she added. "Whether the construction scared her away, she hasn't been around."

Overlooking Forest Park, the eleven-story Chase Hotel was designed by architect Preston J. Bradshaw and built by Chase Ulman in 1922. The red brick building with terra cotta trim was one of the most expensive hotel constructions of its time. Its partner, the twenty-nine-story Park Plaza, was completed in 1929 and featured a two-story lobby designed as an exact replica of the lobby of the Savoy Plaza Hotel in New York. Developer Sam Koplar used to walk the corridors at night during construction, to insure its quality. It was heralded as one of the "most nearly perfect hotels ever built" and served as a template for future hotel designs.

Together the buildings featured nearly 1,600 hotel rooms in the '30s and '40s, and the Park Plaza was eventually converted to apartments due to declining demand. In 1956 the two merged, with grand lobbies connecting the two buildings, and the same year the famed Khorassan Room was built. He received national attention in architectural publications and became a favorite gathering place for celebrities, royalty, and presidents.

In the late 1990s a group of investors launched a $95 million overhaul, including new wiring, heating, air conditioning, and water systems. The grand new hotel now features a movie theatre, three restaurants and two lounges, and apartments and penthouses.

There's also another ghost, a tuxedoed chap believed to be that of the hotel's namesake and builder, Chase Ulman. Ulman, who died at the nearby Chester Apartments, was said to have been seen frequently during recent construction work.

Observers have reported seeing the ghost more frequently at night, when there is less traffic at the hotel, and the curious spirit also has been spotted peeking out the hotel's windows. Gene Scheck, a former director of security for the hotel who now serves as door captain, said he has seen the man, although he doesn't necessarily believe in ghosts.

"I'm the type of person, I believe in them when I see them," he noted.

About five years ago, before renovations, Scheck spotted a distinguished, middle-aged gentleman in a black tuxedo. Hearing a door slam, he looked around and "saw someone behind me, walking about that high off the floor," he said, motioning below his waist.

The man also has been seen on the Park Plaza side of the hotel complex, Scheck said.

"I used to have to go over to the other building and patrol, make sure there were no street people who had gotten in," he said. "It was dark enough that you couldn't see your hand in front of your face in some of these rooms."

But he did see the tuxedoed gentleman, who continued his stroll and walked right through one of the massive pillars in the Park Plaza lobby.

"We believe it's the same stately-looking gentleman over there," Scheck said.

Ghost at Ruebel Prefers River Views

Farther up the Mississippi River, in the historic town of Grafton, Illinois, is the historic Ruebel Hotel, established in 1884 to serve river traffic. Located along the Great River Road at 217 East Main Street, the Ruebel was destined for the wrecking ball when Sandy and Jeff Lorton and their family bought it in 1996.

The Lortons invested nearly a year of work restoring the hotel and its elegant wood stairs, doors, and trim and adding fine period furnishings. They opened the hotel on April Fools' Day 1997.

"Really, it should have had a wrecking ball to it," Sandy Lorton recalled. "Anywhere you stood on the main floor, you could see the sky. It's something that we saved that I'm sure was going to be knocked down. We kept it original as we could. We've got bathrooms in all the rooms, where [formerly] they only had one down the hallway.

"We have twenty-two rooms here, a bar and restaurant," she added. "They're all decorated a little bit differently, all named after something to do with the history of Grafton. They're mostly boat, tree, and bird rooms, like the Blue Heron Room, the Dogwood Room, the Marsh Room—he was the first mayor of Grafton."

The Ruebel also has, some believe, a ghost, if guests and a cleaning lady can be believed.

"Shortly after we opened, three women stayed here who were from Peoria," Lorton said. "It was like the first or second night. As they were going up the stairs, they turned around and looked at me and wondered if the place was haunted.

"And I said, 'Well, I guess, if you want it to be,' so they went to room eleven, and all night long they saw 'Abigail' running around in their room," she said. "That's what they called her.

"Other people who have stayed here have said they felt something,"

Lorton added. "My cleaning lady we first had, she always felt like there was somebody following her all the time upstairs."

But Lorton doesn't believe it.

"No, I don't," she said and laughed. "I think it's an old building, and I think you're going to hear the noises, creaks, and cracks."

A Little Dip, Chief Pontiac?

St. Louis has other hotel ghosts as well, some of whom are inclined to water sports. For example, it is said that the spirit of Chief Pontiac haunts the pool and lower level of the Regal Riverfront Hotel, 200 South Fourth Street, downtown.

Pontiac, chief of the Ottawa Indians, was enraged by the transfer of power to the British in the area known as "French Louisiana." He led an ambush of British soldiers during the French and Indian War and was murdered at Cahokia in 1769. This led to a bloody war between the Ottawa Indians and the Illinois tribes, Charles van Ravenswaay noted in *Saint Louis: An Informal History of the City and Its People, 1764-1865.*

"In 1769 Chief Pontiac sought refuge in St. Louis with his old friend, St. Ange (French Capt. Louis St. Ange de Bellerive)," van Ravenswaay wrote. "Even then, seduced by drink and defeated by the failure of his great plan to overthrow the British, Pontiac was an impressive figure. Shortly after his arrival, he decided to pay a visit to some Cahokia friends.

"At Cahokia he feasted and drank too heavily. That night, while he was reeling about the woods near the village, a Kaskaskia Indian, bribed by an English trader, crushed Pontiac's skull with a war club. The murdered chief's body was brought to St. Louis and buried with honors on the hill above the village (later Fourth and Walnut streets)."

The Medinah Temple, 3541 Olive Street, is said to have a female ghost in its swimming pool. This four-story red brick structure, with terra cotta face, parapets, and finials, was built in 1909 for the Knights of Columbus. It formerly was a union hall for the International Brotherhood of Electrical Workers and now serves as a Masonic temple.

St. Louis Union Station is rumored to be chock-full of wandering spirits, and at least one employee of the grand railroad-station-turned-shopping-plaza has reported seeing a mysterious man in a tuxedo in its corridors at very odd times.

The identity of the ghost would be anyone's guess, because the beautiful Romanesque-style building has served as a stopping-off place for millions of busy travelers through the years. It was designed by architect

Theodore Link and completed in 1894.

The station also is built over a portion of what was known as Chouteau's Pond, a man-made mill pond dammed from a stream by Joseph Taillon in the late 1700s. For years the picturesque pond served as a recreational attraction, a trysting spot for lovers, and a favorite place for housewives to do their laundry, Norbury Wayman noted in *St. Louis Union Station and Its Railroads*. As time went on, however, a number of industries also settled around the river, and the pond was blamed as a source of St. Louis' great cholera epidemic. It was drained forever in 1850 and 1851.

Strange Flying Objects at Webster Groves Theatre Guild

The old frame building that houses the Webster Groves Theatre Guild, 517 Theatre Lane, is known for more than fine performances. The building is believed to be haunted as well, though by what no one is sure.

"We did a little bit of history on the building, and I think it was built in 1927," said Linda Spall, a member of the theatre guild who teaches children's theatre. "At the time, Webster wasn't quite as built-up, at least in this particular area. The person who lived here at one point was the first president of Eden Seminary. I don't think he died here. He sold it and moved. Then his kids owned it and rented it out."

The theatre guild purchased the building in 1951, and at least since then no one has died there, Spall said.

"When I first came here, I was like twenty, and it was 1972 or so," she said. "The officers would love to thrill me with scary stories. They always said that it was haunted. The director, he would sit after rehearsals and tell me horrible tales—just kidding around, of course."

She chuckled. "I'm sure that's why I'm emotionally scarred today.

"It's an older building, and there are drafts that go through. It's not well insulated up on the stage area, so there's birds that get in there," Spall added. "It's always the one corner of the building that gives me the big creeps."

That corner includes the men's dressing room and the stairwell, she said.

"When I talk to other people, everyone feels the same thing in that corner," Spall said. "It's not just me."

One time, a lid from the building's trash can flew off, as if someone had propelled it like a Frisbee, and it sailed along the side of the wall.

"I put the trash can lid on the trash can, and I walked across the lobby," she said. "I'd say it was fifteen minutes later, and that thing just shot across and hit the wall—and it was a good four, five feet from the wall. I shot out of here so fast! Took me like five minutes to get my nerve to come in. It was so out of the blue. And I'm fifty years old; I'm not a baby about this stuff."

Strange sounds can be heard from a back dressing room and the stairwell, she said. And then there was that incident with the plaster cherub a couple of years ago...

"This one the president of the theatre guild can vouch for," Spall said. "They were doing a play, and some guy spent a whole bunch of money on a set—it's his own play, so he really wants it done well. He spends money on a Victorian-type set. One of the things he bought was a plaster cherub that he placed over the set.

"They said the thing didn't just fall, it shot off the wall. They said it was just freaky, because it was up there very well, and how could it have done that? There were actors on stage, and it didn't just fall, it didn't just drop down, it like projectile-dropped."

Fortunately, no one was hurt, she said, "just scared."

Grandel's Ghosts

Today it is a gracious showcase for the St. Louis Black Repertory Company, the St. Louis Shakespeare Company, and the Grandel Theatre Cabaret. But the Grandel Theatre, 3610 Grandel Square, in midtown, wasn't a theatre at all when it was built in 1884.

Designed by Lewis Rice, of Boston, in the Romanesque Revival style, the building began life as a Congregational church and at one point became the Union Methodist Episcopal Church. Somewhere along the line, one of the ministers who served the church lived in the bell tower, and it is his ghost that is believed to haunt the place, Ron Elz said.

The minister's home in the bell tower was left abandoned for years because people came away with a creepy feeling when they went up there, noted Merrell Wiegraffe, facilities manager for Grand Center Redevelopment Company, the owner of the Grandel. It's still unused, although the rest of the building—with its intricately carved newel posts and handsome wood trusses—is most inviting.

Raymond Jones is a believer. Jones, who is in charge of housekeeping at the Grandel, has heard some strange things in the building when no one else is there. That includes toilets flushing by themselves, doors slamming, and footsteps on the stairs. A visitor to the building also heard the piano play on its own.

Lyn/Sun: Teutonic Spirits?

For years a poor stepchild to the big theatres on Grand Boulevard, the Sun Theatre still is empty at 3627 Grandel Square. The Victoria, as it was originally called, was built for the German Theatre Society in 1913 and featured German-language plays such as Goethe's *Faust*, its first production.

However, the theatre had a limited customer range, and when America entered World War I in 1917, it was considered unpatriotic to embrace anything German. Since then, the theatre has gone through a number of incarnations, including the Liberty, the World, the Lyn and the Sun, noted Mary Bagley, author of *The Front Row: Missouri's Grand Theatres*.

But is it empty? Visitors to the theatre have heard the low but distinct sounds of someone murmuring in German, Elz noted. And Wiegraffe has reported hearing inexplicable noises such as banging sounds from the theatre's parking lot.

Kiel Opera House: Is It Chase?

Wiegraffe formerly served as operations manager for Kiel Opera House downtown, and during that time a number of his employees reported seeing a gentleman in tux and tails walking around. Does the ghost of Chase Ulman haunt two places at once, or has some other glamorous visitor decided to take up permanent residence?

According to Bagley, Kiel Auditorium opened at 1400 Market Street on April 14, 1934. The Opera House, which backs up to the auditorium, is one of its five public assembly rooms. Spectacularly outfitted in art deco style, the Opera House retains its elegant, timeless appearance. It, too, is empty right now, with an uncertain future.

Don't Talk To The Motorman

Elz has one last legend, this one concerning the old Garavelli's Restaurant at the northwest corner of DeBaliviere and DeGiverville. The ghost of owner Joe Garavelli was said to haunt it. Garavelli, the story went, used to appear behind the restaurant's steam table, right underneath a sign that read, "Don't Talk To The Motorman."

11 [CIVIL WAR CHILLS]

It was a brutal war that divided individual families as well as the country, and it subjected countless young men to miserable and extreme conditions. Even the food was a challenge.

On the other hand, Civil War–inspired advances in medicine have remained with us to this day, noted George Wunderlich, a former St. Louisan who now serves as director of education for the National Museum of Civil War Medicine in Frederick, Maryland.

"During the course of the Civil War, they developed the first-ever specialty hospital system; for instance, there was a maxillofacial hospital in Georgia that did nothing but tend to facial wounds to the jaw and upper palate," Wunderlich said. "The first neurology hospital in the world was in Philadelphia. Nobody had ever had specialty hospitals before.

"The first use of triage as a system for evaluating patients was developed by Dr. Jonathan Letterman, a Union army major," Wunderlich added. "We never had triage before that. Unfortunately, pharmacology was not something that advanced much during the Civil War. They were still using some pretty deadly poisons to try and treat things, but for the most part medicine probably moved forward fifty years during those four years, and we [the museum] represent that."

Today, thousands take to the battlefields on weekends for living history demonstrations and Civil War reenactments.

"It's a fantasy of mine come to reality, because I always was fascinated with that time period," said Erline Leady, of Alton, who attends reenactments with her husband, Henry. "It seems like it's a part of history some people don't know even happened. I'm proud to be a reenactor, to educate the people and tell them what happened back then."

Doug Harding, of St. Louis, who during the week serves as a park ranger for the National Park Service, agreed.

"If you think about a battle from the nineteenth century, look how much emotion, how much energy you burn off," Harding said. "Charging across the field, trying to get to the other end in one piece...we try to recreate part of that for ourselves, try to see what it's like. You can imagine, what kind of mindset would keep someone standing there when the guy next to him just got killed? Or a cannonball takes the head off one of your officers?

"In a way, you're kind of honoring them, because then you can tell people how it was, drawing from our own experience, putting ourselves in their shoes. I've got chipped teeth from the hardtack."

Given such emotion-packed experiences, perhaps it's not unusual that many people—especially reenactors—pick up on that long-forgotten "energy." Some feel cold spots or hear noises. Others see apparitions.

"Science has shown that our brains create electrical currents," Harding said. "If one believes that a person has a soul, our soul might be that energy. Energy cannot be made or destroyed; it just passes from one form to another.

"As reenactors, we're putting ourselves in the same environment, sometimes with the same mindsets," he said. "I think we're putting ourselves in a position to bump into [strange phenomena] more often than most people. Everyone has psychic ability. Most people don't know it."

Pea Ridge Battlefield

One strange event happened while Harding was attending a living history weekend at Pea Ridge Battlefield, Arkansas National Park. After arriving one Friday night, Harding and his friends decided to chew the fat on the porch of an old tavern in the park, used as a hotel and way station during the war. The original tavern had been burned by guerrillas in the 1860s and was rebuilt after the Civil War.

"The moment I stepped onto the porch, there was a definite change in temperature; it was like going into a cold spot," Harding recalled. "And the rocking chair was rocking very slowly. And the guy right behind me steps up on the porch, and he freezes. And the third one steps up on the porch.

"I looked up and said, 'It's the rocking chair, right?' 'Yeah.' So I said, 'OK, I'm going to check this out.' I was about three steps away from the rocking chair, trying to see if I could feel anything there. Just about that time, the fourth person stepped onto the porch, the temperature went back to normal, and the rocking chair stopped.

"Well, we found out that the rocking chair wasn't old—it belonged to another reenactor who had just bought it from the store. He had just assembled it for his wife, who was going to sit on the porch in costume and tell stories about the battle and what it was like."

Others have witnessed more than that, Harding added.

"One [acquaintance] said he saw a white pair of legs walking across the field," he said, and laughed. "Just the legs."

Comforting Handclasp at Confederate Prison

Leady, who works at a Target store, had an encounter with the beyond several years ago while showing a friend the old Confederate prison ruins, now a memorial, in Alton.

"I made the comment of how tragic the Civil War was and that it should never have happened because it was family members fighting each other," she said. "I was standing there, and the next thing I knew, it was like somebody picked up my hand, raised it, patted it, then put it back by my side in agreement with what I had said. It did freak me out, because I kept saying, 'Did you see that?'"

The friend didn't.

Mysterious Soldier at Pilot Knob

Leady said she has heard many stories from the battlefield in Pilot Knob.

"I've heard Pilot Knob is really haunted," she said. "A friend, Mike, was telling me that he was sitting on the fort...and he saw this soldier in full gear, and he knew that it was a ghost because it wasn't making a sound. When you hear these guys when they have their canteens and all their stuff on, you can hear them clinking. And he said there was not one sound, nothing."

Was that the same ghost Wunderlich observed during a 1980 reenactment?

"That particular year, the state changed the way they were doing the event, and we had to leave all the artillery in the fort, even though we were camped outside of the fort," Wunderlich recalled. "What they decided to do was run a twenty-four-hour guard from the artillery units down there and just walk the parapets and make sure that the cannons weren't touched.

"I was elected corporal of the guard to run the shift from basically two o'clock until six o'clock in the morning on Saturday," he said. "There were three guys who were actually walking the shift. All I had to do was, every half hour [I'd] go out and make sure that if they had to go to the bathroom, someone would relieve them, that they hadn't fallen asleep, things like that."

The third or fourth time Wunderlich went around, he noticed a fourth man clear on the other side of the fort.

"'He must be from one of the infantry units,' was my first thought, because we're all artillerists; we don't have muskets," Wunderlich said. "We're just there making sure nobody fools with the gun.

"I got to within about twenty feet of him—he looked right at me and disappeared," he said. "It was dark, but he definitely had a musket on his shoulder, and he was dressed in dark clothing, which would be commensurate with a Union soldier. The fort has grown up with trees over the years—you're in a pretty secluded place, and there's just not a lot of light that gets down there unless it's moonlit. It was kind of an overcast sky."

Ghostly Goings-on in Grubville

The old homestead of Frank Frost, the first postmaster at Grubville, Missouri, in 1853, was full of unexplained goings-on in the 1930s, noted Jefferson County historian Della Lang in her book *Witchcraft, Wickedness, And Other Wacky Happenings In Jefferson County History*.

Frost had died in 1904. Family members living there in the 1930s had told stories of the bed moving around the room in the middle of the night and chains being dragged up the stairs. A ghost, and a Civil War ghost at that, was thought to be the culprit.

"Frost was a known Democrat and probably sympathized with the South," Lang wrote. "During the war, some Union soldiers once stopped at the house and shot all of Mr. Frost's chickens. In the course of the shooting spree, some bullets became embedded in a cottonwood tree on the property. Many years later, one of Mr. Frost's great-grandsons spent a lot of his spare time digging the old bullets out of the tree. That seems to be about the time the unexplained visitor first made its presence known."

Was it the ghost of a Union soldier coming back to haunt the Frost relatives, as descendant Gladys Lee Castleberry maintained?

"The house is gone now," Lang wrote. "It has been replaced by a new brick home, and we can only assume that the restless ghost who haunted the family at midnight is finally at peace."

Hazel Dell: Victorian Retreat for Confederate Major

He was appointed lieutenant colonel of the Sixty-third Tennessee Regiment by Gen. Robert E. Lee and was badly wounded at the Battle of Chickamauga.

But a coal-black stallion named Great Britain saved Col. William H. Fulkerson's life by returning him safely to his hometown of Rogersville, Tennessee.

And when Fulkerson retired from battle, he and his wife, Cornelia, settled into a beautiful fourteen-room, southern-style Victorian mansion built for them just outside Jerseyville, Illinois, in 1866. Their farm, Hazel Dell, became home to the Fulkersons' five children; a large herd of registered shorthorn cattle; 200 horses, including the beloved Great Britain, who is buried under the buckeye trees at the estate; and many visitors, including "cowboy artist" Charles M. Russell and outlaws Jesse and Frank James.

The beautiful mansion at 1510 North State Street is now known as the Col. William H. Fulkerson Mansion and Farm Museum and is listed on the National Register of Historic Places. Tours are available, and the farm is the site of the annual Jersey County Victorian Festival, held each Labor Day weekend.

Owners Brenda and Larry Nolan purchased the home from Fulkerson's grandson, Will, who is in his nineties. Until recently, Will would help give tours of the mansion and provide fascinating details of life in the mansion. For instance, his father, Frank, recalled secretly taking supplies to the Jesse James gang, which was encamped nearby. And many of the home's original furnishings and artifacts remain, making for an endless supply of stories about the home.

In recent years, tales have sprouted of ghostly events at the mansion, such as chains dragging and the ghost of Great Britain galloping around. Many stories were spread by a family who had planned to buy the estate and operated a restaurant in the home for about three years. The family operates a well-known restaurant in St. Louis, Brenda Nolan said.

"The family started to buy [Hazel Dell] on contract, and they couldn't go through with it," she said. "They started some stories, and they had 'hell at Hazel Dell,' and they had a haunted basement—they dug out some of the basement—and they would truck young people in from St. Louis, trying to make this like what they have there, caverns or whatever. That's when a lot of the stories started.

"Now there's a lot of people who are really afraid of this house," she added. "And that's okay with me. But all I can say is, we have a very good, warm feeling being in this house. I do believe that there's spirits, but I think they are friendly spirits."

Nolan's daughter, Jenny, once heard a distinct knock at her door when everyone else was asleep, and there are the standard noises of footsteps and doors opening and closing, which Brenda chalks up to normal old-house noises.

Not so easy to explain is an experience that happened while the Nolans were still restoring the home and were sleeping in a hideaway bed in the south parlor on the first floor. Another room nearby used to be the servants' room and was opened up and made into two bathrooms during the time the home was used as a restaurant.

"This was the maid's room, and the only way she could exit was directly into the kitchen area here," Nolan said. "We always keep the hall light on here, and of course the rooms are dark in the night. So we have a light here. My daughter's bedroom is upstairs.

"My daughter, who was just seventeen at the time, had a cold, and I'd given her some medicine before she went to bed. It was about ten-thirty, and we went to bed on the hide-a-bed, and my husband was starting to snore. I hadn't been asleep. A lot of times you're half awake, half asleep, and you aren't quite sure what you've seen.

"Anyway, I heard a noise, and I looked across, and I saw this figure come out of the bathroom into the light...I thought, 'Well, Jenny's upstairs, she's down getting some medicine.' So I get up right away, I go through the hallway, look up the stairs as I'm going through. She's not going up there, so I think, 'Well, she's in the kitchen.'"

She wasn't.

"I go through, and there's a chill as I go through. Just a real chill—funny. I come right back out, go upstairs. Jenny's fast asleep. She hasn't been up.

"It was a young girl. I just thought Jenny had a white T-shirt on. She had long hair like my Jenny, but she wasn't."

Was the ghostly guest a maid whose tribulations with an alcohol-abusing husband led to tragedy long ago?

"We know a little bit about one of the servants, and that was a young woman who stayed here. Her husband was abusive as far as alcohol, and so forth," Nolan noted. "He would come out, and he would knock on the door, and Frank—Mr. Fulkerson—would say, 'I will ask if she wants to see you or not.' And he would ask her, and she would say 'yes' or 'no.'

"So on this one occasion he came out, cut the telephone wires coming into the house, and came to the door. He was going to see her whether she wanted to see him or not—and she did not want to see him. Mr. Fulkerson talked to him, the story goes, and told him he was going to have to change his ways and gave him the old sermon. And he went out, put the gun to his head, and killed himself out there."

Whatever the identity of the mysterious figure, Nolan said, there was no mistaking the experience.

"I do know I saw a figure coming out of the darkness into the light, and I had that real uncanny chill, and I wasn't even thinking about anything like this," she said.

Ring My Bell?

Robin Groppel, a Jerseyville resident who cleans a doctor's office next door to Hazel Dell, wonders if one of the mansion's spirits paid a visit to her in May 1991.

"I was cleaning the doctor's office one morning when my children were little, about four in the morning, and was thinking about how nice it was to have a little time to myself," Groppel recalled. "The office has a small bell like you hang on the end of a fishing pole so that patients can ring it if they need anything.

"While I was cleaning, I heard that bell start ringing just like someone had picked it up and stood there shaking it. I was in the next room and in a position to see the bell, but it wasn't moving. I first thought, 'Oh, my God, there is someone in here with me,' but I searched the whole building and never did find an answer to why that bell rang.

"I can honestly say it scared the hell out of me, and the hair on the back of my neck stood up, but I kept cleaning because I figured it wasn't going to hurt me, whatever it was," she added. "I still get an eerie feeling when I clean out there, but I figure it's friendly and just ignore the little sounds I hear."

12 [MUSIC AND MAYHEM]

He started his illustrious musical career playing the windowsill of his family's West End apartment and went on to make seventy-seven appearances on the *Tonight Show* alone.

"I wanted to learn to play the piano, and when my folks had the radio going I'd walk up to the windowsill and play right along with it," concert theatre organist Stan Kann noted with a smile, "until one day I did it on a freshly painted windowsill and almost got killed."

The American Theatre Organ Society hall-of-famer and veteran vacuum cleaner collector is a dyed-in-the-wool St. Louisan, home again after more than twenty years living in the Los Angeles area. The delightfully eccentric Kann now lives in the Holly Hills neighborhood and enjoys a schedule that is as busy as ever, playing at such venues as the "Fabulous Fox," the Bevo Mill, the Jug in Belleville, and special performances all over the nation.

And, like many others, Kann has had some strange experiences over the years that he simply can't explain.

A Distinguished Childhood

At the age of nine, Kann recalled, he was playing piano for real.

"At that time, we belonged to Temple Israel, which was right on the corner of Kingshighway and Washington," Kann said. "There were three churches there—they're still there—it's called the "holy corner." Second Baptist was on one side, St. John's Methodist on the south of Washington, Temple Israel on the north side. The organist at that time used to let me come up into the organ loft and watch her play...I was just fascinated. My folks thought I was nutty. They said, 'Where are you going to learn to play an organ?'"

By age fourteen he had done just that and took classes from Arthur Lieber, an organist at Second Baptist Church, and Howard Kelsey, head of organ studies at Washington University.

"I'd practice sometimes at the church, sometimes at the chapel, and sometimes at Berger Memorial, which was a funeral home around the corner on McPherson. Someone said, 'You practiced in a funeral home?' I said, 'No one ever left.'"

He laughed. "I'd walk over there from Soldan, where I graduated in 1944."

Vacuum Cleaner Collector

Kann also had another love: vacuum cleaners.

"I was always crazy about them," he said. "We didn't have one, but our neighbors did. I hated to eat dinner, hated to eat this, hated to eat that. One of our neighbors had an old Ohio vacuum cleaner. If I would eat my dinner, she'd bring the Ohio over, set it in the dining room, and I'd get to turn it on. If I didn't eat, she would take it home.

"I liked the sound, I liked the bag, I liked everything about them," he chuckled. "I began going around the neighborhood, and I'd walk down the street and hear somebody running a vacuum, and I'd walk up to the door and ask, 'Can I come in and watch you run your vacuum cleaner?' Sometimes they'd let me, sometimes they wouldn't let me. But pretty soon, by ear I could tell what kind they were using. Hoover didn't sound a thing like a Eureka, General Electric didn't sound like a Hamilton Beach—everything had its own sound."

Kann, now professor emeritus of the vacuum cleaner collectors' club he belongs to, said they just don't make 'em like that anymore.

"The new ones, unfortunately, the same thing that's happened to the vacuum cleaners has happened to the cars—they all look alike. Now you don't know whether that's a Eureka or a Dirt Devil or.... They sound alike, too. All made of plastic, and they sound alike, and they work alike.

"We have a big, look-alike, plastic society."

The Fabulous Fox

After a stint in New York, where he heard his first theatre organ, Kann returned to St. Louis and in 1950 discovered the Fox Theatre had one of the largest theatre organs in the country. He asked the management if he and a few friends could try to get the organ to play—it had sat silent since

1937—and was able to coax enough out of it that the management decided to hire a professional organ company to work on it.

So Kann, who was playing for a number of churches at the time, also became the Fox's organist. Even while in California, he returned several times to play for major affairs, including the theatre's grand opening in 1982.

"When I moved back, Mary Strauss, who was now the owner of the theatre, said, 'Stan, you've got to come back,'" said Kann, who also gives special tours of the organ at the theatre. "When this place was built, it was the second largest theatre in the world, not just this country. The larger theatre than the Fox was the Roxy Theatre in New York, built in the 1920s, and that was superseded by the Radio City Music Hall in New York, which opened in 1934. Our Wurlitzer organ was one of the largest Wurlitzers ever made—the original Wurlitzer in its original building—restored exactly as it was in 1929.

"People today tell me they used to come and see [shows] because they wanted to hear the organ," he added. "They didn't care what the picture was. They just wanted to come hear the organ.

"See, the theatre organ was originally invented in 1915 to accompany silent pictures in all the silent movie houses because that's all they had. The year the Fox Theatre opened, sound came in, and there was no reason to have this big organ, because they were showing sound pictures. So they decided to use it in those days to play between shows, between 1930 and 1937, as people were going in and out of the theatre."

Kann credits Strauss with having the foresight not to let the Fox be torn down.

"It's a palace," he said. "There's detail in that place that you never see unless people point it out to you—reliefs here and ornamental stuff there and the carved elephants and the brass on the balustrades that go up and down the stairway. Right above the stage is this huge elephant's head with the tusks and trunk sticking out over the orchestra pit. Why, they've never seen that before, and they've been coming to the Fox for years.

"Even out in the lobby, they spent $650,000 last summer doing more restoration. They had the whole place recarpeted again and all the carpeting rewoven, just like the 1929 carpeting. And they had all the columns in the lobby remarbleized, had the original painting put back on the ceiling that had come down because of rain, and the ceiling was repaired."

For his part, Kann, in 2001, received the American Guild of Organists' Avis Blewett Award for his work on behalf of the theatre organ.

Hoovers on Hollywood

Kann's Hollywood career began while he was living in a Georgian co-lonial-style home on Washington Terrace and playing on the show of lo-cal celebrity Charlotte Peters.

"One of the major guests was Phyllis Diller," he said. "She and I be-came very close friends. In fact, she stayed a couple of times over on Wash-ington Terrace when she was coming through here to appear someplace. She told the *Tonight Show* about me: 'You've got to see his vacuum clean-ers. You've never seen anything like it in your life.'

"On her say-so, they had me on the *Tonight Show* when it was still in New York," Kann recalled. "I intended it to be a very straight presenta-tion, but it turned into a hilarious thing, and then one show after the other started calling: 'Will you be on our show?' Mike Douglas, Merv Griffin, Dinah Shore, all of that. And that started the whole thing."

On one occasion when *Tonight Show* host Johnny Carson was in town, Kann hosted a special party for him at the request of NBC executives. More than 400 people attended the festivities at the Washington Terrace manse.

Washington Terrace: Strange Noises

Strange noises, as well as celebrities, were common around the house. One night, Kann and his aunt both heard the sound of a huge crash, "like a big oil can hitting the concrete."

"I jumped, she jumped. I said, 'My God, what was that?' She said, 'It sounds like it's coming from the third floor.' I said, 'No, it sounds like it's coming from the basement.' She said, 'No, it's coming from the third floor.' I said, 'No, it's coming from the basement.'"

Kann laughed. "I said, 'Well, I'm not going to look either on the third floor or in the basement; I'm going to call the night watchman.' We had a night watchman who would go up and down Washington Terrace all night long. So I watched for Ray in the car."

Ray, in turn, called the city police, and they all went through the house but could find no explanation for the noise.

Another night, after playing until the wee hours at Ruggeri's Restau-rant, Kann wasn't tired and sat down to practice on his big grand piano in the corner of the living room. All of a sudden, he heard a knock on the window.

"I jumped," he said. "I thought, 'Now who in the world at one o'clock in the morning is knocking on a window?' So I hesitated at first, thought maybe it's something I did with the music. I was playing again, and all of a sudden, just as clear as day, *KNOCK KNOCK*. Got up right away to the front door. The whole front porch went all the way across the front of the house and had balustrades going across. I looked out—not a soul in sight on that porch. I went to the edge and looked around the side of the house—the whole house was lit by spotlight. Came back in, and then something came to me.

"My mother, who had died, she'd always get mad when I was practicing late. She'd say, 'Now go to bed! You need your rest! Go to bed! Go to bed!' I figured she was knocking on the window to tell me to go to bed. It was too late to be playing the piano, I guess. And so I went up and went to bed."

Another time, a friend spent the night at the house in the room that had belonged to Kann's late father and was kept awake all night by what he thought was a tree branch rubbing against the window.

"I said, 'Now come on. First of all, there's no tree near enough that side of the house that a branch could possibly rub. Look out this window. You'll see there's no tree anywhere.' He said, 'What kept scratching on my window all night long?' I thought, 'I haven't the slightest idea.' Nothing had scratched on my side of the house.

"He said, 'I wouldn't sleep in here again if you paid me!'"

Flying Pictures

But the most astounding incident happened in the second-floor reception hall, which could be viewed directly from Kann's second-floor office. After returning from Ruggeri's one evening, Kann was at his desk catching up on paperwork shortly after midnight.

"As you come up the stairs from downstairs, the main stairs came to a landing," Kann said. "The continuation was divided—one side went this way, one side went that way to the second floor. It was open between—you could see down to the first floor.

"In between the balustrades on the second floor, there was a lovely commode with a lamp on it—we kept the light burning all night long in the second-floor hall—and then there were some pictures on that chest.

"I don't know what made me look up at that time, but I looked out into the reception hall toward that table.

"One of the pictures just went right up in the air and came right down on the floor and the glass broke in a bunch of pieces," Kann said, forming an arc shape with his hand. "I couldn't believe what I saw. It was on a solid table; it stood on its own little easel—there's no way it could have fallen off the table unless somebody picked it up and moved it."

Going Batty

Several months later Kann was working in the same spot when he looked up in amazement to see a large bat, with a wingspan of about two feet.

"Just standing still, flapping its wings like that," he said. "He was standing there looking at me, and I'm looking out at him. It startled the hell out of me, and I startled it as much as it me because I jumped, you know. And with that it turned around and swooshed and went to an alcove around the whole reception hall downstairs.

"I called the Humane Society—it's now one in the morning— and I told them, 'There is a bat in this house.'"

A man from the Humane Society went to Kann's house. The worker asked for a stool, stood on it, and shined his flashlight into the alcove, which startled the bat. The bat suddenly flew out, and the man fell backwards off the stool, Kann recalled.

"And with that, my aunt hears the commotion and opens the door in her funny little [nightgown] and says, 'What's going on here?' I said, 'Aunt Cora, we have a bat now.' She said, 'Oh! Oh my God! A bat! In here! My hair!'

"The man said, 'Don't believe that, Madam. They don't get in your hair.' And she said, 'Well, I'm not taking any chances.' I said, 'Go back in your room and close the door.'"

Finally the bat was apprehended and placed in a large bag. It was after 2:30, and Kann's aunt came down the steps and asked the Humane Society worker where the bat was headed.

"He says, 'I'm going to take him over to Forest Park and let him go—we don't kill them,'" Kann recalled. "She said, 'You're going to let him go? He's going to come right back!' He said, 'Madam, how do you expect him to find this house from Forest Park?'

"And my aunt said, 'Well, he found it in the first place, didn't he?' She was absolutely a card."

Haunted Carriage House on Portland Place

From about 1968 until he moved to California in the 1970s, Kann lived in an English Georgian-style home on Portland Place, which featured a carriage house with second-floor apartment. He decided it would be nice to offer the apartment rent-free to someone in exchange for help with snow removal or handyman jobs.

"I don't remember how I found this couple—a man and his wife," Kann said. "He went to Washington University. Really nice couple. They were there a really short time, when one morning he calls me: 'Mr. Kann, we can't stay here.' I said, 'Why?' He said, 'That garage is haunted.'

"I said, 'Now come on. What do you mean, haunted?' It had a place for three cars on the first floor, and I collected old cars. I was in and out of there all the time. I didn't spend any time in the apartment, and the apartment had been redone. It was very contemporary.

"He said, 'We were awakened last night. My wife woke up first, and she was scared to death. She reached over and she punched me. There was a figure standing at the end of our bed; it looked like the figure of a man. And it scared her to death. It stood there for a while looking at us, and then it just dissolved into nowhere.'

"He said, 'We didn't want to say anything to you the first time because we thought you'd think we were crazy. After the second time, we knew we were not crazy. We just cannot stay here in this apartment.'"

Kann, who had never believed in ghosts, later learned there had been a murder in the carriage house some years earlier.

"It scared them enough that they wanted to move," he recalled. "Here they were, living in a beautiful place, didn't cost them a penny, and even at that they wouldn't stay in it."

After many years, Kann still hasn't figured out all these strange experiences.

"I don't know; I really don't know," he said. "We won't know until we pass over—and then what will we do?"

[Reading, Writing, and Wraiths]

When we were young, it seemed we couldn't get out of our grade school building fast enough after that final bell rang and the teacher dismissed us. No one wanted to hang around, and those compelled to stay would find that a mere fifteen minutes later, the big, brick building would become really quiet—almost spooky.

It seems, however, that some spirits—or cosmic vibrations or whatever you want to call them—find it pleasurable to hang around the halls of knowledge or feel compelled to do so. And now, if you'll please concentrate on your book, we have an intriguing lesson today on creepy schoolhouses.

Gardenville Elementary School

Gardenville School made its debut as a one-room schoolhouse in the 6200 block of Gravois Avenue during the Civil War era and progressed to a larger quarters at 6651 Gravois after 1876.

"During the Civil War era, Gravois was part of a trail heading west," Betty Tighe wrote in *Heritage of the Bevo Area, Book Three*. "The land, usually 10–20 acre farms, primarily was used for truck gardens by farmers mostly of German descent—thus the name Gardenville School."

The second building was destroyed in the famous May 27, 1896, tornado, Tighe wrote, and a new building replaced it in 1907 at a cost of $89,276. Two wings were added in 1912 at a cost of $146,285.

"Evelyn Detterman Edwards recalls buying a bowl of hot soup from the baker across from Gardenville for 5 cents, the long walk to the outside john and the picnics at Mueller's Park," Tighe wrote. "Mildred (Koenig) Lucker, a graduate of 1914, remembers Principal Ringling (and her strap) and the kindness of a teacher, Ms. Gallegar, the recess games of hop scotch, tag and jump rope. She was one of the fortunate ones who was given a nickel by her father to ride the streetcar to school in bad weather. She lived at Morganford and Bates—a long walk to Gardenville."

Designed by famed architect William B. Ittner, the imposing South Side landmark was closed as a school in 1980, but remained open as a community center and post office in an agreement between the St. Louis Board of Education and the community.

"I was up there on a Sunday afternoon one time, doing some work upstairs with a friend of mine, and I heard footsteps down in the hallway, so I went down to see who it was, and there was nobody there," recalled Bob Hughes, who has served as executive director of the Gardenville Community Center for the last thirteen years. "So I went back up, proceeded with what I was doing, and all of a sudden you can hear the footsteps again.

"So I went down, checked all the doors, and everything was locked, and there was nobody in the building," he said and smiled. "It kind of halfway made me mad, but then I got to thinking about it, and then I thought, 'Wait a minute, what is this?' Very unnerving, after you realize it was something you couldn't put an answer to what had happened.

"Most of the time you say, 'It's the old building, and it's just shifting.' But that building doesn't shift. It has been there awhile, and it's solid masonry."

Custodians at the building, working late at night, also heard voices on several occasions, Hughes noted.

"They'd go into the room where they heard the conversations coming from, and there'd be nobody there," he said. "They'd check outdoors to see if it was somebody talking alongside the building, and there wouldn't be anybody out there. Two different custodians heard the voices at different times, and it was always after they'd closed up and they were cleaning the building, getting the trash out...the building would be empty except for them.

"They couldn't understand what the voices were saying, but they could hear several different voices in a conversation, talking, and they thought that somebody had stayed in the building and hadn't left when everyone else had. It scared them a couple of times."

After investing thousands of dollars into building improvements, including new windows throughout, Gardenville Community Center was forced to leave the old school October 1, 2001, after the St. Louis Board of Education reclaimed it for school purposes. Board officials had proposed reimbursing the community center $178,000 but later withdrew the offer, so Gardenville Community Center now is operating from its bingo hall at 2908 Telegraph Road. Nearly every night of the week, bingos at the hall benefit different charities.

"We still fund the food pantry. We've transferred it over to the Baptist church on South Kingshighway," Hughes said. "We make contributions to local charities—we're not very full-blown yet."

And Hughes hopes school officials don't make the same mistake he did.

"We thought we had a spooky deal one time, and it was right after I had taken over the building," he recalled. "I was down in the basement, and there were some switches in one of the old rooms down there, and I threw the switch—it was on and I turned it off, not knowing what it was.

"The next day we came into the building, and we noticed that all the clocks had stopped at the [same] time, and we thought that was really spooky till I finally realized I had turned the clocks all off," he chuckled. "All those electric clocks were operated off one circuit, which was very odd, as big as that building was."

Cool Valley Elementary School

Who is the little girl lurking in the bushes behind Cool Valley Elementary School?

Bob Schaper, a novelist and former reporter for the *Suburban Journals*, heard this intriguing story not long ago. Just for fun, he went to investigate but never saw a thing.

"There's a line of bushes that separates the playground and school," he said. "Kids walk past there and claim that they see this little girl wearing summer clothes in the dead of winter, and they talk to her. Supposedly this has happened several times."

Cool Valley Police Officer Scott Seabaugh, a five-year veteran of the department, said a call came in one night to another officer, who immediately started making weird faces and put the call on the speakerphone.

"She was asking if we'd ever heard of a little girl being killed or found dead by these bushes," Seabaugh said. "And we're like, 'No, why?' She starts telling about her daughter coming home from school, talking about how she was talking with the girl in the bushes. She told her about it two or three times.

"Then one day, it was snowing pretty good, so the mother and grandmother drove to the end of the walk there by the school to pick the daughter up, and she said as she was driving down the street they could see a girl in the bushes in summer clothes. This is in the middle of winter. They really couldn't see her face, and as they got closer, she vanished.

"So the officer said, 'It was kind of like the *Sixth Sense?*' and she said, 'Yeah, just like that.' She wanted to know if anybody else had ever called about it, and we said no. She didn't leave her name or anything—she was kind of embarrassed about it."

Ghostly Nun at Loretto Hall

Webster University's Loretto Hall supposedly has its own ghostly tale of a pregnant nun who allegedly killed herself after an encounter with a priest.

"No one seems to be sure what the nun's name was, the exact time period she was from, or if she had been raped by the priest," staff writer Tammy Kranz wrote in the Webster University *Journal*. One thing's for certain, though: numerous student orientation leaders have had fun spooking freshmen with ghost stories of the nun.

"The older students talk about ghost sightings and strange occurrences on the fourth floor—creaking boards under footsteps and items in dorm rooms being mysteriously rearranged."

The hauntings seemed to have been concentrated on the second and third floors of the residence hall, which could be due to major renovations that were underway, Kranz noted with tongue firmly in cheek.

The stories began right after Webster University broke from the church and became an independent college, Professor Dennis Klass said.

"That's a piece of Webster history that only some very old people still remember," he said. "How can we say now—she's apparently now a resting spirit.

"In the '60s, students reported feeling some presence. Whether or not there's any relationship [to the split with the church], the chapel was at that point just kind of an open space; now it's the Winifred Moore performing space. Students were more interested in psychological phenomena and less interested in their careers in those days. I think that's probably less interesting to the modern student."

Klass, author of the textbook *Continuing Bonds: New Understandings of Grief,* calls such stories "hocus-pocus stuff."

"I know a lot of people who have active interactions with people who have died, but they're important and not just 'let's scare ourselves with nuns wandering around the halls or with spirits over at the Lemp Mansion.'"

Alton's Milton School

The story is spine-chilling, the building naturally creepy, the ghosts, it would seem, ever present. There's just one question: did the story of a long-ago murder really happen at Alton's Milton Elementary School?

"I'm not even sure how much of that story is true," said Troy Taylor, author of a number of books about ghosts and host of the History & Hauntings Tours of Alton. "I always think of it as 'ghost lore,' where people make up a story to explain the weird things that are happening. It's really haunted, but probably not for that reason."

According to the story, a young student at the school stayed late one autumn afternoon to finish a project, and just as she was leaving she heard a noise behind her, and everything went dark. The girl, who generations of students called "Mary," was brutally raped and murdered, and her body was found the next morning in the girls' shower room.

Police later questioned a janitor at the school about the crime. As rumors began to fly, the janitor, the story goes, hanged himself at the school and left a note saying "I did it."

Since then, people have reported strange shadows, unexplained sounds such as footsteps, and even the apparition of a young girl. Unfortunately, there are no police reports to authenticate the murder story.

Taylor compared this story to similar stories that circulate on college and university campuses.

"Every college has at least one ghost story, and if they've got more than one, at least one of those ghost stories probably has something to do with a murdered coed," Taylor said. "Rarely do murdered coeds show up in any legitimate history. But yet, something's going on there. So again, I think it has more to do with people's need for an explanation."

For a time, the 1904-vintage school was used as the offices for a design firm, and Taylor visited with his tours. One of the hot spots of the building was the lower-level girls' restroom, where a number of people have had strange experiences over the years, he noted.

"Most of the people we get on the tours are not from the immediate area," Taylor said. "This woman was from somewhere around Peoria, and she had come down for the tour, and we were going through the school in kind of a group, and she had gone into this bathroom and all of a sudden just came flying out of there in a fright.

"We hadn't even gotten to the part where we say, 'This is the bathroom where they've had encounters with banging doors and that kind of thing,'" he added. "We hadn't even gotten that far. She went screaming out of there and said, 'There's something in there. There's something in there. I don't want to be in there.'

"Who knew? That place is creepy, I'll be honest with you."

Daruby Enterprises

It was said to have been built originally for one of the owners of the old St. Louis Browns baseball team, but facts on the elegant home at 1301 South Florissant Road are difficult to come by.

With its beautiful wood beams, pocket doors, stained glass, and large fireplaces, the home probably dates to around the turn of the last century. Esley Hamilton, preservation historian for St. Louis County, said that as of 1909 the property was part of the estate of Louise B. Reid, who had nearly eighty-four acres, but there was no mention of a home on the property.

Ruby C. Harriman, the current owner of the building, said she was told the house was built around 1899. In later years it served as a nursing home known as Hilltop and, at another time, under the name of Bellcrest.

Harriman and her late husband, David, founded Daruby Enterprises in 1994. Daruby is an adult learning and early childhood center that offers programs in computer training, certified nurse assistant, computer office assistant and administrative secretary to low-income clients. Clients are taught job survival skills as well as professional skills.

"We provide a lot of services to the low-income, welfare-to-work clients," Harriman said. "We have contracts with the state and also the Department of Labor. We're helping people get off welfare and into the workplace."

Along the way, Harriman has won numerous awards and honors for her management of the business, including the U.S. Small Business Administration's Welfare-to-Work Small Business Owner Award and the National Association of Women Business Owners' Distinguished Woman Business Owner of the Year Award 2000. She is a member of the St. Louis Ambassadors and other organizations. Harriman moved Daruby to its current location in 2000.

"[The home on South Florissant Road] had been vacant for about eighteen months," she said. "We had to spend quite a bit of money to bring it up to code."

Harriman and her staff also learned they weren't really alone in the old house. Lynda Anderson, director of job placement, often hears strange noises and footsteps and sees shadows slip by out of the corner of her eye.

"It doesn't seem creepy," she said. "I know when I'm here by myself and I hear things, I just kind of open up the door and look out. You look up and you have company."

Herb Crenshaw, case manager for Daruby, admits leaving work before he had intended on several occasions.

"The blurring of the eye—you see something pass by, and you look out, and it's not there, walking up the stairs," Crenshaw said. "You hear somebody, and you come out to check—'Hello?'—and nobody answers.

"Sometimes you get nervous. You've already got a lot of things on your mind, trying to do your work, and you keep hearing these things you can't see," he added. "You know how heat reflects off asphalt or a sidewalk? It's there and then it's gone. But the most creepy thing to me is footsteps on the stairwell.

"So I just say, 'I'll take a break now—I'll go home.'"

Crenshaw, Anderson, and Harriman laughed. Harriman acknowledged hearing conversations but said she can't make out what the people are saying. Still, she says she's not afraid to be there by herself.

"We don't pay them any attention," she said. "We just laugh and say, 'A lot of people died in here. They've come back, probably, and they're all friendly.'"

Maybe so, but the strange noises managed to unnerve Cool Valley Police Officer Scott Seabaugh when he was called to the training center after its burglar alarm went off. Several times he was called to Daruby, and each time the door was unlocked, but nothing was amiss, he said. Then the next night Seabaugh heard something.

"I was on the main floor, and just as the alarm quit sounding, I heard some voices upstairs. It sounded like kids, but not kids from the area, you know, because you can kind of tell the black kids from the white kids," Seabaugh said. "There were only white kids up there playing, playing and talking. It kind of stopped me in my tracks."

And soon after the conversation started, the voices stopped, as though they knew they had been discovered, noted Seabaugh's friend, former *Suburban Journals* reporter Bob Schaper, who wrote about the house in an article for the *Journal*.

"As soon as the alarm was silent...it's kind of like talking too loud in a room, and all of a sudden it gets real quiet, and you're the only one talking loud," Schaper said. "He was pretty freaked out."

Seabaugh searched upstairs but found only a vacant building, and all of the computers and equipment were turned off.

"Since the alarm was on, I knew if anybody was up there they would set it off, and it never went off," he said. "I figured if it was kids, they would have had to set it off when they went in, because I did. Most alarms, after a certain time of sounding, they'll reset. If it senses you again, it'll go off again. It never went off again...."

Seabaugh laughed. "It made me a little bit nervous because I knew it was a pretty old house. I went through the basement, too—fairly quickly."

[A Little Local Color]

If God is in the details, then small-town scribes Della Lang, Bruce Carlson, and Joan Gilbert have cubicles reserved for them at the Pearly Gates, right next to St. Peter.

Lang, Carlson, and Gilbert are local writers of the best kind, capturing historical accounts from "regular people" that otherwise might be lost to the ages. And in their travels each has written at least one lively book of ghost stories, from which they have kindly agreed to share some of their stories.

Della Lang

For more than twenty years, those in the know have called Della Lang the "Jefferson County historian," and for good reason. She has completed well over a dozen books including *Along Old Gravois with a Detour or Two: A History of Northwest Jefferson County*; *Reflections: The Legend of House Springs*; *River City: The Story of Fenton, Missouri*; *Pioneer Lady*; and *Country Schools of Jefferson County*.

Lang's illustrious career began when she volunteered as a member of the area's Community Library Association.

"When we started the library, it was a volunteer library— that's all we had," she recalled. "And we ran this volunteer library in High Ridge for fourteen years, I think, before we could finally get a tax passed and have a tax-supported library. Of course, we were always fund-raising. Since people kept asking for material on local history and we didn't have any available because no one had ever done anything on local history, I just decided it was time somebody did. It also provided a nice income for the community library. I've continued over the years; it's just kind of gotten to be a hobby with me now."

From people to papers, Lang combed every source she could find.

"At that time, when I did *Along Old Gravois* (1983), there were still some old-timers left to tell stories," she said. "Most of them have died since then. In fact, I recorded a bunch of them, and they're all gone now. You go to records, newspapers—I get a lot from newspapers. Luckily for us, somebody in the state decided to put all those on microfilm a good many years ago.

"You get a lot of it from just little stories that they put in the newspaper," she added. "During that time, they had these writers that just did local columns, you know, in every little town like Rush Tower and Murphy. They all had their different columns and oh, say, like once a month, they would print something from that area."

In 1995, Lang penned *Witchcraft, Wickedness, And Other Wacky Happenings In Jefferson County History*, which is available from the Jefferson County Genealogical Society, P.O. Box 1342, High Ridge, MO 63049 (www.rootsweb.com/ ~mojcgs/orderpubs.html).

Stories from the book include the ghost of an abandoned two-story house on McKissock Street, in DeSoto, that was later demolished:

The windows had been broken out by vandals and the house was crumbling with decay. No human being could possibly live in the house in that condition, and none did. Yet time and time again, passers-by witnessed the image of a woman carrying a coal oil lantern down the stairs. She would go into the former kitchen of the home, and then return back up the stairs and disappear.

The DeSoto ghost story came from an old newspaper account, Lang said.

"It was just a collection—it wasn't mine—that I happened to get together and do a little booklet on," she said. "And it's been really successful. I think we have reprinted that thing about ten times. It was just some little thing I decided to do on the spur of the moment. You know how that goes."

Lang, who also enjoys traveling, is at work on a sequel to *Along Old Gravois*.

Bruce Carlson

If you're looking to meet a real character, look no further than Bruce Carlson—although you shouldn't take seriously any photographs he sends you.

"Some [reporter] wanted a photograph of me for I don't know what," the veteran writer explained. "It was several years ago. So I didn't cut, but I tore, a picture out of some seamy magazine that showed a barely-clad, extremely muscular, young, stud-looking guy, OK? Of course, on the reverse side was some writing...and stuff that just made it obvious it was tore out of a magazine. I told her, 'This is a picture of me, and they made a mistake in the developing facility, and they got stuff on the backside, too,' but she shouldn't pay any attention to that.

He laughed. "I had a lot of fun with that one."

One gets the idea that the native Iowan has a lot of fun wherever he goes. Formerly a product engineer for the Schaffer Pen Company, Carlson wrote a history book at the request of his father and liked it so much he began writing on the side. A few years later, he opted for early retirement and launched his publishing company, Quixote Press.

"I'm certainly not the least bit sorry that I did it," he said.

Many of Carlson's books have a midwestern focus and feature ghost stories collected from around the region, including St. Louis; outhouse stories; roadkill recipes; and more. Among his earlier classics are *Ghosts of the Mississippi River from Keokuk to St. Louis*, written in 1988. Carlson's books are available at outlets ranging from gift shops to farmstands. For a catalog, write or call Quixote Press at 1854 345th Avenue, Wever, IA 52658, (319) 372-7480.

"Those are some of the first ones I wrote. As you might have noticed, they are in the book typewritten," Carlson chuckled. "From an old manual, no less."

Not inclined to be holed up in a library for any length of time, Carlson relied on unique methods to research his books.

"I took off down the highway one time, hitchhiking, and I had two front pockets in my Levi's and two back pockets," he said. "At the time, I was writing books of ghost stories and also the outhouses and roadkill and the hooker books, all at the same time. As I hitchhiked down the road, I would inquire of the person who picked me up or anybody I met along the way, 'Do you know any good ghost stories? Do you know any good hooker stories? Do you know any good outhouse stories? Roadkill stories?'

"They would tell me, and I would make some quick notes and stuff them in the appropriate pocket. When the four pockets were evenly full, I turned around and came home."

Carlson lives in Fort Madison, Iowa, with his wife, Marilyn. The couple have two grown children.

Although a firm nonbeliever in ghosts when he started out, Carlson said he is no longer so sure after he made a visit to his family's farm near Sioux City in the summer of 1999.

"I was raised on a farm, and we chose to live a hundred years earlier, so when I was a child we had all horse-drawn equipment," he said. "I know exactly what a horse-drawn farm wagon sounds like as it goes down the road. I was on that farm, and I heard this wagon coming down the lane. I thought, 'Well, that's strange, who's driving a team of horses with a wagon coming?' And I waited for them to come around the bend, and I heard the sound as it progressed toward me, and when the sound came around the bend, nothing else did. I heard the sound progressively coming closer and over the culvert, you know, and there was no mistaking it. It wasn't a matter of 'Gee, that sounds like a horse-drawn wagon.' It was very definite. I heard that sound come past me and continue out toward the barn, and at no time would I ever see anything.

"I was just totally mystified," he said. "I was alone and had no one to substantiate my experience, but it was remarkable."

Carlson chuckled. "Now I'm not sure anymore. It was kind of a neat experience, certainly one I'll never forget."

Joan Gilbert

A native of Dixon, Missouri, in Pulaski County, Joan Gilbert spent much of her time listening to stories, including ghost stories, when she was growing up.

"I belong to a generation in which conversation was a great recreation, before television or anything, and people used to spend a lot of time sitting around talking, exchanging their experiences and speculations and all that stuff," she said. "I heard people exchange a lot of ghost stories and strange stories, so I grew up with an interest in the unexplained."

Gilbert went on to write nearly 700 pieces of short fiction and nonfiction as well as five books, including *The Trail of Tears Across Missouri*, published by The University of Missouri Press in 1996. The historical account won her a first prize from the National Federation of Press Women, and she has captured twenty awards for her other works. Her books of ghost tales include *Missouri Ghosts*, which was recently republished in an expanded second edition with ten new chapters, and *More Missouri Ghosts*. Both are available in local bookstores and from MoGho Books, P.O. Box 200, Hallsville, MO 65255.

"I really started this as how interesting it is, as folklore, that we've got all these stories," Gilbert recalled. "As I went on with it, I was really amazed

110   SP|R|TS

at how many people came to tell me something had happened to them. It makes a person feel that there certainly is something that we don't understand, and it's got a lot of different branches and a lot of manifestations, because some people have seen things, some people have just felt things in an overwhelming way.

"I don't know if it's a time slip," she added. "To me, the time slip [concept] doesn't apply to all the things people tell me but it could apply to a lot, and to me that's the most attractive and exciting thing because I believe that someday we will understand time better than we do now. [Time slip] is a term that is applied to anything weird that happens with time, just like the idea that something can happen that has such intensity that it just stays there—it's ongoing.

"I think it was Einstein who said it's like you're going down a stream, and you pass through different villages and camps by the river, and you keep on going on the river, and you pass by them and they're gone, they're over, as far as your experience is concerned, but they're still there, and they're still doing what they're doing. It is just fascinating to me the different ways that people have looked at time."

An animal lover, Gilbert is completing work on her newest book, *Missouri Horses*. She lives near Hallsville in a home with many trees, books, and pets, and she tries to keep an open mind on the subject of the paranormal.

"I have a lot of friends who are in the, quote, 'scientific' field, and people like that take great pride in rejecting the idea that there could be anything they don't understand," Gilbert said. "That's what science is all about, trying to understand what you don't understand."

Gilbert referred to a story in *More Missouri Ghosts,* in which the late Leonard Hall of Caledonia was awakened from his tent while on a float trip on the Current River. He reported seeing campfires attended by Indians in breech clouts. Around the fires sat men wearing armor, which he recognized as Spanish by the helmet style. Hall, too embarrassed to call anyone else to look, feared he had hallucinated.

"It seemed so strange, and then research indicated that DeSoto or somebody was in the area with soldiers and with Indians that were acting as their guides," Gilbert said. "It sounds strange that anybody would be sitting around a fire eating supper with someone with armor on, but they were afraid there might be Indians shooting at them from outside the light of the fire. It seems rather logical that they might leave it on.

"The thing that really interests me is little details like that that seem out of place or weird," Gilbert said. "And when you think about it, well, maybe they would have been doing that. It would not have been like the suits of armor we see in castles, but it was metal stuff that they had over their backs, chests, and some sort of headgear that was metal. I have seen pictures of people wearing that kind of armor. As I remember, it leaves their arms free."

15
[River Views]

Although located miles apart, the subjects of the next two stories have in common a lovely river view and a history of entertaining St. Louisans during their leisure time. The venerable Goldenrod Showboat now makes its home along the Missouri River in St. Charles, and yesteryear's Castlewood resort area borders the Meramec River a good distance south. Both share decades of history as well as some colorful stories of an unexplained nature.

The Glorious Goldenrod: An Entertainment Legend

As of this writing, the Goldenrod Showboat faces an uncertain future. One of two remaining historic entertainment barges in the country, the grande dame has been laid low with a cracked hull and is closed until further notice. She is owned by the city of St. Charles and rests at a dock in Frontier Park as her fans try to have her saved and restored in a basin that would protect her from the future whims of the river. A preliminary study is also afloat to give or sell the boat to the city of Alton, Illinois.

"Eighty-eight showboats were built during their heyday from 1880 to 1909," noted Steve Powell, director of the Greater St. Charles Convention and Visitors Bureau. "This is pretty much the last of those boats, although there is one other, the Majestic, built in 1927."

Powell was instrumental in bringing the Goldenrod to St. Charles in 1989 and supervised its restoration. He's also seen the ghost of Victoria, the elusive woman in red who is said to haunt the boat.

"It's probably been five years ago," he said. "I was on the boat about eleven at night, and I was there with the general manager, who also saw the ghost. We were closing the boat up, and we walked down the gateway to the gate, and we were locking the gate up, and we both sort of looked up.

"We saw a figure of a woman in a red dress—at least it appeared to be red, or a dark, dress—with long brown hair, peering out at us from the upper deck of the boat. It was a long dress where the shoulders were kind of puffed up. I'd say it looked like a Victorian type of dress or at least an early- 1900s type of dress.

"We both said, 'There is nobody else on this boat,' and she just looked at us and sort of turned and walked away," Powell recalled. "We were probably fifty yards away or so—it was clearly visible."

The legend of Victoria dates from a stopover in St. Louis during the showboat's early years, Powell believes.

"The story that I've been told is they were visiting St. Louis, the showboat was, and she and her father had an argument because she wanted to be an actress, and he basically said, 'No way, it's not gong to happen,' and she got angry and ran off the boat and was murdered that night," Powell said. "And forevermore, she's haunted the boat—not malicious things, just there occasionally."

From 1937 until it was purchased by St. Charles, the boat was moored at the foot of Locust Street in St. Louis.

Last of the Old-Time Missouri River Showboats

The largest and finest showboat ever to travel the inland waterways, the Goldenrod was launched in 1909 by the Pope Dock Company of Parkersville, West Virginia, for W. R. Markle, at a cost of $75,000.

The envy of all showboatmen, the Goldenrod measured 200 feet long and 45 feet wide, according to a 1965 thesis paper by Walter J. McCormick, which is now in the convention center archives. It had an auditorium 162 feet long with twenty-one red-velour–upholstered boxes and a seating capacity of 1,400. Its interior was patterned after that of the Majestic Theatre in Denver, Colorado, featuring 2,100 electric lights hung in attractive clusters over a richly carpeted floor. The layout and hull have been modified over the years, and the boat now seats 400.

"The Goldenrod was equipped with hot and cold running water, steam heat for the winter, a cooling system for the summer, and electric lighting," McCormick wrote. "The energy was provided by the towboat's steam engine system. The calliope served as a condenser for producing drinking water."

Back in 1963, Augustus H. Edmonds of Miami, Missouri, recounted to

McCormick his memories of the shrill whistle that signaled the boat's return:

> When the showboat rounded the bend you could hear the calliope playing, and it stirred the blood. It was the boat's ballyhoo, advertisement and come on, suggestive of amusement to come. It got the population in the mood to prepare to be at the show.... There was hardly a spot in the little town where I lived that the sound of the calliope didn't reach. After all these years I can recall in my 'mind's ear' the thrilling sound.

The festive calliope, along with an advance agent who traveled by automobile ten days ahead of the show, were phased out in 1927 because of rising operating costs and because the incorporated towns began objecting to the loudness of the calliope.

In the meantime, the Goldenrod was sold at auction by a federal marshal in 1913 when Markle went bankrupt. Ralph Emerson made a successful bid of $11,000 on the boat, and in 1922 he sold it to Capt. J. W. (Bill) Menke and his brother, Charles Menke.

That's when the boat really took off, traveling through more than fifteen states. Capt. Bill Menke recalled the 1924 route in an old newspaper interview:

> We would go from Pittsburgh to Fairmont on the Monongahela, then down the Ohio to Cairo, Illinois, and up the Illinois River. Returning to Cairo, we would go north as far as St. Paul, then down the Mississippi again and up the Missouri to Kansas City and sometimes Omaha. The last long leg took us down the Missouri and Mississippi to New Orleans.

Gradually, the preferences of showboat audiences changed, as people tired of straight dramas in favor of the more comedic melodramas. By 1930 Captain Menke was playing only city landings offering "Old-Time Melerdrammers."

They paid their actors $35 to $50 a week, based on the importance of the role. Actors received free room and board, and spent the daytime hours fishing, swimming, talking, and rehearsing.

"Red Skelton got his start on the boat as a dockhand," Powell noted. "One of the actors fell ill, and Skelton was called in in his place. That was the start of his acting career."

Ted Mack in his early days played an offstage bloodhound in one of the shows. Bob Hope played there, as well, while on tour.

"A good example of the audience's acceptance of the Goldenrod occurred the season Captain Menke was near the mouth of the Osage River," McCormick wrote. "He tried to take the big craft up that river to play

Bonnots Mill. The Goldenrod was too large for the Osage, and Captain Menke had to turn back. He moored the showboat five miles from Bonnots Mill and sent a man into the town to assure the people that a performance would be given that night. When night came, not even standing room was available.

"Farmers and merchants, white and Negro, mothers and fathers, grandparents and children all came to the landing for the boat show. As an audience, they were so quiet, a pin, if dropped, could be heard. The audience in those days took their entertainment seriously. Entertainment for them was rare."

The Goldenrod served as inspiration for the popular musical *Showboat*, Powell said.

"They were basically the infancy of theatre in America," he said. "The rivers were your highways; you had roads, but they weren't very good, and showboats were the birth of American theatre, at least out in the west. They would bring out the actors and actresses and do a parade down the town, tell everyone that the showboat was there, and get people to come to the boat."

Both Powell and Charlie Nichols, a street supervisor and part-time mooring expert for the city of St. Charles, have logged some strange experiences on the boat.

"I hear things like people walking upstairs, and there ain't nobody there," Nichols said. "I'm not scared."

Powell recalled an incident during the Great Flood of '93, during which officials had placed a generator on the boat while trying to keep it afloat.

"We had a gentleman servicing the generator, and he was there by himself, no one else on the boat, and all of a sudden a big plate glass mirror comes down and flies around the corner and lands down there in the middle of the deck, smashed right beside him," he said. "It freaked the guy out so much he wouldn't come back on the boat. We just wrote it up to Victoria."

Victoria also is credited for all hell breaking loose one night after a chef cursed the boat. Much of the contents of the kitchen—food, pots and pans, and knives—began flying everywhere. There were no disturbances elsewhere on the boat that evening, and the river was calm.

Other phenomena have included phantom music playing on an otherwise empty boat, doors opening, and lights coming on by themselves. And the spirit of venerable Capt. Bill Menke is thought to be aboard, as well.

"Captain Menke was quite a character and actually operated the boat for a number of years," Powell said. "What people will smell occasionally is cigar smoke, and he was notorious for walking around with a cigar in his mouth all the time."

Given some of the stories about Menke, a post-mortem return makes sense, Powell said.

"Negotiating the Missouri River was quite treacherous with the trees and tree stumps, and this would be before the river was actually channelized," Powell said. "Showboats did not have engines. They were pushed by a steamboat, and with a steamboat behind you, it's hard to see in front of you. They hit a log, which punctured a hole in the boat.

"The story has it that Captain Menke, to keep the boat from sinking, basically inserted his body in the hole, smoked a cigar, and drank whiskey all night while they headed to port to repair the boat."

Castlewood: Michigan Weekend for Yesteryear St. Louisans

There were two hotels, a multitude of little wood cabins, and a stop for the railroad near the Meramec River. For thousands of St. Louisans nearly a century ago, the area known as Castlewood, near Ballwin, was the "poor man's Michigan."

That's how Chris Canepa, a rehabber in the Castlewood area, describes it.

"That place was in its heyday in the teens, '20s, and '30s," he said, "and everything was pretty much gone by the '40s or '50s.

"People who went to Michigan bought houses in Michigan. St. Louis folk didn't have air-conditioning in the teens and '20s, decided to go out and get a country place, and there wasn't a lot of activity going on. Subsequently, a couple of hotels were built. There's pictures of the hotels. There's pictures of people in bathing suits playing in the Meramec, and lots of canoes out there. There was a church—big, brown, wood-frame church with white trim and mullioned windows—all that kind of stuff, very Michigan-y. The style was three-inch siding, probably creosoted black with white trim or pink."

Today Canepa owns several of the old cabins, which he rents.

"I rehab them, keep intact what I think is worth keeping intact," he said. "These were simple, simple buildings originally—basically the way they were sixty years ago—wood floors, wood walls, no insulation, exposed wiring, the whole deal. A lot of the real estate out there was very characteristic of the type of building that was going on in Michigan: dark wood, white trim, that kind of a look....upstairs were these metal beds and springs and mattresses, like a bunk, where the kids would hang out. I guess Mom and Dad maybe had a little spot downstairs. It was simple stuff, a way to get cool in the summer, before TV and everything else."

Bootleggers and the Chicago gangs also seemed to enjoy the area, he said.

"There was a lot of talk about bootleggers. St. Louis had their group, and the Chicago boys liked coming down here, too," Canepa said. "They'd get out their wooden boats and get on the river and do their fun thing. There was one little place that used to be a speakeasy in the '20s, right across from the lake in a little blue house—it's an apartment house now. Originally it was just a speakeasy, had a little restaurant, a little sneaky booze. The sheriff from the area—Manchester, Ballwin, whatever—would come out there and get his shot of booze. Those guys would play the game, and they were having a pretty good time—they were all in bed with the booze guys. They took care of each other."

Despite their colorful past, Canepa couldn't recall hearing any ghost stories from the old properties—except one.

"There's a million-dollar house up on Holland Road that's very intimate," he said. "It's on the edge of the bluff at the cliff, a contemporary type of house, lots of glass, big view. My buddy, Craig Cervantes, lived out there and thought it was haunted."

Castlewood Home: Great Conversation, But No One There

Built in 1977, the home had beautiful views but many bizarre happenings that couldn't be explained, Craig Cervantes recalled.

"I'm a composer and a producer, so I would write a lot of music at that property," Cervantes said. "I had a big grand piano near this window that would look out over the bluffs of the Meramec River.

"I would hear voices and conversations coming through what I thought was the air vents of the home, and I knew I was the only one there. I could hear distinct conversations. That was about 1989, 1990, that that happened.

"I had a horse that I kept up there, as well—there's a barn—but I could not ever get the horse to come up to the house. It would turn around and run away as soon as it got anywhere close. I'd even try to hand-walk it, you know, lead it, and it would just rear up and turn around and run away on me."

He chuckled. "There was always kind of a mystique about it. It's such an unusual place.

"At one point—this was when that small earthquake hit, because I remember the house kind of shook its foundation a little bit—I woke up about three-thirty, four in the morning and heard an incredible symphony going on in the house: violins playing a distinct melody. And I went upstairs to see if my stereo was on, or why it would be on. I thought maybe my brothers had come in while I was asleep and were partying upstairs, because the property basically starts from the top and was built down the cliff, so the bedroom was on the lower level.

"I ran all over the house trying to figure out where the music was coming from. And again I put my ear up to the vents where I thought I'd heard the conversations, and that's where the sound was coming from. I thought, 'Boy, that is really bizarre,' and it didn't last very long. Once I got up, turned the lights on, and started stirring around the house, it just kind of shut down. But it brought me out of a deep sleep. So that was pretty spooky."

Intrigued, Cervantes opted to do a little research and turned up some fascinating facts.

"The house [property] that I owned apparently was, back during the '20s, a retreat for Al Capone and his gang," he said. "They would come down to Lincoln Beach by train from Chicago, and the Castlewood area was an ideal getaway because it was so secluded. They had a winery up on the hill, too, and I think there was an old hotel that sat on the site back in the '20s.

"I found out from a farmer whose land I'd sold close by, some of the stories, how they got up there. It was an old logging road, and they would come from the river and get off the train at Lincoln Beach, and then ride horseback up to the lodge.... apparently somebody was murdered there back during the time that it existed."

The son of late St. Louis Mayor A. J. Cervantes, Craig now divides his time between St. Louis and Los Angeles. Many of the songs he has written over the last dozen years, including those composed during his ownership of the strange Castlewood house, recently were released on a new CD called *Carmelina by Craig Cervantes*. To hear the music, visit Cervantes' Web site at www.craigcervantes.com.

16

[Memories for Sale]

Is it possible for inanimate objects, such as an old Victrola or a brass bed, to be haunted? Some authorities on the paranormal say it is. They call it psychometry.

Psychometry is the theory that objects absorb the "emotional vibrations" of their owners and those around them, and retain and reflect those emotions indefinitely. As the following stories show, it doesn't matter whether the object is a comfortable old bed, an odd Victrola, or a house full of not-quite-forgotten treasures.

Sleigh Bed For Sale: Free Ethereal Owner With Purchase

Cathy Bagby and her husband, Brian, brought home an antique sleigh bed several years ago. The midtown Alton residents soon learned from Antoinette Eason, a psychic and host of Antoinette's Haunted History Tours, that they had received a ghostly bonus.

"Antoinette is a good friend of mine, and she investigated my house," Cathy Bagby recalled. "There's a woman here that Antoinette believes came with an antique sleigh bed that we have. Back then I was like, 'Oh, come on!' But Toni gave me a name, and I went to the library the next day, and there was a woman who lived in Alton by that name, who was married in 1905. And Antoinette said she felt the woman had a child in that bed, or something very important to her, that she was connected to it. Back in 1905 is when you had your kids in your bed at home."

Bagby, a patient accounts customer representative, credits the ghost with the disappearance—and eventual return—of sewing scissors, a curling iron, a brand-new bra, and other things. And when her oldest son, Ian, was a toddler, she used to tuck him in the bed before anyone realized it was haunted. The family also has a male ghost (see Chapter 22, Happy At Home).

"[Ian] was two years old, and he would cry—he would be frightened of this," she said. "This was before I realized what was going on. We had to lay down with him every night before he fell asleep, because he would point. He's always been more sensitive to things."

"Only once in fourteen years have I seen the figure of a woman at the bottom of the steps," she said. "She was very transparent, very vague, and there for a second and gone. From the moment we moved here, I saw around the corner right in the same spot like a blur, a white shape, not the same shape all the time, and not a human shape. It's like a blur, like if car lights would zip through your house or something.

"The stairs have always been one of the hot spots," Bagby said of their 1918-vintage, Prairie School-style brick home. "We've got a couple cats, and sometimes the entertainment is to watch them watch something—they stare up the stairs at something. We've got one of those electro-meter things, you know, and it goes nuts on the third or fourth step up all the time."

The female spirit is a kindly one, she believes.

"Sandy [another local intuitive] said the woman that's here checks after the kids," Bagby said. "She makes sure everything's okay, so that's good to know."

Clock Radio: Who Loves Janis?

Although she grew up in the Central West End, Nicole spent many hours in her grandmother's house near Fairgrounds Park in north St. Louis, a home that was considered by the family to be haunted. Nicole, an employee of a software company who asked that her last name not be used, remembers a strange incident involving a radio.

"I had a little clock radio in my room, and I would spend vacations here—spring break or Christmas break—from school," Nicole said. "I used to play the popular station, and I'd always have that one before I went to sleep; I'd sometimes set the alarm, so it would be on that station when I woke up.

"On several occasions, this radio would actually switch from FM to AM, and the dial would be on an entirely different station. I would turn it to 104, and it would end up on, like, 92. I would wake up to this weird station and—this is the weirdest thing—it would play the [Janis Joplin] song "Oh Lord Won't You Buy Me a Mercedes Benz." It happened over and over. It was always that song; it would either be the beginning, the middle, or the end."

Nicole first wondered if someone was playing a trick on her.

"I sleep through thunderstorms, but if somebody walks into the room I'm wide awake," she said. "So I know somebody wasn't messing with my radio. I'm only guessing that there was a ghost in here that really loved that song, or really loved old music, and would switch it. I know I didn't do it. I remembered feeling more annoyed than anything: 'Put it back on my station!'"

Antique Victrola: Bad Vibes in Ferguson

Shelley Romo and her family have lived in their older home in Ferguson for nearly nine years without incident—except for one brief period seven years ago.

"We bought an antique Victrola at a Lafayette Square sale," Romo recalled. "That night we were going out, and I felt a little funny about leaving our fourteen-year-old [son] home. There was a very unusual, frightening feeling in the house. I was uncomfortable all night, and we came home early.

"When we arrived, I went to my son's room, and as soon as I opened his door, he said, 'Oh my God, I'm so glad you guys are home. I thought somebody broke into the house! I kept hearing slamming and things moving. But I couldn't tell where it was coming from.'

"That night our six-year-old son began being afraid of the spiders in his room at night and of the dark," Romo added. "He was terrified of his room for months.

"Several days later, I was taking a shower, and both of my cats ran in and stayed in the bathroom with me. Their eyes were huge and their ears were pulled back. They kept looking at the door. As I was getting out of the shower, I could hear either the Victrola or one of the wooden-legged chairs moving back and forth across the floor. No one else was home."

Romo also heard her son and her husband calling for her two different times, and when she went to talk to them, both were sound asleep.

"On several occasions, we heard heavy, angry footsteps coming down the stairs and abruptly ending," she said. "We also heard, almost nightly, something that sounded like a very heavy book being dropped onto the wood floor downstairs."

The Romos have since sold the Victrola, and the strange noises have stopped.

Cleaning Can't Erase Bed's Tragic Past

Back in the 1950s, Joyce Holsen bought an antique brass bed at an estate auction in Florissant and cleaned and shined it like new. But her bedroom was never the same.

Author and publisher Bruce Carlson interviewed Holsen while researching his book *Ghosts of the Mississippi River from Keokuk to St. Louis*. The first night after buying the bed, Holsen woke up with the feeling she was not alone.

"When she flipped on the lamp at her bedside table, she saw...an old woman standing at the foot of the bed looking down at [her]," Carlson wrote. "It took a minute for her to get her voice back. 'I asked the woman who she was and what was she doing in my bedroom.'"

With that, the old woman turned and walked through the wall, an exterior wall on the second floor of Holsen's St. Louis home.

"There was no window or door on that part of the wall at all, but she sure enough walked out through it," the mystified buyer recalled to Carlson. "I know I wasn't dreaming. I was just as wide awake as I am now."

After repeat performances several times over the next few weeks, Holsen went back to the woman's estate and did some research. She found that the woman who visited her looked very much like the woman who died and that the bed had belonged to the woman's daughter, who died at a tender age after an illness. The mother, family members recalled, was never the same.

"I'm sure that the old woman in my room was the ghost of that girl's mother," Holsen told Carlson.

Joyce Holsen then sold the bed at a consignment house and bought a new one. No one seems to know what happened to the old brass bed.

"If it is being used, it's probably occupied by someone who is a very sound sleeper or doesn't mind having someone watching them through the night," Carlson noted.

The Ettmann Home: Clayton Time Warp?

It wasn't a single item, but a whole houseful of nostalgic things, that gave Ron Elz the creeps more than a decade ago.

Elz, a.k.a. radio personality and trivia expert Johnny Rabbitt, handles estate sales every so often. He was called to the Wydown Avenue home of the late Henry and Kay Ettmann, a veritable treasure-trove of old, untouched things.

"Ettmann was a scientist, inventor of things," Elz recalled. "He had a high position with the A. S. Aloe Company here in St. Louis, and he created a lot of things [such as] different types of film. He had his own laboratory in the basement—it was a full-fledged lab like you would see in a Frankenstein movie, without the electronics, with dissecting tables and tables where the blood would drain, and all of the vials and beakers and tumblers and spinners and things to mix and coagulate stuff. Spooky-looking knives, tiny to very long. Those were scalpels, really, and surgical knives. And he had all these chemicals down there...there were pictures of monkeys being operated on and things like that. You'd think, 'Oh, Geez.'"

After his death, Henry's wife, Kay, left everything as it was until her own death several years later.

"I worked full time during the day, so I had to spend nights there," Elz recalled. "And I'll tell you, that was an eerie place. It was a very nice house, but nothing had ever been updated for many years. It looked like it could have been the late '40s, early '50s, as far as how everything looked. And everything was still there—all their clothes, lots of old furniture...."

The attic, especially, was a virtual toy store from the past, Elz remembers.

"At A. S. Aloe, in [Henry's] position with all these suppliers or buyers or whoever he dealt with there, they were always wanting to give him a gift," Elz said. "He would say, 'Just give me a toy for my son, Henry Jr.'...Henry Jr. had so many toys it was incredible. Most of the things hadn't even been opened, or if they'd been opened, they were put right back in the box. I spent a lot of time in the attic.

"That's when I first started hearing noises down there," he added. "It didn't concern me too much at first. I remember the first time, I went down, looked around, didn't hear anything, went downstairs to the first floor. Then I heard something upstairs: 'Oh boy, somebody's gotten in.' But I tried all the doors, checked the windows...I kept having this creepy feeling that somebody or something was there. It just sounded like somebody moving around. After I had checked again, I decided I'd had enough. It was pretty late, two in the morning or something."

Over the next few nights, the noises continued.

"The owner's son and friends of theirs swear it's the mother, who never wanted any change, never wanted anything to be taken away, to be moved—she was upset, and she was a very strong-willed and domineering person," Elz said. "That was Kay's way of showing that she was unhappy.

"So I started talking to her, just talking out loud as if she were right there, that all of this had to be: the house was going to be sold, and her son's not going to live there. He didn't want to live there—he wanted to get out and get away—it was too overpowering."

Elz's "discussions" with Kay made him feel better, but it didn't quell the racket in the house. Sounds of doors creaking open, heavy objects sliding across countertops, bottles clinking together, footsteps, and other noises pervaded the house.

"There, I was really trapped in a time warp, so to speak," he said. "I was there in a place that hadn't changed for years, that had some very strong personalities in it. They did a lot of entertaining there. They had a lot of people there, lots of parties, lots of dinners, a lot of life. If you reach a point where you feel your life is going to end, you look back at these kinds of things, and you certainly don't want to leave it behind. A lot of people may wish to stay in some way. Whether you could will your spirit that way, I don't know. I guess anything's possible."

Over the years, Elz has done estate sale work in a number of houses he would have sworn would be haunted but weren't.

Grimm Costume Shop

"Anna and Otto Grimm had this old costume shop they'd opened right at the time of the World's Fair, and they moved to 3838 Olive Street in 1938," Elz recalled. "He'd been dead for years, since the '50s, and she ran it. A very, very sweet person. She was known as the Angel of Olive Street. She was very small, very diminutive, had the most beautiful blue eyes. Unfortunately, time had passed her by, and she lived alone. Finally, she froze to death—hypothermia got her. She had lived next door, upstairs, but unfortunately some neighborhood character raped her. She was 80 years old, she was afraid to go up there anymore, so she lived in the store."

Elz handled her estate about fifteen years ago.

"You'd find these wonderful costumes, but most of them were just rotten from dry rot," he recalled. "I loved the sign—they had a wonderful sign in the window, Transformations Made Here. I remember one time I was just literally sitting on top of a mound of stuff that I'd just gotten out from walls and cabinets and shelves, where I must have been fifteen feet in the air, sitting on this stuff to go through, because they had just saved everything."

The family was sure the Grimms had stashed a fortune someplace, but nothing ever was found. All in all, it was a bad experience, and the building was infested with rats, Elz said.

"The hookers would be working out in the front, the rats would be in the back, and I'd be in there with dim lights, the old-time light bulbs," he said. "I would have thought that would have been a haunted place, but there were no ghosts there. Just ghostly memories. Maybe she was ready to go."

Timeless Treasures on Botanical Street

Elz also bet he might meet up with some ghosts when he handled an estate on Botanical Street in the Shaw neighborhood in 1970. The Krembs, Herman and Ed—two reclusive brothers—had lived in the home for years.

"The sister, Alice, she had died in 1941 and had lived upstairs, and everything was still the same in 1970 as it was in 1941," Elz recalled. "They just closed it. All her clothes were still laid out where she was going to get dressed that day. They still had an ice box, and all the food was still in the ice box, all the medicines were still in the cabinet.

"These people were very wealthy—certainly by my standards and even in those days by theirs," he added. "Their estate was well over $600,000, and there you would find boxes with gold coins and money. The last one to live, Ed, was half shell-shocked, as they say, or something had happened in World War I, and he was never quite right. His brother, Herman, who was in charge of the purse strings, always told Ed, 'If you see something come in here that's got a lot of zeroes, that doesn't mean anything—that's zero. If you see a two with five zeroes behind it, that's just $2, not $20,000.'

"And poor Ed lived like a hermit. He wound up his old Victrola, and he rendered meat, and he lived on about fifty cents a week. He had all this money—he could have had everything he wanted. They still had a 1925 Lincoln in the garage, hadn't been started in years.

"But no ghosts. Nothing."

[ALL IN A DAY'S WORK]

Ghosts and workplaces—particularly *old* workplaces—seem to go together very well, for some reason. Perhaps it's because the workplace was once home to these spirits, as in the old Schubel House in Hillsboro; because they used to work there, as in the old Federal Reserve Bank downtown; or because they died tragic deaths there, as in an old officers' quarters duplex at Jefferson Barracks.

The Schubel House Ghost: Just My Type (writer)

For years the house at the corner of First and Maple in Hillsboro has been known as the Schubel House, a two-story white brick house with a front porch, green shutters, and a green roof.

"It was in the Schubel family when I was a small child, and I delivered the *St. Louis Post-Dispatch* to them," noted Audrey Vreeland, local historian and community leader who is working to save the home from demolition. "I am seventy-one years old...So I go back a long way."

The house dates to the early-to-mid 1800s and is owned by Jefferson County, which operated its purchasing and recreation departments out of the home for several years, ending in 2000.

"So when I learned that the county planned to demolish this house because they needed the space, I said, 'Well, could it be moved?' and that's how it started. We are now a corporation, and we're called Monticello First, and I'm trying to raise money to move the house. If you know of a very kind philanthropist, I would be most grateful."

Many people are not aware of Hillsboro's historic legacy, Vreeland noted.

"The name Monticello was changed to Hillsboro because there was another county seat, in Lewis County, Missouri, that had that name, and of course this was in the days before zip codes, so there could not be two," she said. "So they changed the name to the English version, Hillsborough, meaning of course hills, which of course Hillsboro is quite famous for. The English spelling was dropped through the years, either by poor penmanship or the slur of the tongue or whatever, and it was just called Hillsboro.

"However, Hillsboro...never had anyone try to preserve the old main street and the old history, and there are a few buildings left, and I'm trying to do that before I'm not here anymore or can't do it. Hillsboro was incorporated in 1839, and we have the Governor Fletcher House here—he was the first native-born governor for the state of Missouri. The stagecoach went right through here. It stopped here from St. Louis and spent the night and went on, so it's kind of rich in history."

There also are tales of ghostly presences at Schubel House that Vreeland said she discounted until she heard the stories from two different Jefferson County employees.

Tabitha Conner, general services assistant for the courthouse, is a believer.

"I started working there in August 1991," Conner said. "Everyone that's worked over there [knows] there's something there. It's not threatening, but when you first encounter it, it's kind of eerie and you have the prickles, that feeling, you know. You would walk through a cold spot just out of the blue. We've all experienced it."

One winter night, Conner, of Festus, returned late after her car had gotten a flat tire.

"Later on that evening they had come out to get it to repair the tire," she said. "It was late at night, and everyone was gone, and we always made sure we turned the lights off in the evening, because my boss was a real stickler about leaving the lights on. When I came back to get my car, up in the window it looked like the light was on."

But there was something strange about the light.

"It looked like it was an old-time light," she said. "We have fluorescent lighting throughout the building now, and it wasn't the same type of lighting. It was real dim, about a twenty-five-watt light bulb, you know. It was on and it was swinging. That gave me the creeps."

Employees also have heard footsteps walking around upstairs when there was nobody there, sensed a shadowy darkness out of the corner of one eye as though someone were standing there, and witnessed things inexplicably moved to a new location, Conner said.

"We always assumed or got the feeling that it was a little old lady because when you would see shadows or something she wasn't very tall, and the footsteps sounded like old schoolgirl boots, like Laura Ingalls boots," she said. "She wasn't threatening or anything; you knew that there was something there.

"The housekeeping girls would make someone come with them when they went over at night and cleaned, because they were spooked."

Loretta Fox is secretary for the Jefferson County Parks and Recreation Department, which used to occupy the top floor of the Schubel House. Fox recalled an eerie park board meeting at the home.

"It was storming, and the wind kept blowing the front door open," said Fox, who lives outside DeSoto. "So our director, Mike Ginger, went down and bolted the door, and during the board meeting the door opened and closed, and we just kind of looked at each other. He ran downstairs, and the door was shut and bolted."

Ginger also was there one evening when he heard somebody typing at the typewriter downstairs.

"No one was down there," he recalled. "It was right before a board meeting."

A student intern named Drew also had a run-in with a typewriter, Fox noted.

"One night he was at the office trying to type a letter, and he calls me," she said. "He says, 'When you hit a letter on the typewriter, does it do weird things?' I said, 'Like what?' He said, 'It just takes off and starts typing. I'll just strike one key.'"

Fox laughed. "I told him, 'Just turn it off and go home.'

"There was one occasion when I was leaving from work, and I saw the figure of a woman up in the attic window," she added. "It was about four-thirty. When I looked again, naturally it wasn't there."

Like Conner, Fox also was unnerved by the footsteps.

"There were a lot of occasions where we would hear footsteps coming up the stairs, and I would walk completely around trying to find who was coming up the stairs," Fox said. "Purchasing was downstairs; we were upstairs. I'd run downstairs, and I'd ask them, 'Did somebody come up?' 'No, nobody came up.'

"After we heard the footsteps and things, I went downstairs and asked one of the ladies in purchasing if someone had ever died there," Fox added. "They said they didn't know if a man actually died there, but they had his funeral in the front room."

You Can Bank on Our Presence at the Federal Reserve

Elegant and imposing, the Federal Reserve Bank of St. Louis spans a whole city block downtown. The older, southern section is where a number of strange phenomena have occurred, according to a bank employee who asked to remain anonymous. The newer section to the north used to be Gamble's Department Store and is relatively quiet, the employee said.

For the record, however, Federal Reserve officials don't believe there's anything ghostly going on in the building.

"I've been here seven years," public affairs officer Joe Elstner said. "We're here sometimes twenty-four hours a day, sometimes almost that much, so it just couldn't happen. If you were a ghost, I don't know where you'd hang out at the Fed."

Built in 1923, the Federal Reserve Bank of St. Louis is the oldest bank in the twelve-bank federal reserve system.

"We do check clearance: when people write checks, they all come through here to clear. The old currency, we shred it up down here," the employee said. "This is the Eighth District. We cover Memphis, Louisville, and Little Rock, Arkansas. Kansas City has one that covers out west."

The employee has seen what are believed to be three deceased former employees of the bank. The first, a housekeeper named Willy Kirby, died at the bank near the end of his shift.

"He was cleaning up here, and he wasn't feeling good that day," the employee said. "He sat down on a chair back there, because it was kind of walled-off...and it was getting near the end, and he got up to leave, and he fell over dead. And they turned the place upside down looking for him that night, because normally we all walk out together, and he wasn't there."

The employee wasn't around when Willy Kirby had his fatal heart attack around 1990 but saw Kirby last year nonetheless.

"I turned around and looked at him and said, 'What are you doing here?'" the employee said. "He turned and looked at me, solid as could be, kind of gave me one of those 'Who are you?' looks. It was just a few seconds, but you could tell he was disoriented. Had on a uniform, receding hairline, black shoes, blue pants, light blue shirt—that's our uniform. I thought maybe he was someone from days. Didn't recognize him from days."

A lightbulb from an adjacent building caught the employee's eye, and when the employee looked back a split second later, the housekeeper was gone.

"So I grabbed my keys, ran around the corner here, because I wanted to know who it was in our uniform," the employee said. "I never found anyone. I described the man to Bob [the supervisor], and he said, 'That's Willy Kirby.'"

One night while turning the lights off on the third floor, the employee heard the sound of keys jingling in a back hallway and assumed it was a security guard.

"I thought it was Roger and decided to play a joke: turned off the lights and went this way, because there's a key down there to turn. I thought, 'I'm going to jump out and scare him when he comes back up.' He never came back up. I went down there, but there was nobody there. The only ones who have keys are the guards."

The employee's good friend and co-worker, Carol, was fatally injured in a car accident a few years ago. Since then, the employee believes she has returned to help find missing objects and provide assistance.

"About a year or so after she got killed, I think she was saving my butt all over the place," the employee said. "One of the guys ran off and left his radio someplace. Radios are expensive, and I looked all over, had just about given up, and then I hear this ka-BAAM!!! big crash, like someone had knocked over a shelf full of glass."

But nothing was amiss.

"I came around the corner. There's the radio sitting right there on that table. It was probably there all along, and it was the last place I would have looked. I think it was Carol telling me to come over and look that way."

Carol also makes sure the trash is taken out.

"One of the employees is always in a hurry to get out of here, so he doesn't always make the last round like he should," the employee said. "One night we were getting ready to leave. This elevator came down, the door opened, and there was a big bag of trash sitting there. Nobody called it—it just showed up. Another time, I got on at the eighth floor and pushed three. Instead of three, we went all the way to the basement. Opened the door, there's trash sitting there by the elevator.

"I think she's saying, 'Hey! Don't leave yet.'"

Why would people be so loyal to their bank jobs that they would return after death?

"I don't know," the employee said. "I've seen people—they literally despise the place, but they work here for thirty years. Recently, we had a lot of construction going on, and a lot happened. I think that's why a lot of them do come back—they see the area being torn up, or [they] come and check in, and things aren't like they were. And around here, as much construction as they do, things are never like they are."

The upstairs auditorium used to be home to the data processing department many years ago.

"You can come up here late at night and stand outside, and there'll be sounds like there's computers running—the machinery with the big old IBM punch cards," the employee said. "You listen, and you hear a department working; you open the door, and it's an auditorium."

And what's inside the auditorium gave one of the housekeepers the creeps.

"She was vacuuming, felt somebody watching her, turned around, and there was a man standing between those two pillars, watching her. She said he was just white, your traditional ghost, transparent and kind of misty. She just stared at him, and he eventually vanished.

"She'd get that kind of feeling when she did other stuff, and she felt him follow her all the way to the elevator. She finally just turned around and said, 'Look—leave me alone when I'm working.'"

The employee laughed. "She never saw him again."

But the auditorium is a creepy place, the employee said.

"One night I came up here to talk to the lady who cleaned up here, and she said, 'I'm not going back in there. That door decided to open on its own.' There's a door for the projection room that's always kept locked—nobody has a key, really, except for the guards. I was up here maybe a half hour beforehand, and it was shut, locked. And I come up here, and it's standing wide open."

Dying to Please at Jefferson Barracks

Walking around and using the bathroom was one thing. But when an otherworldly office occupant kept setting off security alarms, Michael Pierce had to put his foot down.

"About ten years ago, I was employed by an organization that has its headquarters in a converted officers' quarters duplex at Jefferson Barracks," recalled Pierce, of St. Louis. "These buildings went up in the late 1800s."

One Saturday morning Pierce was working alone in the building in a small office on the second floor. At the end of the hall was a bathroom.

"I heard the toilet flush, the door close, steps go down the hall and down the steps, then the sound of footfalls stopped," Pierce recalled. "I got up from my desk and went to take a look around. The doors were locked, no one was in the building. I guess I was mildly bewildered."

Company employees also had problems with the building's security system.

"Our security system was always going off several evenings a week after the office was closed and we had all gone home," he said. The security company came out and checked the motion sensors numerous times. Nothing was found that could be setting off the alarms."

Intrigued, Pierce—who is studying full time for a B.A. degree in history at Webster University—decided to learn more about the building.

"In my research, I found out a young army officer was killed in one of the upstairs bedrooms by his wife," he said. "She found out he was messing around with one of the nurses on the base, so she stabbed him to death."

The next time Pierce received a call about the alarm going off, he was ready.

"I went out to check, as usual, and everything was okay," he said. "I stood in the middle of the downstairs room and said, 'Listen, you can have the run of the building when we're not here. JUST STOP SETTING OFF MY DAMNED ALARMS!!!'

"They never went off again."

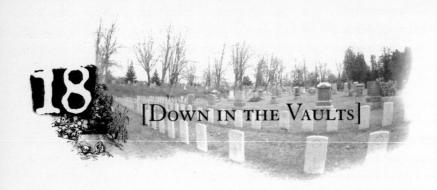

[Down in the Vaults]

It doesn't get much spookier than this: a wet, overcrowded, disease-ridden slum, closed off underground for more than a century, and reopened as a tourist attraction in 1997 amid countless reports of ghostly presences.

The place is Edinburgh, Scotland's, South Bridge Vaults, which have acquired an international reputation for being one of the most haunted parts of Scotland's capital city. The time is April 2001, and the players include parapsychologist James Houran, of Springfield, Illinois, who was asked by colleague Dr. Richard Wiseman, of the United Kingdom, to help set up and monitor what became known as the "Edinburgh Ghost Project," part of the Edinburgh International Science Festival.

"Richard has clout in the United Kingdom; he's a well-known public figure and a well-established parapsychologist," Houran noted. "He was able to get permission to bring groups of people down into these vaults. I was called over to help with the experiment because I had a lot of experience doing on-site investigations and how to design experiments where you're testing psychological variables in connection with these experiences."

The Vaults: Traumatic History

"Edinburgh is probably one of the most famous cities abroad that has haunting activity," Houran said. "And of course, Edinburgh Castle has a long history of violence, death, disease, poverty, famine—just the whole area. Being a city that was so large, there were areas of town where we would consider slums, certain parts where large numbers of people died, certain parts where people were sequestered or quarantined so disease wouldn't spread. It has a very intense history of violence, disease, and death. It's not a surprise, therefore, that people report experiences in parts of the city."

Edinburgh's South Bridge was built in the late eighteenth century to ease transportation problems in the city. Constructed of nineteen stone arches supporting a wide road lined with several three-story buildings, the arches housed a series of "vaults," or rooms, and corridors built inside.

"The bridge was so large that they actually could build little compartments in the bridge for workers to have their workshops, people to live, storage rooms," Houran said. "That worked out fine until they realized they didn't waterproof the bridge properly, and water seeped into these work areas, and people couldn't live there anymore, people couldn't work, and they abandoned them. And then they filled it all with earth, and people pretty much forgot about it until about twenty years ago they were rediscovered.

"So they started digging out these compartments and vaults—they were actually labeled and numbered—and taking people through them, and people started having experiences," he said. "People started hearing voices, seeing people in period clothing. People would feel someone touch them on the shoulder. [You'd get] the feeling that you're being watched or sense a presence when no one is there. Some of these experiences were so intense that people would refuse to go down there alone, and some tour guides that took people through there refused to go down there. It was on a series on the Discovery Channel called *Haunted History*.'"

Into the Vaults

People attending the science festival in Edinburgh were invited to participate in the investigation, to date the world's largest and most systematic haunt investigation, Houran said. Participants were taken to a room where they received a presentation on the historic significance of the vaults, and then were taken into the vaults, first to a meeting room and then, individually, to one of ten rooms. Five were haunted; five were non-haunted, or "control," rooms.

"Now, the person didn't know which room they were going in; in fact, they weren't told there were five haunted rooms and five unhaunted rooms," he said. "They were just told, 'We want you to participate in an investigation of the South Bridge Vaults today. We're going to be taking you down, and you're going to spend ten minutes alone in one of these little rooms. And I have a questionnaire for you, and I want you to write down any strange thing that happens that you notice.'

"They weren't allowed to talk to anybody, [although in] some of the rooms you could see other people. We had investigators in each of the hallways to make sure there was no contact or communication among the participants. And the [facilitators]—I was one of the people to help facilitate this—also did not know which rooms were haunted and which were not haunted. So we were all uninformed as to what was happening."

Some Startling Reactions

"After the ten minutes, people would write down things like 'I was being watched,' 'There was a strange odor in the air,' 'I felt I was being touched,' maybe they saw apparitions; we have a wide range of experiences people reported," Houran said. "Some people didn't report anything. At the end of the ten minutes, they came back out, they filled out their questionnaires, and they also took back a packet of psychological tests that I gave them."

Of those who went through the vaults, about 60 percent, or 134 people, actually followed up with the questionnaires and the tests.

"Without the research subjects knowing which rooms were haunted or not haunted, sure enough, people tend to report experiences that happened where people previously reported things," he said. "We kept getting this effect of focusing. Only certain areas in a haunted place will people report something. It's only certain locations. There's something special in certain environments that people are responding to.

"In Scotland, the people reported more experiences in the five haunted vaults versus the five control vaults, without them knowing which were which. And again, this is different levels of belief [in the paranormal]. It's not just strong believers. It was mostly the believers that reported things—that's predictable.

"Sixty-six of the 134 people reported some type of experience—often, more than one," he added. "Some experiences were very subtle, such as change in temperature, which was the most common one. Other people reported very dramatic things: full-blown apparitions in period clothing talking to them. My background as a clinician actually is very helpful, because sometimes these experiences can have such an impact on people they freak out. They don't know what to do, they just break down, start crying.

"One woman even refused to leave the room because she was in such a trance. She was literally engrossed, and other experimenters tried to tell her, 'The experiment's over; it's time for you to leave.' She wouldn't respond to that, so I had to come in and ease her out [of the trance]. I first had to get her to come back to her normal waking consciousness, and then I had to ease her out and talk to her about her experience. There were some very intense things—there's not just things we can easily disregard, but some very dramatic things."

Psychological Variables Involved

Of the 134 people who took the tests, 66 had an experience, and 68 did not. That's a high number, but participants also knew they were part of a haunted investigation, Houran said.

"They were going down into vaults which were dark and dreary, looked the part—they really looked scary—plus they were alone, so that kind of heightens your anxiety," he said. "So we have the atmosphere right there."

Participants were questioned on a number of psychological variables such as absorption, how strongly someone can become involved in an experience; hyperesthesia, one's sensitivity to environmental variables such as light levels and sounds; synesthesia, the unusual ability to experience things such as colors or sounds in more than one sensory mode; whether the participant expected, before going in, to have such an experience; belief in New Age philosophy, including having dreams that come true later or thinking of a person who calls the next minute; and transliminality, how easily one can summon up images, fantasies, emotions, or memories from one's inner (unconscious and preconscious) mind.

"People who are high in transliminality have a very fluid gateway," Houran said. "They are very easy to get in control with their inner selves. These are fun-loving people. They're open-minded, they're willing to try new things, they're open to new experiences, they have very good memories and are very creative...artists are good transliminals; accountants are people with low transliminality."

Not surprisingly, the people who had experiences scored higher on all these variables, he said.

"What this study in Scotland revealed for the first time...was that people's sensitivity to the actual physical environment plays a major role," Houran said. "So the type of people that see ghosts, we know from a psychological-profile point of view, they are expecting to see something, or at least they know the possibility of it. They're believers, but not just any believers—they're the kind of believers in the paranormal that need to feel they're in control of their environment. If something strange is happening, they need an explanation for it. And they tend to be people who are very sensitive to the environment, so they're going to notice more things happening.

"So it's a certain type of person, but also in a certain location," he said. "We're still trying to figure out what it is in those locations that people are responding to. They're responding to something. They're very sensitive to something. They're reporting similar experiences in the same parts of the building, and these reports are all independent. People don't know that other people reported similar types of things in that room, yet they are experiencing sort of the same thing. So there's something systematic going on, and it's just not the person anymore. There's something in certain environments that's just there. Maybe it's electromagnetic, maybe it's cues in the environment, maybe it's just a ghost—I don't know. But there's some element in the environment that really is there, for people to report this trend."

Strong electromagnetic fields influence the brain to simulate paranormal events, Houran said (see Chapter 1, Searching for Answers).

"What's happening is natural sources of magnetic activity—electromagnetic fields—can influence people's minds, influence people's brains, and cause experiences that are what people have been reporting as hauntings, ghosts, UFOs, alien abductions," he said. "And it influences a particular part of the brain called the temporal lobe. The temporal lobes are the ones that facilitate our rich complex of memory and fantasy. So if I stimulate your temporal lobes, your brain kind of goes haywire, and you start reliving past experiences, things that you are perceiving now become much more rich and meaningful than they did before, and you start getting a lot of emotional changes. So basically you're producing experiences in people that parallel hauntings and poltergeists and alien abductions, all these weird things that people report. Whether that individual presence is an angel, a demon, an alien, or a ghost depends on the person's religious and cultural backgrounds and suggestion."

But that doesn't account for the details: why ghosts have clothing, why they are talking to the person, what they're saying, Houran noted.

"The psychological part comes from context," he said. "In other words, if we stimulate someone's temporal lobe in a saloon in a ghost town, they're going to see western figures. Now, early on, psychical researchers and amateur ghosthunters say that, well, ghosts are tied to a location. That's why you find cowboy ghosts in a haunted saloon. Well, this other research says, no, it works the other way, again, just like the EMF: the environment tells you how to interpret ambiguous stimuli. So you'll never see phantom elephants in a haunted saloon."

No Ghosts Yet

So far, Houran said, researchers haven't found any ghosts, but in learning the tremendous role psychology plays in these manifestations, they've found something just as interesting.

"We're very far along in understanding haunts," he said. "We haven't solved it all—of course not. It's very expensive to do these large-scale studies, like in Scotland. The mathematics involved in this are just awful, *awful*. But it's doable. And we've learned something very important about how people work, how sensation and perception work, how emotion works, and how people's beliefs interact with their behaviors. We learn more about the living, by studying ghosts, than we do about the dead.

"It's amazing what our minds do with just a little bit of information," he added. "But that just shows you—that doesn't mean we're crazy. When people hear I'm a mental health worker and I also gain insights into imagination, hallucinations, and delusions by studying these experiences, I explain to them that it doesn't mean I believe they are crazy at all for having these experiences. What it means is your brain is doing what it's supposed to do, and that is [to] make sense of things we don't understand.

"In fact, I'm giving you a compliment," he added. "I'm saying you're a creative person whose mind is working wonderfully."

There is still much to learn, Houran said.

"We don't want to jump to conclusions of unexplained phenomena being paranormal," he said. "When there really is something strange, parapsychologists and healthy skeptics will admit it. That is, they will concede there is an anomaly that needs an explanation: 'So let's try to figure out under what conditions it happens. Can we duplicate that in any way? What information can we get to tell us about the nature of that anomaly?'

"That's what we do. We don't try to jump and say, 'It's paranormal.' All we say is, 'It's unexplained.' We don't know. That's why I'm investigating."

[HISTORIC HAUNTS]

From antebellum mansions shaded by cypress trees to solid stone fortresses, historic homes in St. Louis have, over the years, come in an array of shapes, sizes, and locations. Some are still standing, others have been demolished, but all offer a fascinating glimpse into our area's history. And once in a while they treat the observant visitor to a glimpse of previous residents, as well.

Thomas January Residence: Pride of Ferguson

During its final years, it was a mere shell of its former glory. But fifty years earlier it was a beautiful country estate, a large brick mansion built in 1842 by Thomas January in what is now known as Ferguson, Missouri.

Spectacular views of the countryside were possible from the two-story porch that ran across the front of the home, which for years was shaded by two Mississippi cypress trees. A private racetrack and a small spring-fed pond graced the grounds.

"Thomas January, among other things, was the first treasurer of St. Louis County," noted Ruth Brown, a member of the Ferguson Historical Society. "He was also one of the reasons why Ferguson became a community...he was on the site selection committee for what was then the North Missouri Railroad when the railroad was trying to establish a commuter path from St. Louis to St. Charles. And he made sure that they came very close to his property. In addition, he talked another fairly large landowner, William B. Ferguson, into sort of agreeing with this plan."

The house was breathtaking, Brown said.

"It was quite large, quite opulent," she said. "A person who saw it described a very grand staircase up through the main entrance, and so forth.

Mr. January raised blooded horses, and that's why he built this little spot that had a spring into January-Wabash Lake, and so forth, and then it was enlarged. Mr. January's lake fed the water tank for the steam engines down at the depot, so he arranged to have that happen, too. He gave grand parties up there. I know that he had threshing contests or something, where farmers came up there and, I guess, showed off their tractors or whatever from really quite a large region."

There were weekend-long gambling parties at the estate, and Brown's grandfather, Frederick Bindbeutel, was selected to hold the purse for those parties. Bindbeutel founded the Bank of Ferguson (now United Missouri Bank) in 1906 .

After Thomas January died in 1886, his son Charles did his best to spend the fortune.

"I don't know what Charles did," Brown said. "He got pretty busy going through his dad's wealth. I even have a little old letter where he's asking my grandfather for a loan for Christmas of one hundred dollars because he'd like to buy his kids presents for Christmas. I think his house was on North Florissant Road. Another son, Machir, built a house because he wanted to be away from town. The humor on this, of course, is that it's the busiest drag through town now, up on Airport Road."

Thomas January's once-lovely mansion burned down in 1925 and became a legendary haunted house.

"After it burned, it had been unoccupied for a few years, and [the ruins were] a favorite place for teenaged kids who had recently acquired cars to take buddies up there and try to scare each other, you know," Brown said. "I'm not sure there are any legitimate stories, but it was used as a scaredy-cat, daring one another to spend the night there and all, and supposedly hearing chains rattle in the basement and all that kind of stuff."

Still fairly far out of town in the late 1920s, the property was used as the city dump for a time, and in 1936 the Ferguson School District acquired the land and built Ferguson High School with WPA funds on the site, Brown said. It opened in 1939 at 701 January Avenue.

"People came from all over the north region to go to Ferguson High School because it was the one that was closest," Brown said. "When I was in high school in the last half of the '50s, kids got bused in from the way far reaches of Florissant and all. Nineteen sixty-two was the last graduating class of Ferguson High School. Then they moved to McCluer. Then it was called the junior high, but later they called it the middle school."

Scrubby Dutch In Kimmswick: The Ziegler House

One of Kimmswick's restored buildings, the Ziegler House is a charming white frame house with a white picket fence in front. In the summer of 1978, former Webster Groves resident Doug Harding spent the summer there with his friend John, who was renting the house.

"One summer between semesters when I was at school, I was working as a seasonal down here," said Harding, now a park ranger for the National Park Service. "When Old Man Ziegler first built the house—he was a German immigrant—he was a very unusual-looking character. He was a captain in the Union army during the Civil War, and they even have a photograph of him—big, tall black hat pulled up on one side, and he's got this big black beard that he parted down the middle (and separated into two parts).

"But he also was a jeweler, a watchsmith, so when he built the house, he had the shop in the front room, and so he had these cases built," Harding added. "My friend John is a reenactor, and he also is a dealer in goods and supplies that reenactors use—small things like buttons and photographs, toiletry supplies. So he had *his* shop in the front room, with the glass cases, so it was kind of like bringing it back to the way it was used originally."

Old Michael Ziegler used to take long walks around town, and every now and then, early in the morning, people have reported seeing him around town, Harding said.

Ziegler's wife was reputedly very immaculate about her house, and strange things often happened after the house was cleaned. Harding believes he saw Mrs. Ziegler himself one night while typing an application for a seasonal Park Service position at the kitchen table.

"I'm typing away, and I get this really, really creepy feeling," he said. "I look up through the doorway toward the basement stairs, and I see this kind of smoky shape of a woman standing there. I said, 'Oh, hi, Mrs. Ziegler,' kind of half-jokingly, went back to typing, and it went away.

"I smoke cigarettes, but I wasn't smoking in the house. John didn't like me smoking in the house—I had to go outside and smoke. So it wasn't cigarette smoke that was hanging there. It looked like this cloud of cigarette smoke, but you could just see the silhouette of a woman standing there. That's the first time I ran into Mrs. Ziegler. She would come out every now and then, only I never saw her after that, but I could always feel that she was there. Usually, it was right after we cleaned, like she was inspecting our work."

And old Mrs. Ziegler may not have cared for cats, particularly one who liked to mess up freshly Windexed glass display cases.

"John had a cat, a black cat, that he called Kitty Popcorn," Harding said. "It comes from an old Henry Clay Work song from the Civil War period, about a black cat that was adopted by the Union soldiers. When we would do our weekly housecleaning, this cat would watch us clean the glass counters, and as soon as we got done he would jump up on the counter and walk across it and leave little pawprints on it. Very mischievous cat.

"One night Kitty Popcorn was being a little bit rambunctious, but no more than usual," he said. "We were back in the kitchen, and we heard this crash in the front shop. Just about that time, Kitty Popcorn comes tearing into the kitchen and jumps up on the chair under the kitchen table behind the tablecloth. His eyes were like this big. We went out in the shop area, and a rocking chair had fallen over.

"Obviously, the cat did something that scared the heck out of him. We tried to figure out how could the cat knock the chair over? Even if the cat was on the mantel and it jumped on the back of this rocking chair, he wouldn't have enough weight to actually push it all the way over like that. So the only conclusion we could come to was that Mrs. Ziegler was upset with the cat for some reason and tipped the chair over on the cat or threw the cat across the room, whatever."

He laughed. "We did notice his pawprints on the glass cases."

Old Mrs. Ziegler may not have liked Earl, either. Earl was a Civil War reenactor and avowed atheist, who stayed in the home for a few weeks one summer a couple of years after Harding moved out.

"Earl was on Social Security, had a physical handicap, and couldn't work," Harding said. "He would buy a bus pass from Greyhound and travel around the country and live off reenactors until they got tired of him. He was really good at reproducing clothing, footwear, and things like that to sell to reenactors."

One night Harding came to the home to visit John, who was out on the town.

"I knocked on the front door; no one answered," he recalled. "I'm walking back toward the picket fence, the door slams open, and there's Earl. His eyes are this big, he's got scissors in his hand, and he says, 'Don't you ever do that again.' I said, 'What?' He said, 'You scared the heck out of me.' I said, 'What are you talking about?' He said, 'These scissors flew across the room at me.'

"He was doing some sewing, and evidently Mrs. Ziegler was trying to get his attention one way or another," Harding chuckled. "He made me stay there with him in the house until John came home."

Myers House: Many Incarnations, A Few Apparitions

John B. Myers, it is said, planned his home in the perfect location in 1869—so perfect that at least one of his immediate family members remains there today.

Nancy Quade, owner of The Weaving Department, has had her shop at Myers House in Florissant for fifteen years. She also served as a volunteer at the house for five years before that.

"Mr. Myers was a land speculator, a farmer from Illinois," Quade said. "His wife [Adaline] came from Pennsylvania and Illinois. He knew, obviously, where to build this house, because it's just a perfect situation here. As one of my friends says, it's cool winter and summer, breezy. He contracted pneumonia and died during the basement excavation. Mrs. Myers completed the building of the house, but during the Victorian era it was not proper for a woman to deal with tradespeople, so the people in Florissant helped her do that.

"Ten years later the walls were [decoratively] painted, and the doors were grained," Quade noted. "It was a grand mansion. Mrs. Myers had two girls, and she was pregnant with a little boy when her husband died. She was a very determined lady, and when you see pictures of her you know that she's going to complete the house."

Once part of a fifty-acre farm, the home sustained two fires, both caused by lightning strikes. One of the Myers daughters was killed during one of the fires, Quade said. Since then, the house has gone through several commercial transformations: it has been a church, a retirement home, a boarding house, and more. And during the construction of Highway 170, the home barely escaped demolition. But then-owner Hazel Ivancich urged the Florissant City Council to declare the vacant home a city landmark.

"She was very congenial to the fact that someone should take it over," Quade said. "Eventually it was recognized as a landmark by the U.S. Department of Transportation, so that prevented the highway department from destroying it. Then Historic Florissant Inc. was born and took over the house, and they did the renovation, and the people that they rented rooms to for antiques or for crafts did the renovations, and Eagle Scouts took all the white paint off the stairway and found walnut underneath. I came shortly after Historic Florissant was established.

"The community was very generous. We had fundraisers, and they'd send in ten dollars and twenty-five dollars and a hundred dollars. It really was a community effort."

The only drawback is the roar of the highway not far beyond the front porch.

"One of my friends said, 'You just pretend that's the ocean; it sounds just like the ocean.' She lives in Seattle, and it does," Quade noted with a smile.

And the noise hasn't stopped either Mrs. Myers or the daughter killed in a fire, one of whom is believed to appear in the house from time to time.

"I used to dress up in a long dress and bonnet, and one of the antique dealers who was here said she saw me in the hall one morning, and I was not here," she said. "It was a woman in a long dress. People have only seen her in the hall, to my knowledge."

Legend has it that a woman walks back and forth along the widow's walk atop Myers House, but Quade said she had no information to substantiate the tale. And Historic Florissant Inc. volunteer Margaret Archambault, while walking around the property once, heard a voice say, "It's a miracle you've saved this house!" (see *Spirits of St. Louis: A Ghostly Guide to the Mound City's Unearthly Activities*).

"Other people have sensed coffee being brewed, and there is no coffee," Quade said. "Little things like this that make you think, well, yeah, there's something going on. My husband claims that tools have been missing when he comes up [to work]. He finds them elsewhere, but he's very careful with his tools, so I tend to give him the benefit of the doubt on that.

"Some of the other people who have worked here hear footsteps coming up the stairs. Now that's old house stuff—everybody who lives in an old house hears footsteps coming up the stairs—so that could be a presence or not. A couple of my people have even gotten up and gone out to look, and there aren't any people."

An unidentified man also greeted an antique dealer at the home early one morning, Quade said.

"He had a shop downstairs, and he was bringing things from a sale in another state at, like, two o'clock in the morning," she said. "After he had unloaded a few things, there was a man standing on the stairway in a uniform, an old uniform, like Civil War."

She laughed. "So he dropped his things and went. He did not finish unloading. That's the only story about a male I've ever heard here. It's always the females drifting down the hall and disappearing."

Having a ghost legend to call one's own is nice, Quade said.

"It's a very friendly place to work—we've been here all hours of the night and morning," she said. "We were talking the other day about how southerners have so many wonderful stories about their houses, and northerners are so cynical, and we don't believe any of those things and don't pass along or even partake of them. So it's kind of nice to have these things."

Landmark House: Jefferson County's Rough-Cut Gem

A Jefferson County panorama surrounds the third-story cupola of Pevely's Landmark House, offering views of the Mississippi River, the area's rapidly declining farmland, and a rich historic legacy.

Legend has it that one of the home's long-ago residents hanged herself in the cupola and now haunts it. But Chuck Banks, who owns the home with his mother, Bernice Banks, has trouble believing that one.

"Everything's pretty short, so for Mrs. Ziegler to have hanged herself, she would have had to have been very short," Banks chuckled. "The Zieglers probably lived here until 1912, and it went through several owners before we bought it."

The spectacular views, however, he can vouch for.

"It's great from up here when there's a big storm coming in; you can watch it come," he said. "On that property is where Bartholomew Harrington had his stagecoach stopover on the El Camino Reale, which is the road from St. Louis to Ste. Genevieve, and it came right up the Old State Road here and went on down to Herculaneum and south. Bartholomew Harrington was the first settler here. He came over in 1789, 1790, something like that, and across the street from the bottling plant you can see the Harrington family cemetery where he's buried. He's a Revolutionary War veteran. Over there is the Dunklin gravesite, the smallest state park in the state—just a gravesite. It overlooks the river, and Governor [Daniel] Dunklin is buried there. Dunklin lived in Herculaneum."

Banks's parents, Charles and Bernice, purchased the Landmark House property along Old State Road in 1961 for the 150 acres it contained. They built a subdivision, Cha-Bern, and a mobile home park, Landmark Manor. The limestone house, in service as a four-family flat at the time, was a bonus.

"It's kind of used as a community center—Cub Scouts, Boy Scouts, Girl Scouts, Lions Club, Community Chest have met there," said Banks, a Pevely resident who is employed as Congressman Richard Gephardt's Jefferson County coordinator. "It was built around 1851 by Dr. William Clark. We don't know if he was a medical doctor, but he acted as a medical doctor.

"He went west with the Gold Rush of 1849, came back with enough cash to build it—that's the story the family passed to us," he said. "He was a strict Southern supporter, staunch Confederate. When the Civil War ended, he died. The family said he got distraught and died because the South lost. It was sold to riverboat captain Alexander Ziegler in 1868, and there was an old story that Ziegler's grandmother hung herself in the cupola. We've never been able to confirm that."

Other legends have it that a tunnel ran from the house to the Mississippi River nearby and that the home was a stop on the Underground Railroad.

"We've never been able to find anything for sure," Banks said of the tunnel. "There's supposedly a bum that froze to death in the mouth of the tunnel, which is supposedly over on the river side. We've looked for it many times without success."

And of the Underground Railroad, he said, "I find it hard to believe, if Clark was a Confederate. If they were going any way, they were going south, not north."

Over the years, the Federal-style stone house has been used as everything from a funeral parlor and brothel to a hospital, courthouse, and warehouse. In the basement of the home, Banks made an interesting discovery.

"We don't know why there's these brick pilasters, one in this room and one in the front room," he said. "And if you look back here, there's an indentation in the wall that is actually laid up that way; it's actually a hole in the wall. We don't know why that's there—that's not common construction practice. There's a lot of caves around Pevely, and there's a good chance when they were digging the foundation, they hit a cave. And they could have shored this up or basically laid up pilings."

Is the strange, cavelike entrance responsible for the a string of unexplained events at the home? As far back as the '60s, apartment tenants in the home complained of moaning noises and chains rattling, Banks said.

"It was probably other tenants—I don't know," he laughed. "But there's something about the house that doesn't like to be painted. When we paint the house, strange noises occur. A fellow wanted to rent these two rooms and was in here one night painting his office. It was summertime, the windows were open, the doors were open, and he heard someone walking upstairs from the front of the house to the rear of the house. So he went up to check it out, and nobody was up there. He locked all the doors, shut the windows, went back to painting, and then he heard the footsteps again from the front of the house to the back of the house. He left and didn't paint there at night anymore."

Banks painted the house again, including the woodwork, around 1998.

"I had a group of Cub Scouts meeting in there, and on the mantel in the one room there are pictures of Dr. Clark and his wife, Lily Ellis—two pictures," he said. "I came in, and the two pictures were on the floor. Dr. Clark's glass was broken, and the leader assumed that the kids might have knocked it off at the last meeting, though there were no kids there. So she got new glass, we talked about it, and I put them back on the mantel. The next day, they were back on the floor again. There was no meeting the night before."

Banks and his wife, Mary Ann, plan on renovating the home someday to include a tea room and a couple of bed-and-breakfast rooms. For now, however, the all-purpose Landmark House will go on with its myriad duties, including a stint as the Boy Scouts' haunted house each fall. And that leads to another story....

"As you go down the basement stairs, there's a small room, and it's not part of the haunted house; they don't want people going in there," Banks said. "Last year, I took a long wood screw, and I screwed the door shut. I put a screw in it right here into this framework, and I locked the front door and left. I was the first guy in the next evening to open up, came down the steps, and that door was busted open and [the wood framework] was split. Nothing in the house was disturbed.

"Now, there was nobody in there unless somebody broke in—didn't steal anything—and there's no way into that room except for the way it was broken in. If one of the kids broke in, there was no sign of that."

Little episodes like that are common around the Landmark House, Banks said.

"It's something about the house," he said. "At night when you go home and you turn the lights off, something kind of quickens your step as you head for the door and get it locked."

He laughed. "It makes your hair rise."

20 [Spirited Souvenirs]

Take a St. Louisan out of St. Louis, and what do you have? For starters, there's Barbara Stanwyck's old digs in Hollywood, where the ghostly antics startled composer Craig Cervantes and inspired the movie *Poltergeist*; a visit to a Denmark castle that earned Shirley Blaine a not-so-secret admirer; a tour of England's Warwick Castle, complete with the ghost of honor for a young Bill Wunderlich; and a strange encounter with a young soldier on a desolate Gettysburg battlefield for Civil War reenactor George Wunderlich.

Haunted Hollywood Hijinks—*Poltergeist* Style

"I moved to Los Angeles, California, in the summer of '75, and I got a room in a home; the third floor was available for rent," noted Craig Cervantes, a music composer, producer, and real estate broker who now divides his time between St. Louis and Los Angeles.

"It was the former residence of Barbara Stanwyck, who had sold it to the Theosophical Society. The Theosophists are, I guess, some sort of Christian theological group," he said. "And the home had a chapel in it, and the owner was the president of a bank in Los Angeles named Don Jolly. We became friends, and he said that his incentive for renting out the third floor was that he was scared to be there by himself because all these occurrences were happening. My brother Barry can verify the story."

One notable evening, the Cervantes brothers learned Jolly wasn't joking.

"We had witnessed a head of cabbage flying through the room with a crucifix in it while a dinner party was going on. It flew against the wall, hit the wall, and we knew that there was nobody else in the house, other than the people who were at the dinner table," he said. "That was kind of strange.

"Then there was a whole wall of stained glass by the dining table that had an image in it of Christopher Columbus and a ship and crusaders and that kind of thing. We walked into the living room to study the cabbage head and the crucifix in it, and when we turned around, all the chairs in the dining room were toppled over each other like dominoes, and the stained glass was clear—there was absolutely no color in it whatsoever."

The partyers heard a knock at the front door. When they got there, all the wrought-iron furniture from the kitchen was stacked on top of itself at the front door, blocking the entrance.

"Then we saw the chandelier swinging in the foyer, and we ran up the steps, and there was smoke coming from underneath a door in the bathroom on the second floor by the chapel," Cervantes said. "We're thinking, 'my God, there's a fire in the bathroom,' so we knocked the door open, and there was a trash can on fire in the bathroom. I picked the trash can up and put it in the shower and reached to turn on the shower, and the knobs were missing off the shower—just the spikes the knobs go on—so that you couldn't get water."

He laughed. "I couldn't make this stuff up if I wanted to. So everybody kind of checked out of the house for the night. That house ultimately became the idea for the story *Poltergeist*, because the owner of the home went to the University of Southern California and recruited Steven Spielberg to come up and film these occurrences. So there's some truth to that movie, although the home was never sitting on top of a cemetery and all that kind of stuff."

One last crazy encounter capped the night.

"Before that evening even started," Cervantes said, "my brother had just graduated from college, and he bought a used Alfa Romeo, and he was coming up to see me, and I was going out to get provisions. Somehow, we both hit each other head-on in front of the property and totalled our cars out. And my dad [former St. Louis Mayor A. J. Cervantes] was in the insurance business and had us both insured, so you can imagine how upset he was."

Someday My Prince Will Come
Shirley Blaine's illustrious career as the Belleville Ghostbuster never would have gotten its start had she not taken a trip with her family to Denmark more than a decade ago.

During a three-hour walking tour through an immense castle, Blaine found a secret admirer perched in one of the rooms.

"My eyes scanned the room, and they kept getting pulled back to this chaise lounge," she said. "And there, formed in front of me, was a prince with long, dark, curly hair. He had a maroon velvet suit on, and it scared me—I had no idea what that was, so I ran out of the room.

"We continued on the rest of the tour and went down into the basement, and they had turned it into a sauna back in the '50s. We were touring that, and all of a sudden it was like all these things were trying to communicate with me—coming at me, talking to me. I felt like I was being attacked.

"So I ran out, and as I looked back, up in the window my Danish prince was waving bye to me. I swore I'd never go back in that building."

Confused over what had happened, Blaine made some phone calls when she returned to her Belleville home. That's when she learned she was sensitive, or psychic, and began taking various lessons from psychic Terry Engle, whom Blaine later adopted as her surrogate mother.

"You know, I can't wait to get back to Denmark," Blaine said. "I can't wait to get back into that castle."

A Picture-Perfect Likeness

"When I graduated from St. Louis University back in 1959, I went to Europe with a Jesuit priest from the university and some other students," recalled retired insurance broker Bill Wunderlich, of Chesterfield. "As part of our trip, we went to Warwick Castle.

"We were guided around the castle, and the last place we went was the keep. Now, the keep is a tower where people go as the last stand—if the castle's been taken over completely, they go there and fight to the last drop of blood. And there's only one way to get to it, and that's a spiral staircase up to it, and then a room at the top."

The students ascended the staircase and were admiring the art collection for which the castle is famous.

"The guide, who was standing by the door, said that this painting that I was standing next to was one of the earls of Warwick, who died in the castle," Wunderlich said. "And there was a gentleman standing next to the painting who looked enough like the guy on the painting to be his twin brother. And the guide said, 'If you will come down the stairs, we will meet in the courtyard, and I'll dismiss you.'

"Father Martin was standing by the door looking at a cabinet," Wunderlich recalled. "I was standing in the room. Everybody else had gone, except this other gentleman, myself, and Father Martin. So I said to the guy, 'You know, you look awfully like the painting on the wall. Are you related to the earl of Warwick?' And he smiled, and he said, 'Many people have noted that.' And I turned around to Father Martin, and I said, 'Father, does this man look like the painting?' Father turned around and looked at me and said, 'What man?' The guy had disappeared."

As the years went by, Wunderlich realized just how famous the ghost really was.

"My daughter was in grade school, and she was reading *A Connecticut Yankee in King Arthur's Court*, and she said, 'Dad, you know, your ghost is in that book.' I said, 'Oh, you're kidding.' So she read it to me and, sure enough, the ghost is in the first part of the book."

And about eight years ago at a dinner party, Wunderlich learned he wasn't alone in his observations.

"I started to tell the story of the earl of Warwick, when two young ladies who were sitting at the table with me said, 'Stop. You were at Warwick Castle, weren't you?' I said, 'How did you know?' 'We met the ghost, too.' Which just about blew my mind.

He chuckled. "The funny part about it, if I were the only one, I could say, 'Maybe it was a delusion.' But to have the kind of confirmation that I had at Ken's party just absolutely shook me, because here were two young ladies who had the almost identical experience."

Goosebumps in Gettysburg: A Soldier Returns

Bill Wunderlich's son, George, grew up to have an otherworldly experience of his own in 1992. He was a Civil War reenactor on a trip to Gettysburg, Pennsylvania, with two friends. Wunderlich now lives in Frederick County, Maryland, and is director of education for the National Museum of Civil War Medicine.

"We went up there for what is called Remembrance Day, which is the commemoration of the dedication of the national cemetery in Gettysburg," George Wunderlich said. "We went up to the parade and everything, and that evening we were all dressed in our period clothes.

"My friend in the back seat says to my buddy in the front, 'Hey, you want to go feel a cold spot on the battlefield?' Typically, as you probably well know, cold spots are related to ghost sightings or whatever; they say that's where a spirit is. And Bob says, 'I know of a couple; let's drive out there.' And the park doesn't close until ten o'clock. This was probably nine, nine-fifteen.

"So we pulled off the main road and went up through the battlefield to a place called the Triangular Field, which is near another spot on the battlefield known as the Devil's Den, which has nothing to do with ghost sightings. It was always called the Devil's Den because it was this large outcropping of rock that you can't plow around; it was no good for anything."

Feeling ill, Wunderlich declined the adventure.

"I couldn't tell if I had just eaten too much dinner, which is quite possible," he chuckled, "or if something was going on. I said, 'You know, I'm going to stay in the car.'

"I have to set the scene: It's a beautiful, crisp, clear night, about thirty-five degrees, a full moon—not quite, but close. You can see about a mile up the road, all the way to the National Park Service visitors' center building—it's that clear. You can see across the field three-quarters of a mile and see every detail of Little Round Top rising up from the valley floor.

"The car was running, the parking lights were on. You can see, if you look behind you in the rearview mirror, all the trees and everything behind you are kind of lit up red. In front of me, the trees and the road are yellow because of the parking lights. And the engine's running, and the heater's on, and the radio is turned on, but the volume is turned off, so the numbers of the stations are lit up."

The longer his buddies were gone, the worse Wunderlich felt.

"I've never had anything happen like that before or since, but I began to get the sense that somebody was with them," he said. "But I couldn't see them because they had gone past the stone fence on the opposite side of the road and down a hill.

"I look up toward Little Round Top, and I see headlights. And my first reaction is—I didn't know at the time that the park didn't close until ten—'This is great; it's a national park service ranger; we're all going to be arrested.' And this guy is coming down the very same path we had taken to get where we are. He's like a mile and a quarter up the road.

"I'm looking around for my friends, and I thought, 'They have been gone an inordinately long time. I can't see them anywhere.' Now this other car, I can see the headlights right down in the valley on the other side of Devil's Den below me, and all of a sudden the temperature on the inside of the car drops fifty degrees, it feels like, instantly. It starts with my left arm and works its way across my body to the right, so it feels like a cold breeze blowing from my left to my right."

Wunderlich, who is six feet eight inches tall, didn't move. He couldn't: he was sitting in the front passenger seat of a Chevy Corsica, with a banjo between his feet.

"Also, it's got a floor-shift automatic transmission, so I really can't move," he said. "When I felt this cold, I looked to my left and noticed that the numbers were moving on the radio. So that was kind of weird. And as the thing passed to the right, it sort of drew my attention off to the right. And as I look out the window, there's a Federal soldier standing there, two feet outside the car, staring through the window.

"Him I can see clearly because he was lit up by the lights from the car. There's a dome light on in the car, there's the red lights behind and the yellow lights in front, plus this sparkling moon. He's actually picking up reflections from the window of the car from the moon. Young guy, under twenty years probably, no facial hair, forage cap, blue sack coat, what appeared to be an artillery pass box or a large black haversack over one shoulder, sky blue trousers, couldn't see his feet. He was literally so close to the car that I couldn't see his feet. And he's just staring in the car. Clearly a Union soldier, probably a private—I didn't see rank."

The sighting rendered Wunderlich speechless—as well as immobile—for quite a while.

"I couldn't say a word, which is very unusual for me," he said. "He stood there for what seemed like twelve hours, and I'm sure it was probably like twelve seconds. And all of a sudden around the corner behind us comes the headlights. And when the headlights hit the car, this apparition disappeared. As the vehicle passed, it wasn't a park guard. It was a black Chevy pickup truck with a couple of reenactors probably doing the same thing as we were doing out there, looking for ghosts.

"Within five seconds, my two friends get back to the car. And the one says that they couldn't find the car, that they came out of the field, and they thought at the time that I had moved the car as a joke. They assumed that I must have followed the black pickup truck because once the black pickup truck passed the vehicle, they saw their car.

"I didn't tell them I couldn't move until we had gotten to the Eisenhower [Conference Center, site of a dance that evening]. My friends said they felt a presence on the battlefield, which I had felt, and they said at some point the presence left them. And I think it came through the car. And while that presence was looking at the car, they could not see the car. And they couldn't see that car until the pickup truck came around and hit it with the headlights and passed it.

"When we got to the Eisenhower, my friend Bob said, 'John, something's not right—he's not talking.' And I finally said, 'You were followed; it left you, came to me. I didn't move the car.' We all kind of put the story together. I was stunned—stunned is a real good way to put it."

Telling the story to other patrons of the Eisenhower, Wunderlich also was flabbergasted by some of the questions.

"I love it, because somebody came over and said, 'Why didn't you roll down your window and ask him a bunch of questions?' At that point," he recalled and laughed, "I was doing everything I could not to soil myself. Asking him questions was the last thing on my mind. Someone asked, 'Were you scared it was going to hurt you?' I said, 'No, not at all. It was just the complete otherworldliness of it that took my breath away.'

"There are four books written about the ghosts of Gettysburg, and the number of tourists who have seen things on the battlefield must be astounding in number," he added. "It's funny, because some people obviously see them, and some people don't. I know people who have worked there for long periods of time who have said they've seen all sorts of things. I've talked to other people who have worked there twice as long that have never seen anything the whole time and don't even believe it."

Wunderlich is not ashamed to admit he doesn't have a clue what is going on.

"This is going to sound like a chicken comment, but I don't care that I don't have a clue," he said. "It doesn't bother me. I'm a fairly curious person by nature, but in the same way that I don't worry about the nature of black holes—I take their existence as a scientific fact, but I don't worry about where they come from. And I don't worry about what they would do to me if I was in one, because I never will be."

Portal to Eternity in Arcola?

Before they purchased their current home, Hazel Dell in Jerseyville, Brenda and Larry Nolan lived for about twenty years in the historic Jacob Moore House in Arcola, Illinois. The couple bought the 1873-vintage home from the builder's granddaughter, who was seventy at the time. Sixteen years later, something strange happened in the master bedroom at about three o'clock one morning.

"I was real restless that night, and there was a real disturbance—kind of a filmy-type thing in the room, and our windows were shut," Brenda Nolan recalled. "It wasn't smoke, and the French doors to our bedroom were closed. I thought, 'Oh, boy, what's going on here?'

"Next day at work, I was telling the girls, 'Boy, the spirits were restless last night.' We were just kind of kidding about it, because this was the first real experience I had had like that. On the way home, I stopped at the little grocery store in Arcola. They said, 'Did you hear what happened to that woman last night that they found dead?' I said, 'No, who was it?' They said it was the woman who sold us the house. They found her that morning, but she had died at 3:00. And she had a flashlight in her hand, and she was fully dressed."

Surprised, Nolan soon put two and two together.

"She had told me that she was born in that room. Her grandfather, who built the house, had died in that room. And so it just seemed to me that it was kind of a portal-type thing. She died on Jacob Moore's—her grandfather's—birthday. So it like all came together."

[A Painful Past]

Thousands of pundits have said it in one form or another: those who escape this world without a scratch no doubt slept through their existence.

Life is often cruel and unfair, to say nothing of being a royal pain in the derriere. And undoubtedly it was even more so in the nineteenth and early twentieth centuries, when tyrannical relationships were common, poorhouses were in fashion, and small children often died of their illnesses.

Missouri Bottom Road: A Long Road Home

For chilling and heartbreaking legends, Missouri Bottom Road, near Lambert Airport, is the place to be, according to Randy Bibb.

"We used to like to go up Missouri Bottom Road because it was so dark and scary," noted Bibb, a Hazelwood native who now lives in Belleville, Illinois. "It's the place where all urban legends have happened: Hook Man, the hitchhiking girl in the prom dress, all that stuff. There are also mysterious lights that bop around. I don't know if it's marsh gas or what it is, but several of us have seen the lights."

Hook Man and Vanishing Hitchhiker, at least, are easy to explain away. The hitchhiker story goes like this: a beautiful young woman hitches a ride, borrows her benefactor's coat, and then mysteriously disappears from his car. The jacket later is found neatly folded upon her gravestone.

That legend, and its numerous walking and wagon-riding derivations, was making the rounds of American folklore back in 1876 and is even popular in China, noted Jan Harold Brunvand, author of *The Vanishing Hitchhiker: American Urban Legends and Their Meanings.*

"In an interesting counterpart to the American legend, the Chinese girl walks behind the man (just as the hitchhiker almost invariably sits in the car's backseat or rumble seat), so that he must turn around in order to notice her disappearance," Brunvand wrote.

"Hook Man" also is a very common urban legend, according to Brunvand. A teenage couple pull into their favorite "parking spot" to do some necking and hear a radio report that a dangerous escaped convict is in the area. They become frightened and drive away, and when they arrive at the girl's home, they find a bloody hook on the handle of the car door.

"Teenagers all over the country knew about "the Hook" by 1959, and like other modern legends, the basic plot was elaborated with details and became highly localized," Brunvand noted.

However, the lights don't seem to have a legend behind them. And there's another tale, one of a tragic fire.

"There were stone steps along Missouri Bottom that several of us heard [led to] a home there where girls lived," Bibb said. "And it was probably in the '20s, from what I understand, rumor had it that the house had caught on fire and that these people died.

"Several people said that often, when they went by, they heard screaming coming from the steps."

Carolyn Avallone, a registered nurse-turned-full-time-mom who lives in the area, did some digging and turned up one possibility: the Fee Fee Baptist Children's Home had a home for smaller children along Missouri Bottom during the late 1940s.

Oddly enough, she learned the home was on property that belonged to her own aunt.

"The Baptist church had it from 1948 to 1950, and the land belonged to [my aunt's] father, Louis Plass, who passed away, and her mother had to sell it, and apparently in the process of that it burned," Avallone said. "Everybody was saved, though. It was for toddlers and children not quite ready to go to school."

In *These Little Ones: The History of the Missouri Baptist Children's Home*, author Jo Colay Ray mentions two farms. The first, Hilltop, included an old house and a forty-acre farming operation, started in the 1950s, near the children's home in Bridgeton. The second, Valley Farm, took in thirty-eight acres of land on Missouri Bottom Road, "located in the shadow of the Wabash trestle where it crosses the Missouri River into St. Charles," Ray wrote. The home housed six boys and harvested 838 gallons of strawberries. Both homes had been sold by 1960, one to the highway department and the other to a real estate developer.

In the account, Ray did not mention a fire at either home. Judy Teson, a lifelong resident and local historian in the Missouri Bottoms area, said she could not remember any girls' home along the road and was not aware of any stories of the strange lights. But she does know of a haunted house in the Bottoms area.

Veil of Tears

"That would be at the corner of Teson and Aubuchon Road," she said. "That was an old Teson house. Thibeau first, then Teson, then back and forth through the Tesons and Thibeaus. That one I can verify."

The house was built around 1900, or shortly thereafter, on a site formerly occupied by an old fur-trader's cabin that had burned down, Teson said.

"The French used to have a lot of parties down there—many, many parties—and each party would last anywhere from two to three days nonstop," she said. "And the women would cook almost constantly around the clock. And they would invite everybody, from all over, to come. They would even invite the Germans on the other side of Missouri Bottom Road, but they didn't get along, so the Germans never came.

"Anyway, they had to work. Life was hard down there, cooking, cleaning. Sometimes there was abuse by the men toward the women. There was quite a bit of that, and it was just an extremely hard life down there. With the mosquitoes and the bugs...it just was not pleasant.

"There was a baby born down there and...the priest from the priest farm up there came and got it—I could get into a lot of things but I'd best not. Anyway, the baby was taken away for various reasons, and then the mother supposedly never had her right mind after that. It was pretty tough. Back then, it was the end of the earth. Nobody was looking, nobody cared, you could do what you wanted. There was just nobody living down there except the French farmers."

After the original Teson family moved out, the house was purchased by Andrew Teson and his wife, Mary Thibeau.

"This Andrew was my husband's great-uncle, his grandma's brother," Teson said. "They had a daughter, Bernice. She's the one who told this to me, and she lived in the house all her life. When the family died, they sold it to another group of family, who lived in it just as it was for a while.

"From what I understand from Bernice, they would hear crying, a woman's cry, at night when they were trying to go to sleep," Teson said. "I think it was coming from the upstairs—I'm not certain—but it was a female cry, profound, horrible crying. It was a very heart-wrenching cry. They would also hear footsteps going up the stairs to the top floor, and there were other ghostly goings-on, but I can't remember all the descriptions."

Around the 1990s, the family that owned the home decided to gut it as a last-ditch measure, she said.

"They decided they could not stay in that home," Teson said. "They wanted to tear the house down, but if they tore it down they couldn't rebuild, because it's in a flood plain. What they decided to do was gut the entire house, take everything out and just leave the walls standing. When you went past the house, you could see through the windows from one side all the way to the other. It was gone—flooring, everything—gone. They rebuilt the entire house inside, and at that point all the crying stopped. Nothing happens anymore.

"If Bernice were alive, we could go back and talk to her, but she died about five years ago. She had a sharp mind, and it was where she lived all her life."

Ghostly Building Blocks Circa 1880

Little Ralph Cobb didn't have much to look forward to—he was a sickly young child, and his family was poor—but he loved his little building blocks and used them to build all kinds of structures.

And his family carefully wrapped them up and brought them along when they moved from a farm outside Palmyra, Missouri, to St. Louis in the 1880s, hoping to provide a better life for Ralph.

"The Cobbs apparently sensed that little Ralph wasn't going to make it," Bruce Carlson wrote in *Ghosts of the Mississippi River from Keokuk to St. Louis*. "Their granddaughter, who told me this story, understands that they encouraged the child to play with what few toys they could afford, foreseeing that Ralph would die at a young age."

They were right, Carlson noted. Shortly after their move, Ralph died, and his body was returned to Palmyra for burial. Within a couple of years, the family moved back to their farm.

While still in St. Louis, however, Ralph's mother observed some strange things happening with the blocks after Ralph's death.

"Those blocks, along with his other toys, were packed away in a leather-covered steamer trunk and stuck under a shelf in the kitchen," Carlson wrote. "The first time the trunk was opened again was in 1886, a few months after Ralph had died...the toys were pitched in the box, pretty much at random, with one exception. Those building blocks were all neatly arranged to form a miniature house, much like one that Ralph used to build."

Ralph's mother was brought to tears by the sight, but figured one of the other children had built it while browsing through the trunk. She ended up dismantling the little house as she dug around to get a doll for one of the girls.

"A month or so later, she had occasion to get into that trunk again," Carlson wrote. "There, again, she found the blocks arranged into the form of a little house. She thought this was a bit strange, because she knew the children weren't in the habit of playing in there. It was simply too inconvenient to do so under that shelf, and the trunk was far too heavy for them to move it out. She mentioned this to her children and asked who had been playing in the trunk. All denied even opening it."

Before their move back to Palmyra, Mrs. Cobb opened the trunk a third time and found the blocks carefully arranged in a house shape.

"Once again, she dismantled the little house, this time to make room for a few more toys," Carlson wrote. "She was home alone at the time and had the trunk moved out into the middle of the kitchen floor...She had shut the lid and was wrapping some items in paper to add to the trunk. When she reopened it a few minutes later, it was a totally different story.

"Those blocks she had knocked down into a random pile just a few minutes earlier were once again arranged into that familiar little house."

When Mr. Cobb came home, the couple conferred and decided there was only one thing to do:

"They carefully wrapped the blocks in paper, tied the bundle with thread so that little fingers could easily open it, and took the package to Palmyra with them," Carlson wrote. "There the couple buried the package beside the grave of their little boy.

"Perhaps, today, those blocks are neatly stacked again, forming that little house under the sod there in Palmyra."

Greene County Almshouse—Ghost of an Era

It's a tall, imposing, L-shaped, building. It was built in 1870 in the Italianate style with arched windows and period detailing. There's also a third-floor tower that was used by its residents as a lookout of sorts.

With windows broken out and its lovely second-floor banister broken to pieces, the vacant Greene County Almshouse is truly a pitiful ghost of its former self. It's sad, because just a decade ago this local landmark outside Carrollton, Illinois, was a proud reminder of the almshouse system of relief in the United States. It served the poor from 1870 to 1932 and is listed on the National Register of Historic Places.

"By the onset of the Civil War, 'indoor relief'—aid given to individuals residing outside an institutional setting—was the predominate relief system," read the National Register of Historic Places' nomination file for the almshouse. "This type of assistance was first channeled through locally administered almshouses. Almshouse care 'became the primary provider of relief throughout the nation.'

"The functions of almshouses varied from community to community, as well as over time. Ideally, the function of an almshouse was to provide relief to the local poor; in reality it was frequently used as a jail for tramps and vagrants, a work-house for able-bodied poor, an old people's home, an insane asylum and an orphanage."

Located on 160 acres of land, the Greene County Almshouse complex was an average-sized poor farm, according to the National Register document. Another 200 acres were added to the site in 1908, and further renovations were made as the years progressed. Several of the buildings on the grounds have since been demolished, and there are various outbuildings such as a pump house, hog house, granaries, barn, and sheds throughout the site. A pauper cemetery is located a quarter mile northeast of the almshouse.

In 1898 the County Farm planted an orchard of apple, cherry, plum, pear, and peach trees as well as currant shrubs. Grapevines, blackberries, and raspberries were added in 1901. Paupers also raised crops and livestock including hay, corn, oats, cattle, pigs, and chickens. These farming operations helped make the farm self-sustaining.

"Typical pre-1900 era paupers included vagrants, the physically and mentally ill, the elderly, orphans and other dependents," the nomination read. "The turn of the century witnessed the highest influx of insane and feeble-minded patients. As state-supported institutions relieved the county facility of the insane and other special classes, the elderly remained.

"In 1928, 90% of the residents were over the age of 61. These individuals were destitute because, in their old age, they were unable to look after themselves."

The paupers' stories are fascinating and sometimes heartbreaking, recalled Wilma Chappee of Carrollton. Chappee and friend Mary Steinacher are former Greene County board members who led a three-year effort to place the almshouse on the National Register in the 1980s.

"You read the pages: this lady came in with so many children—husband abusive," Chappee said. "One older gentleman that we read about, I think he was of German descent, said he had been in the military, and it talked about how he walked erect and was tall and slim. He went out there because he willed his property to his children, and they kicked him out. So he ended up with nothing—a nice how-do-you-do.

"Some of the children were adopted, and there was one lady who was telling me about a couple who came out to adopt a child. This little girl came out, and she had a hole in her dress, and she took her dress and covered up that hole, and the couple said their heart went out to her and melted, so they adopted this child. Good stories came out as well as a lot of bad things that happened. There was even one lady who met her husband out there, and they got married out there."

Not everyone lived in the main house, Chappee said.

"The tenant houses—they actually worked on the farm and were paid to work—that was part of the pay," she said. "Most of them had worked in gardening and stuff like that. The tenant houses were like a small, plain house. The main house, the front part, was where the overseer lived, and it had a beautiful staircase; we have pictures of that. [Vandals] knocked the staircase down. You went up, and there were three rooms on one side, a living room on the other side. Most of the time they ate in the basement. They built on a sunroom site on the side—sometimes they'd sleep up there. And then on the little cupola thing up there, that was kind of a lookout post where they could look out over the farm area, ring a bell or something."

After much research, the Greene County Almshouse was placed on the National Register. And with the help of area teens who worked out there all summer one year, the old almshouse was turned into a showplace of sorts and was on display to the public at the annual Greene County Days event.

"All the board members that were on at that time worked hard, said we'll take turns going out there," Chappee recalled. "That's the best summer I ever spent in my life. Even our florist here brought flowers that we hung around. We had one room set up with different things in it, and pictures on the walls. We all took tools, and I took my little utility tractor out, and the kids were very, very good. One day it was raining bad, and they couldn't work, and we made quilt blocks for the Greene County Days event.

"The boys cut out the quilt blocks and sewed them on the machine—I took my machine out there," she said. "They had tomato plants out there, and they were so proud of those and the flowers. They learned a lot."

Greene County owns the almshouse but moved it to a back burner, so to speak, after giving it a few years in the limelight, Chappee said. After a brief stint as a senior citizens' center, the house was allowed to fall into disrepair. The place is boarded up now, but vandals tear off the boards and go in anyway.

"Maybe five years after they hadn't been showing it anymore...I went out there and showed these people, and I had tears in my eyes that day," she said. "It was so sad to see what had happened."

The home desperately needs a rescuer, Chappee said.

"To me, they'd be better off to sell it for a dollar and let someone go in there," she said. "The foundation and the walls are still good, but the last time I was out there every window in the place is out, and the animals are just taking over."

The farm and its accompanying pond are popular with kids who like to party, and some of those young people have seen strange things on their visits, said Neil Bushnell, of Jerseyville.

"There's a lot of people who go up there and party—kids around Carrollton and a lot of the Jerseyville kids go up there," Bushnell said. "They said they've been in there, just one or two at a time, and they'll hear voices and see people walk through the house—apparitions, I guess. They say they don't really bother anybody; they'll just see weird things. It gets kind of creepy, and they'll take off."

The place needs to be torn down, Bushnell said.

"The kids have just trashed it," he said. "The worst part was, it was probably a pretty nice house, but kids went down there and busted a bunch of the stair rails, punched holes in the walls, took the wiring out, spray-painted the walls. We just go up there and walk around."

If there are ghosts, they are the vandals who are destroying the house, Chappee said.

"That's really the ghost," she said. "The last time I was out there, I saw what I would call satanic graffiti on the wall."

[Happy at Home]

There's no place like it, to paraphrase Dorothy. Depending on the prose, it's the place you hang your heart, or the place where they have to let you in, or the place where the heart is. Or just plain sweet.

Is it any wonder, then, that so many self-respecting shades are loath to leave home when their time on this planet runs out? From sitting in their easy chairs to dictating silly prose to perching on the beds of subsequent residents, they just can't find it in their hearts to move on—just yet.

Grandma Cora—Look for the Big Red Chair

While growing up in the Walnut Park neighborhood, Betty Crossno lived two blocks away from her grandparents' house on Genevieve. Eventually, just her Grandma Cora and her Uncle Henry lived in the big frame house.

"Grandma died in February 1954," noted Crossno, of Kirkwood. "We had just always called that 'Grandma's house,' because Henry was still living there, although he'd come to our house for his meals and stuff.

"I guess I was about fifteen when Joan moved in the neighborhood a few years later, five houses down the street from my grandmother's house," she added. "I don't know why I never told her my grandmother was dead— you know, at that age, it just didn't come up. I said, 'That's Grandma's house' and left it at that."

About a year later, Betty went over to Joan's house one evening.

"She said, 'Oh Betty, I saw your grandmother today,'" she recalled. "And I said, 'You what?' Joan said, 'She was sitting in the window, and I waved at her, and she waved back.'"

Betty was stunned, but the more she thought about it, the more it made sense.

"Grandma had this big, red armchair, and she had fallen and broken her hip when she was in her early fifties," she said. "She had gotten heavy from lack of movement and had gotten to the point where she couldn't get around at all. And that's what she did all day—she sat in that big red chair by the window and just waved at people as they went by."

The same Grandma Cora would one day demand an automobile ride from a later tenant of the house (see Chapter 9, On The Road).

Charles: Keeping Tabs in Alton

Cathy and Brian Bagby are only the third owners of their large home, a two-story brick foursquare, Prairie School-style house built in 1918 in midtown Alton.

"Antoinette [Eason, the psychic] is a good friend of mine, and she investigated my house, I guess, back in '92," noted Cathy, a patient accounts customer representative. "The name 'Charles' she picked up in this one room. There was a Charles that lived here, so I'm just assuming that's him."

The Bagbys' younger son, Patrick, was only three when he saw Charles for the first time, sitting at the edge of his bed.

"Patrick is the only one who has seen the full apparition of the man," Cathy said. "He said, 'Tell him to go away.' Just last year I asked him, 'Do you remember saying that to me?' And he said, 'Yeah.' He said he had a beard, sort of a long beard, and wore a hat, and had sort of a stern look on his face, and that he stood up and just disappeared. And Patrick told me to tell him to go away."

But the apparitions—which also include a little boy who sits on the steps and a woman who was brought in with an antique sleigh bed (see Chapter 16, Memories For Sale)—don't frighten the Bagbys.

"They've sort of become part of the family, to tell you the truth," Cathy said. "It's really not frightening. I've never awakened to see someone standing at the end of my bed or stomping up and down the stairs or anything like that."

Cool Valley: Unhappy at Home

The house is just a little bungalow on Redwood Avenue in Cool Valley, but the legends about it loom large. It supposedly was the only farmhouse in the area originally, and members of the family who owned it are buried on the premises.

"This old woman used to live there," noted Bob Schaper, former reporter for the *Suburban Journals*. "Evidently it was she and her husband's home for decades. She would be outside sitting on the porch all the time. She [would say], 'I don't like being in the house because it's too scary, because they're in there. She was talking about spirits in the house that bothered her. She could have been senile, from all we know, but…'"

The woman no longer lives in the house, and the empty home burned last summer, said Cool Valley Police Officer Scott Seabaugh.

"It was being rehabbed, so we weren't sure who burned it or how it started," Seabaugh said. "[The bomb and arson squad] said it smoldered for a couple hours."

But the night it burned, some of the neighbors came out and mentioned how haunted the house was, he said.

"As it was burning, some of the neighbors were talking about the last residents to live there," Seabaugh said. "Her husband worked evenings. He didn't get home until one in the morning, and his wife would sit on the front porch until he got home, because she would hear like glass crashing upstairs, glass breaking. So she'd sit outside every night. They had two sons, the last residents. The neighbors were saying that both of the sons died—not in the house, but of weird causes—and they didn't know if that was in connection with the house or not."

Kindly Visit: Old Lady in Shawl

While growing up in north St. Louis, Nicole's mother had an experience she'll never forget: the apparition of an old lady would come and sit on her bed and talk to her, in unintelligible tones, when she was six or seven. Nicole, who asked that her last name not be used, also lives in north St. Louis and works for a computer software company.

"She said at first she was afraid; she just got stiff, thought she was dreaming," Nicole said. "It would kind of wake her up, this presence. I guess she just wanted to communicate with her, this presence, because she would sit and talk. You couldn't hear anything; you could just barely see her mouth move. And when she was finished, she would just fade away, like when cigarette smoke, or any type of smoke, dissipates. My mom said she got to the point where she could sit up in bed and still see her, so she knew she was awake—it was definitely not a dream."

The old woman was wearing a very tattered dress and a shawl.

"If she could use a word to describe her, it would be almost like a witch, the stereotypical, storybook kind of witch," Nicole said. "But there was nothing mean about her face. It was a very kind face, from what she could make out.

"Have you ever seen *Star Wars*? The only way we could think to describe it is...there's a holographic image of Princess Leia telling them about the Droid and everything in the first *Star Wars*. She said it's almost like that, this image that's not like flesh—just this gray, hazy image, but a distinct outline of her face and her shawl and her arms."

Nicole loved to hear her mother tell the story again and again.

"It tried to communicate with her. I think that is so cool," she said. "The lady would come back just on occasion. There would be some nights when my mom would sit up and wait for her, but she'd end up falling asleep because she just wouldn't come that night. It was always at night."

One night when the lady appeared, Nicole's mother called for her own mother to come see.

"She started out real quiet—'Mom, Mom'—and then she got a little louder, so she could hear her," Nicole said. "And the lady faded away. She never came back. That was the last time she saw her. She said she'll never forget her."

And what was it that the lady wanted?

"I wonder, too," Nicole said.

American Legion: Good Friends Stick Around

Mark Croghan doesn't mind if a few spirits hang around Goff-Moll American Legion Post 101, in Brentwood. But he does wish they'd pitch in once in a while and help with the cleaning.

"I've seen what looks like people just standing at the end of the hallway. When I set the hall upstairs, set up trash cans, I come back, and they've been moved," said Croghan, of Rock Hill, who works as caretaker for the building. "Sometimes I walk through cold pockets, and it's kind of weird. I'm not frightened to be here—I wish they'd grab a mop or broom. If you're going to be in the building, let's get with the program."

Are these fleeting shadows detected out of the corner of the eye or something more? Croghan isn't sure. Perhaps because of all the people who have passed through the doors, the building has picked up its own kind of "life force," as opposed to a traditional haunting, he said.

"I couldn't stand up in court and tell you I actually saw something," he said. "There are days when I see all three of them—at least I think I do. Like I said, it's always out of the corner of my eye, and there's not any distinct features. They stand in three different places.

"Ted [Ganahl] has said he's even heard things in the kitchen when he was closing up at night, and I think even Jim Reilly has said he's heard things," Croghan said. "I've got to work. I don't have time to be afraid."

People joke about it, saying the pink elephants will be coming soon, but Ganahl truly believes that the presences of some old members remain in the building. A Rock Hill resident, Ganahl is a thirty-one-year member of the post and also manages the building, which was dedicated in 1962.

"A friend of mine had passed away, and I was sitting here feeling sorry for myself, and it sounded like somebody threw a tray of glasses against a wall," he said. "All the hair rises on the back of my neck, and I look around—there's nothing there. I just figured, 'Time to stop feeling sorry for yourself and get the hell out of the building'—which I did. I wasn't going to stick around and see what was going on.

"I've had situations where I've been up at night sometimes," Ganahl added. "It's an old building, and it makes the creaks and the moans and things like that, and you'll be sitting here watching the bar by yourself at night, and you feel something's inside, and you turn around—you somewhat see a shadow, but nobody's there. Little things like that."

Ganahl said he is a firm believer in the hereafter.

"We've had such great friendship and camaraderie here, and you make such dear friends, and then they're gone," he said. "As long as you're remembering somebody, they're still with us, is the way I feel about life. It keeps their spirit alive, and they just like to come around and say hi every now and then."

The Ellsworth: Gladys Makes a Show

Her name was Gladys, and she was one of the original Rockettes when the group was still based in St. Louis. While still a showgirl in the late '20s, Gladys rented an apartment at the Ellsworth, West Pine and Newstead Avenues, and despite her recent death, she wasn't ready to abandon the place when Randy Bibb moved there in 1988.

"She never married; she had a niece and a nephew, and she lived there all those years," Bibb said. "And when I first saw the apartment, what was the last of her possessions—she had died, but did not die in the apartment—there was a rollaway bed and some stuff, and a crystal chandelier in the dining room. She sat under that chandelier for what?—fifty, sixty years, something like that—smoking, and that chandelier was just as yellow as could be from cigarette smoke."

Faced with an unhappy living situation at the time, Bibb couldn't wait to move in—so much so that he immediately grabbed some cushions from his sofa and brought them to the Ellsworth.

"I was just getting used to working nights at the Hyatt-Regency in Union Station—it was the Omni at the time," Bibb noted. "I worked night audit at the front desk. And so I came home from work, and I guess I had been asleep for about an hour when I woke up with this intense, *intense* fear that someone wanted in my apartment. It was so intense it woke me, and I went over to my door and bolted it. I was awakened out of a sound sleep, and it just terrified me."

The Ellsworth did have, and still has, a security door, and Bibb admits feeling somewhat sheepish about bolting the door, when locking it was probably sufficient. But bolting the door allowed him to sleep comfortably.

"For several days after that, I would be awakened with this same feeling, and I really didn't understand," he said. "One day I was standing at the elevator, which was right outside my door, and I felt this, this presence, staring me down. I could feel it just as plainly as I could someone in the room next to me."

Bibb asked Suzanne, the building manager, about the apartment, and she told him about Gladys, the woman who had lived there for decades. Shortly thereafter, he began hearing three loud raps on the wood portion of the door—so loud that the brass door knocker could be heard bouncing.

"My mother heard it, friends heard it," he said. "Every time I would go out and answer the door, but there was nobody there. The stairwell and the elevator were right there by my door, but the stairwell was very loud, so even if you were going down the steps in your socks, you could hear it. The elevator was one of these old elevators with the grate doors that closed. So if somebody was in the elevator I would have certainly heard that."

One time a neighbor even noticed the distinct knocks, which had a different sound from when a real person knocked.

"He said, 'Did you just knock on your door from the inside?'" Bibb recalled. "I said, 'No, I didn't.' He said, 'I heard a knocking on the door. As a matter of fact, when I looked up I could see that the vibrations were causing the knocker to move.'"

One day Bibb's friend Charlotte came over, and the two were playing piano when the regular three knocks sounded at the door. Charlotte asked why Bibb wasn't answering the door, and he told her the whole story.

"She went to the middle of the room and said something like, 'Gladys,

I want you to know that this is still your home,'" he said. "'There'll be a lot of music and a lot of singing and a lot of dancing and a lot of love in this house, and any time that you want to come, we want you to know that we want you there.'"

It worked—sort of.

"It would be really dramatic for me to tell you that the knocking stopped right there," he said. "It didn't, but it slowly faded out, became less and less, until finally it quit. The last year or so I lived there, there was no more knocking."

Was Dad Watching?

When Bill Wunderlich and his wife, Terry, were building their home in Chesterfield, Terry's father died.

"He was just crazy about this house—he really wanted to move into this house," recalled Wunderlich, a retired insurance broker. "After the funeral, we came out to the house to walk through what was essentially the unfinished house. It had the roof up and the walls up, but that was about it.

"And I turned to Terry, and I said a nonsense poem, the words of which I cannot tell you anymore, but it was that [Lewis Carroll] kind of a poem, where the words don't have any sense to them, it's just that they kind of rhyme. And I went through that entire poem to Terry, and she said, 'Nobody's ever said that poem to me except my father.' Her father used to recite it to her when she was a little kid.

"I've got to believe that he was there, watching over the house."

[MYSTIFYING ORACLE]

For some, the simple Masonite board with letters and numbers and a planchette-like pointer is a pathway to the spirit world. For others, it's a date with the devil and evil forces.

Many believe the "mystifying oracle," or Ouija talking board, picks up messages from discarnate spirits or ghosts. Others say it is merely a tool that collects instructions from the users' subconscious minds through a process called "automatism," similar to automatic writing.

"Ouija boards are perhaps best thought of as tools to gain access to unconscious material," noted James Houran, an expert on the paranormal. "There has never been any scientific evidence that they are 'gateways' to contact the dead. Rather, any movements of the planchette are caused typically by the unconscious movements and motivations of the sitters. These are not paranormal events, but rather in the same ballpark as Rorschach ink blot tests, in which an individual projects unconscious impulses onto an interpretation of an ambiguous figure."

Predecessors of the Ouija board and its cousin, the writing planchette, date to before the birth of Confucius in China, around 551 B.C. They were considered a nonthreatening way to communicate with the spirits of the dead, Stoker Hunt wrote in *Ouija: The Most Dangerous Game*. Named for the French *oui* and the German *ja* for "yes," the current-day Ouija board was patented by Elijah J. Bond more than a century ago and purchased by William Fuld and patented again in 1892.

"William Fuld made a fortune from the board, but he was not an addicted Ouija user," Hunt wrote. "'I'm no spiritualist!' he said. 'I'm a Presbyterian. I built this factory on Ouija's advice, but I haven't consulted the board since. Things have been moving along so well I didn't want to start anything.'"

Over the years, a bevy of factual—and non-factual—messages have been received, including one by a twelve-year-old girl that indicated her life would end at age thirteen. Although she didn't die a year later, the ominous message managed to traumatize the girl who, in the meantime, dreaded everything from routine trips to the common cold.

"In 1956, the last will and testament of heiress Helen Dow Peck provided that the bulk of her $180,000 legacy was to go to a certain John Gale Forbes," Hunt wrote. "A judge invalidated the will. No John Gale Forbes could be found, for he was merely the creation or invention of Mrs. Dow Peck's Ouija board."

The board was closer to the mark when a seventeen-year-old woman heard from it that her soldier boyfriend had been shot at by another GI in Vietnam.

"The board was specific in its details: it was night, Gary was riding in a Jeep with another soldier, the flashlight Gary had been holding in his hand was hit, Gary had not been hurt," Hunt wrote. "She wrote Gary about this, half-thinking she was crazy. But Gary, shocked, verified that the story was true. The details were accurate; he had been shot at—while the letter was in transit."

Perhaps the most intriguing messages to come from a Ouija board did so under the guise of "Patience Worth," a supposed spirit who broke through to a middle-class housewife on a steamy summer night in St. Louis in 1913 (see Chapter 24, A Charming Spook).

Playing with Ouija boards remains a popular yet much-feared pursuit, fraught with all kinds of superstitions, as a unique Web site belonging to the Museum of Talking Boards notes (www.museumoftalkingboards.com/ouistit.html). If the planchette repeatedly makes a figure eight, for instance, that means an evil spirit is in control of the board. A Ouija board also will scream if one tries to burn it, and those who hear the scream have only thirty-six hours to live. Oh, and never, ever use the board in a graveyard.

Lois Andrews, of Jerseyville, Illinois, has played with a Ouija board from time to time, and during a fruitful session at the 518 South Restaurant some years back, she turned up some information on a boy who had died there many years before (see Chapter 7, Victorian Visions, Part II: Jerseyville Landmarks). She also has her own little Ouija folklore.

"This Ouija board, the lady that owned it, it was her grandmother's, and she always kept it in a white paper sack or a white plastic bag," Andrews recalled. "And I said, 'Why in the world do you have it in a white bag?'

She said, 'Because Grandma told me it should always be covered in white—that will keep it from working.'

"I said, 'Oh, yeah, okay.' She told me, 'Lois, I didn't believe her at first, but I had it in a nightstand next to the bed, and every time I would go in there, the drawer would be open. Ron [her husband] and I both, at different times, would shut the drawer—nobody would be in there—we'd go back in, and the drawer was open. So we decided Grandma must be right!'

Andrews laughed.

"After I had [the Ouija board] for a few weeks, I decided it needs a much better home than a plastic sack, so I actually took a white pillowslip out of my linens," she said. "I said, 'Ouija, would you like to have a new white pillowslip? Can I put you in a new house?' It told me YES. So I returned it that way. I told [the lady who owned the board] Ouija wanted a new home.

"My husband sometimes thinks I'm kind of strange, but I very much believe in the spirit world."

Some years ago, Dan and his friend became believers, too, after a strange incident involving a Ouija board at Dan's family's old farmhouse outside Millstadt, Illinois. Dan, who asked that his last name not be used, now lives in Belleville and is a customer service representative for a St. Louis company.

"We had just gotten out of grade school—he was fourteen, and I was thirteen," Dan recalled. "We started asking [the Ouija board] questions, and I started getting a little more scared. It started answering all these questions, answers my friend would never have known, like my grandparents' initials, stuff like that. Then we asked if it would show itself, and it said it would show itself in the stairway. We said, 'Which stairway?' And it said the upstairs.

"My friend starts walking down the hall to the door that goes upstairs, and just as he opened up the door he slammed it, screamed, ran into my mom's room and jumped on her bed. She was like, 'What is going on?' He was just white, pure white. He said, 'I saw it.' He saw this white figure walk right across the stairway and kind of stopped, then kept on going. He was like a Rambo kid, played in the woods and everything...to see him petrified—he was so pale, it was unbelievable."

Dan and his family later heard that there was a death at the farm many years before, that of a hired hand, whose body was found hanging from the rafters of the barn.

"We've tried looking into it, and we've never found any proof on it, so I don't know," he said.

Many years ago Susie Schulte, of Jerseyville, had another strange experience with a Ouija board.

"I totally will not have anything to do with [a Ouija board] anymore, but we would use it, and my brother asked it how old he would be when he died. And it said twenty-one. And the interesting thing is, when he was twenty-one he was in a very bad accident where they thought he was dead a couple of times. It was just horrible. And when he died three years ago, the cause of death was that accident. It was actually because his spleen had been removed, and he died very suddenly."

Schulte's sister, Debbie Hotz, picked up the story.

"He had a bacterial infection get into his bloodstream, and he just went quickly, very unexpectedly," Hotz said. "The coroner or the medical examiner asked me about it, asked me if he had been in a wreck, because he could tell. Said that that was the cause of the death. That was very eerie."

Table-Rapping: Conjuring up Philip

Table-rapping, -turning, -lifting, -tilting, and -levitation are all forms of Ouija-like automatism. In table-rapping, experimenters ask the table questions, and the table "answers" by tapping a leg or legs against the floor: one rap usually means no, two raps mean yes, and there's usually a code pertaining to the alphabet.

Table-rapping enjoyed great popularity in the United States, western Europe, and the Far East beginning around the 1850s. In 1961, spurred by a more scientific purpose, local author-poet John Neihardt founded The Society for Research on Rapport and Telekinesis (SORRAT).

"The original SORRAT group consisted of Neihardt and students from the University of Missouri at Columbia," James McClenon wrote in *Hauntings and Poltergeists: Multidisciplinary Perspectives*, edited by James Houran and Rense Lange. "After about three months of meeting regularly, the group reported experiencing anomalous rapping sounds and table movements."

Neihardt was assisted by Dr. J. B. Rhine, the founder of modern parapsychology. One of Rhine's assistants, William Edward Cox, also investigated the SORRAT case and built a "mini-lab" made of a sealed, inverted aquarium, secured by a lock onto a wooden board with metal bands.

"The mini-lab was designed so that no object could enter or exit while the locked bands were secured," McClenon wrote. "If an object moved inside the minilab it triggered a microswitch activating a movie camera for 30 seconds."

About four hours of film were produced, taping phenomena that included "two leather rings linking, balloons inflating and deflating repeatedly, candles lighting spontaneously, and objects moving, levitating and passing in and out of the front of the locked and sealed mini-lab," McClenon wrote. "Some films portrayed coins exiting a special mini-lab permanently locked and sealed by a professional locksmith."

A Canadian group took a similar approach to the original SORRAT group in 1973, but decided to create their own ghost, so to speak. They named him Philip and gave him an entirely fictional history and biography. That way, no one could later claim that Philip actually existed at one time and had really come back from the grave to visit their table-rapping sessions.

The eight members of this group, the Society of Psychical Research in Toronto, included an accountant, an engineer, an industrial designer, a scientific research assistant, and four housewives. None claimed to be a medium, noted Iris M. Owen in her book, *Conjuring Up Philip*.

The group made up this story, Owen wrote:

Philip was an aristocratic Englishman living in the middle 1600s at the time of Oliver Cromwell. He had been a supporter of the king and was a Catholic. He was married to a beautiful but cold and frigid wife, Dorothea, the daughter of a neighboring nobleman. One day, when out riding on the boundaries of his estates, Philip came across a gypsy encampment and saw there a beautiful dark-eyed, raven-haired gypsy girl, Margo, and fell instantly in love with her.

He brought her back secretly to live in the gatehouse near the stables of Diddington Manor—his family home. For some time he kept his love nest secret, but eventually Dorothea, realizing he was keeping someone else there, found Margo, and accused her of witchcraft and of stealing her husband. Philip was too scared of losing his reputation and his possessions to protest at the trial of Margo, and she was convicted of witchcraft and burned at the stake. Philip subsequently was stricken with remorse that he had not tried to defend Margo and used to pace the battlements of Diddington in despair. Finally one morning his body was found at the foot of the battlements where he had cast himself in a fit of agony and remorse.

A typical session involved everyone greeting each other and sitting down around the table. Then each person would say hello to Philip and begin asking questions, which were answered in a simple code with a rap on the table. The table at times also flung itself around the room, followed members, and displayed a unique personality—so much so that interested physicists came to observe.

"To measure the intensity of the rappings, an electrically wired metal plate was hung in the room, and the group was asked to try to transfer the responses from the medium of the table to the metal plate," Owen wrote. "The quality of the recorded sounds is acoustically different from other noise. The force has not been identified, nor has it been explained. But something exists."

Philip had certain personality characteristics that were obviously not those of any one individual member of the group, Owen noted. The personality was a composite, presumably projected by the group.

"Group projecting might well offer one explanation for the traditional ghost story," Owen wrote. "The historical ghost behaves just as one expects that it should, even to the idea of Ann Boleyn carrying her head tucked underneath her arm. The family ghost in the haunted mansion appears always on the same staircase, in the same dress, and with the same expression points in the same direction, because the family members all know that this is just as it should be."

It might also explain why prayer services or exorcisms often put a ghost to rest.

"In this situation what the mind can create, it can also, when it wants to, destroy," Owen wrote. She compared the Philip phenomena favorably to poltergeist disturbances.

"We should hasten to add, however, that we do not for one moment believe that this one theory accounts for *all* the reports of hauntings, ghosts and apparitions that one reads about," she wrote. "We believe it's quite possible that a large proportion of such cases could be accounted for in this way. Neither are we saying...that spirits do not exist. Still less are we denying the possibility of any form of existence after death. We feel, however, that our theory offers a scientifically verified alternative to the accepted belief that spirits of the dead are responsible for all hauntings as well as for poltergeist phenomena."

The Philip group, although it would inspire many more such groups throughout the world over the years, never managed to conjure a full-fledged apparition of Philip himself.

"This would provide complete proof of our theory in their eyes, and the group is still hoping to pursue this," Owen wrote. "If this happens, Philip will indeed be a true 'thought-form.'

"Neither do we yet understand how composite group-thought can be transformed into a noise that can be heard and recorded, nor do we yet understand the mechanism. We are inclined to believe in the possibility that the instances of hearing a voice alleged sometimes to occur in mediumistic circles might be a variation of the rapping phenomena."

Over the years, various SORRAT groups have reported a wide variety of phenomena, including a few apparitions, McClenon noted. This includes thousands of pages of text allegedly written by spirits. However, all effects reported by SORRAT could be duplicated by magicians using accomplices, he wrote.

Members of the Philip group believed their phenomenon could be repeated by any determined group, and this theory was borne out during a Christmas party in 1974, during which several people put their hands on a table and conjured up Santa Claus, Owen noted.

"'Are you Father Christmas?' asked someone. One rap followed," Owen wrote. "The answers to questions about reindeer, presents, chimney pots, and the climate at the North Pole were all entirely 'in character.' The episode was a perfect example of the childlike approach to the phenomena that we recommend, and a beautiful illustration of the fact that in these situations 'you get what you expect.'"

24 [A Charming Spook]

Companioning is a strange, strange thing.
We may sit together,
Each inclined to the other,
Each intimately in contact,
Each with one accord,
Listening with the same wisdom.
Yea, but this is but the flesh
Of companionship!
He who would know a fellow—
Must know his dreams!
Must see his soul through that parted curtain.
　　—Patience Worth

She made her debut in St. Louis through a Ouija board on a toasty summer evening in 1913, launching a writing career that would include nearly four million words, thousands of poems, seven books, short stories, dramas, aphorisms, and witty conversation.

Before it was all over, she would attract worldwide attention that included English royalty and Hollywood film stars—as well as many beloved and distinguished backers and a few critics intent on denouncing her as a fraud.

"I shall play with words like castinets," she once said. "I shall set them twinkling like stars, yea and make them pale and langorous. I shall burn them of passion and wreak them dizzy of twisting. He who keepeth apace shall find him a lout at the prancin'."

Who—or what—was Patience Worth?

Whatever she was, she was impressive, recalled J. Richardson Usher, of

Webster Groves, whose parents, Roland and Florence Usher, heard Patience through the voice of Pearl Curran at her West End home in the early 1900s. Scott and Agnes Cady MacNutt, the parents of Usher's wife, Alexandra, also visited the Curran home, and all four had special poems written for them by Patience Worth.

"Dad wasn't so much into the mysticism stuff, but he said it's awfully convincing," J. Richardson Usher said. "There's just no question of the range of her capacity for detail [in the books]. The interesting thing would be, you'd have nine people in a room, and she would write something for each one of them that applied to that person. It wasn't a general thing."

An Inauspicious Setting

"In the parlor of a comfortable, upper-middle-class flat in the 6000 block of Kingsbury Avenue in the city's West End, three women fanned themselves and gave their attention to a Ouija board that rested between them," wrote Irving Litvag in *Singer In The Shadows: The Strange Story of Patience Worth*. "In the dining room nearby sat the husbands of two of the women. They smoked cigars and played pinochle.

"Mrs. John H. [Pearl] Curran was tired and hot—and quite bored. Across the table from her sat her guest and close friend, Mrs. C. Edwin Hutchings. It was Emily Grant Hutchings who had persisted in this Ouija-board business. Pearl Curran didn't believe in it and was tired of it. The third woman was Mrs. Curran's mother, Mrs. Mary Pollard, who sat alongside with paper and pencil ready, in case the board produced anything interesting."

That night it did. "Many moons ago I lived. Again I come—Patience Worth my name."

Patience would work exclusively through Curran, who has been described as a charming, witty housewife whose own education was limited. Born in Mound City, Illinois, on February 15, 1883, Curran recalled being left to her own devices much of the time while growing up.

"I collected broken china and bits of colored glass, and spent hours worrying 'doodle bugs' with a stick," Curran recalled to psychic researcher Walter Franklin Pierce in *The Case of Patience Worth: A Critical Study of Certain Unusual Phenomena*. "I did not like dolls...preferred live toys, and dressed my cats in doll clothes and wheeled my dogs in the doll cart. I did not name my pets, nor did they seem specially dear. I don't remember any playmates at this period or much else than some of my doings. I was quiet and quite healthy."

Pearl was the only child of George and Mary Cordingley Pollard and spent many of her formative years living in Missouri's Lead Belt, around Potosi and Bismarck. For several years she took voice lessons in Chicago for part of each year, working at a music company addressing envelopes to pay for her lessons. She married John H. Curran, a well-known and respected businessman with a daughter from a previous marriage, in Bismarck, when she was twenty-four.

The Currans lived in a red-brick, two-family home with a wide porch across the front in their well-to-do neighborhood. The enchanted memories of the Louisiana Purchase Exposition were fading, and World War I would soon begin in Europe.

"So although the *St. Louis Globe-Democrat* on that July day carried the headline SERVIAN LINE OF RETREAT MENACED; SOFIA CONFIRMS MOVEMENT OF LARGE BULGARIAN FORCE, a more prominent display was given, with front-page pictures, to the problems of a young couple, aged nineteen and seventeen, fighting to marry despite the objections of his older brother-guardian," Litvag noted. "Readers of the sports page on that day got scant consolation from the fact that the St. Louis Browns had won the final game of their series with Detroit—both the Browns and Cardinals were mired in sixth place in their respective leagues."

Praise From Publishers, Professors

Initially considered a novelty, Patience's "visits" soon attracted the attention of editors Casper Yost and William Marion Reedy. Yost had been on the staff of the *St. Louis Globe-Democrat* for twenty-five years and was Sunday Editor when he met Curran. He was described by many as a man of unimpeachable honesty and integrity, and in 1916 he wrote a popular book about Curran and Patience Worth, *Patience Worth, A Psychic Mystery*.

Litvag described Reedy as "a sloppy, fat man, a boozer," who nonetheless became "one of the most colorful and perceptive figures in American literary history." With a national circulation of more than 32,000, his literary magazine *Reedy's Mirror* could take credit for such literary "finds" as Emily Dickinson, Theodore Dreiser, and the poet Edgar Lee Masters.

Though deluged with other examples of so-called "spirit communications," Reedy became convinced that Patience Worth was the genuine article and of sufficient literary merit to profile. He featured articles about Patience for three months straight in 1915–1916. One article was appropriately entitled "Chat of a Charming Spook."

Roland Greene Usher was a brilliant young historian with a doctorate in history from Harvard, and while still in his thirties he had become a full professor of history and chairman of the history department at Washington University. His 1913 book, *Pan-Germanism*, had accurately foretold events leading to World War I and the arrangement of power on both sides, which differed from what experts had projected. His special fields of interest included Tudor and Stuart England, which included the period in which Patience supposedly lived.

Usher and his wife attended occasional sessions at the Curran home, but Usher, a calm, unemotional man, declined public comment. In 1917, however, after reading Worth's book *The Sorry Tale*, Usher penned an article for the July 6, 1917, issue of *Reedy's Mirror*.

"If you know *The Sorry Tale*, it's the story of Jesus' birth and a Roman child who was the equivalent, and the trajectory of their two lives, which crossed," J. Richardson Usher noted. "The 'sorry tale' is that both of them go bad—literally. Jesus is crucified, and the Roman child goes bad.

"Dad said you could smell the camels in the reading. It's a long book, it's an older writing...but it gives you so much of a picture of the Holy Land, life at that time."

Usher, who wasn't afraid to take odd or unusual positions, was a proponent of women's suffrage at the time, a cause his wife championed. He also made no secret of his admiration for *The Sorry Tale*:

"I am convinced of Mrs. Curran's absolute innocence of any conscious attempt at authorship or at deception," Usher wrote. "There is local color totally unlike that of the encyclopedia-crammed author of the usual novel of the Holy Land.

"One thing impressed me particularly. I have been told by travelers that the most characteristic thing about the Near East, as about the Orient, is the smells. From these one is never parted in *The Sorry Tale*; the reek of the camels, the acrid taste of the sands, the stink of the kennel are unforgettable because they are a part of the story, not mere lumber dragged in by the struggling author...Unquestionably this is the greatest story penned of the life and times of Christ since the Gospels were finished."

Usher wasn't alone in his praise for *The Sorry Tale*. For a number of years, Patience would become a cause célèbre for her works.

"It was a big phenomenon," Usher said. "Sometimes [Curran] would have a home séance, or she'd come to your house. You'd have a party, and people would ask her, and she would give answers that were relevant to the people that were asking the questions. She also did several down at Soldan High School. They'd have a large audience and questions from the audience, and there immediately would come an answer or a statement or a poem, whatever was relevant."

Of course, Patience was not without detractors. These included Dr. Morton Prince, a specialist in neurology and abnormal psychology from Boston, who met with the Currans during a trip east. Prince said he could get no further in his questioning of Patience unless Mrs. Curran consented to hypnosis, a request flatly rejected by the Currans. They said they feared hypnosis might permanently impair Pearl Curran's ability to communicate with Patience.

And James Hyslop, longtime college professor and director of the American Society for Psychical Research (ASPR), declared the case of Patience Worth "a fraud and delusion for any person who wishes to treat it seriously." Among other accusations, Hyslop charged that the language of Patience was not really archaic, but dredged up through Curran's contacts with Ozarks people who had spoken an archaic dialect. Two decades later, an article in the ASPR's *Journal* would rebut Hyslop's arguments.

Was Patience Real?

Patience gave few clues that she had ever been alive in the first place. "About me you would know much," she told those who asked about her. "Yesterday is dead. Let thy mind rest as to the past."

The details she did give are these: Patience was born in England in the seventeenth century; lived there and worked in the house and on the fields until grown; left for America and, soon after, was killed by Indians. When asked her birthdate she was uncertain, alternately providing "1649" and "1694." She also alluded, in a roundabout way, to the town of Dorsetshire, where Yost later traveled and found a number of similarities between the landmarks there and Patience's statements.

Patience describes the sea many times in her poems, and Curran had never seen the ocean. And the pattern of correspondence, in brightly lit rooms with plenty of action going on, departed from the dark, serious, secretive séances popular at the time.

Although it began with the arduous process of letters on a Ouija board, Curran was later able to get the correspondences through mental pictures, and she eventually used a typewriter as Patience "dictated" to her. She told Prince that when a poem was about to be given she felt a slight sense of pressure at the top of her head.

"I shall never forget it—Mrs. Curran sitting, perhaps twirling a cigarette and taking an occasional puff, her attention a little abstracted as it must necessarily be to hear the inward voice and watch the inner panorama, but ready at any moment to stop and answer a question or make a remark or answer the doorbell," Prince wrote. "To think that subject after subject was being fired at her, and within a few seconds after each Patience Worth was dictating a stream of words so fast that every little while the lady...had to pause, and perhaps to repeat, in order to permit the recording to catch up!"

A Real Ham

In one single evening Patience was known to deliver thirty-two short poems and seven sayings, each within seconds from the time someone in the audience called out subjects. Books often were interspersed with talk and short poems, and one night in 1918 the result was nothing short of genius:

"She dictated 100 words of *The Merry Tale*, then immediately gave 200 words of *Samuel Wheaton*, then about 50 words of *The Merry Tale*, and finally 1600 of *Samuel Wheaton*," Prince wrote. "But the most peculiar thing was that, as the record informs us, she 'tried to make the breaks between the stories fit so closely that one character in one story seemed to reply to the character in another story, which caused a great deal of amusement and pleasure.'"

For the most part, Patience Worth was eager to please her curious audiences. Agnes MacNutt was a ballet dancer who taught dancing to low-income children on the public playgrounds of St. Louis and often helped them to buy shoes and supplies their families couldn't afford. For MacNutt, as for many others, Patience composed a special poem:

> *To dance...*
> *And what is dancing?*
> *Fancy in action...*
> *Wisdom playing...*
> *Music concrete...*
> *Color wedded...*
> *Rhythm*
> *The honey of the universe*
> *Binding the many atoms.*

"I never really talked too much with [Mother] about it, except she thought it was remarkable what happened there," Alexandra Usher said.

"Whatever it was she did, apparently Mother felt that she really hit the nail on the head. Mother felt that they were really quite interesting."

Another time one of the guests, a Judge Corliss, gave Patience the word "sockman" and asked her what it meant.

"No one else in the room had ever heard the word before, presumably including Mrs. Curran," Litvag wrote. "Yet she was immediately given a vision by Patience of a man walking behind a plow with blood running down his hands. Patience went on to write a poem about the workman. Judge Corliss...was astounded. The word was so terribly obscure that he was certain no one, even the ubiquitous Patience Worth, would know it. He explained that in feudal days a tiller of soil was called a sockman. Such men often worked so hard in pushing a plow, he said, that it was not uncommon for their hands to become raw and bloody."

Patience also wasn't afraid to chide her guests if she felt they deserved it. During a program at the St. Louis Artists' Guild on November 9, 1919, Patience challenged poet Edgar Lee Masters to come up with a topic for her. He asked her to wait a minute while he thought of one.

"Patience Worth laughed. 'Ah, me, what a dullard!' which was speaking with scant respect," Prince recalled. "'I'm a little out of key,' confessed Mr. Masters, but after a little thought he suggested a subject, and Patience Worth produced her result in less time than it took him to think of a subject."

During Walter Franklin Pierce's six-year study of Curran, he grilled Patience and asked her to hand back the sharpest retorts she could. A portion of a conversation follows:

DR. PRINCE: *I cannot believe in you, since mind is but a function of the brain. Your brain died long ago—if you ever existed.*

PATIENCE: *Weel, better a resurrected dead than a dead living, eh?*

DR. PRINCE: *If you once lived, you are now nothing. How can nothing remember?*

PATIENCE: *Thee art less than naught, and thy memory is retained. I am as much as thee, and the trick even so is mine.*

Questions about ghosts and haunted houses also dismayed her. One night a guest mentioned an episode in which friends in Michigan had reported seeing a white figure after being awakened by a cool wind. Asking Patience for an explanation, they came up dry.

"Look ye," she snarled, "I be nay dealer in wraiths!"

Patience wasn't always happy with her human dictating machine, either. Once, when Curran had a cold, she lamented, "I put [compose] amid a fog." And she was quick to object when the words that Curran used weren't what she intended.

"'How be it,' she exclaimed, 'that she setteth this thing "portions" when I say me not so? Tis bits,'" Prince wrote.

Patience Wee and Difficult Times

In 1916, Patience urged the Currans to adopt a baby girl and name it Patience Worth, and she helped them find a baby born into a "broked" home. The baby would be the joint responsibility of all who came to talk with Patience and listen to her words, Patience stressed. Soon they learned of a mill worker, killed in a recent accident, whose widow had just given birth to a baby girl and wanted the child to have a better future than she could provide.

"Those who ascribed supernatural qualities to the Patience Worth case often cited this moment as providing powerful evidence of the paranormal," Litvag wrote. "The baby was found to have red hair and brown eyes, which fit the description that Patience Worth previously had given of herself. And it was also found that the child's father was English and the mother Scotch, which conformed to the heredity that Patience had announced for herself."

Although legally named Patience Worth Curran, the child was known as "Patience Wee." Poems by the dozen were dedicated by Patience to the baby, whom she often called "mine own bairn [baby]."

The death of John Curran in 1922 was the beginning of the end of the Patience Worth saga. Curran had always kept careful notes and painstaking details of each session. Six months after his death, Pearl Curran gave birth to a baby girl, which she named Eileen, and faced a difficult future with two children and her mother to support.

As her husband once noted to a reporter, the activities of the past few years — including travel and book publishing — had left the family drained from the experience, rather than richer for it.

A devoted friend came to the rescue. Herman Behr, a wealthy New York admirer of Patience, and the publisher of her books, provided Curran with an income of $400 a month for a number of years.

"There was another reason for the disappearance of the Patience Worth literature from general attention during the early 1920s," Litvag wrote. "It seems quite apparent that many critics and anthologists turned away from Patience simply because they feared becoming involved with a writer of such questionable, controversial origin. The case somehow seemed to bear a taint—of what? fraud? sensationalism? lunacy?...Even in her home region, Patience was ignored. *The Missouri Historical Review*, journal of the state historical society, in 1924 carried a lengthy two-part article on 'Missouri Verse and Verse Writers.' There was no mention of Patience Worth."

Curran eventually heeded the pleas of her old friend Dotsie Smith and moved with her family to California in 1930.

"Mrs. Curran had not been in ill health," Litvag wrote. "According to Mrs. Smith, around the middle of November 1937 Mrs. Curran said to her: 'Oh, Dotsie, Patience has just shown me the end of the road and you will have to carry on as best you can.'"

Curran caught cold on Thanksgiving Day, and pneumonia later developed. She died at a Los Angeles hospital on December 3, 1937. Since that time, others have claimed to have made contact with Patience Worth, but there has been no convincing evidence.

"The official record of Patience Worth, which was begun in 1913, was closed on Dec. 6, 1937, after 4,375 pages, with these final words, spoken at Mrs. Curran's grave: 'And thus it is that we take leave of her, knowing well that her head is resting upon the bosom of Patience, whose words are as arms that would cradle the world,'" Litvag wrote.

Spirit or Subconscious Marvel?

The jury's still out on this one, although nearly everyone agrees that Patience Worth was never a conscious effort on Curran's part. Was she really a spirit, or some marvelous working of Curran's subconscious mind?

"Is it conceivable that some sort of involuntary line of communication had been set up between Pearl Curran and the subconscious mind of a noted, living writer, who was producing these materials—perhaps in his sleep—without even being aware of it?" Litvag asks.

"This idea doesn't seem very persuasive...but it deserves consideration along with theories offered by many persons over hundreds of years of a universal unconscious—a sort of grand, collective mind on which Pearl Curran may have been drawing, which she somehow had discovered how to tap without even being aware of her power," Litvag wrote. "The great majority of persons...would subscribe to the solution that...Patience Worth was entirely a figment of Pearl Curran's subconscious."

Each possibility has its weaknesses, Litvag pointed out.

Dr. William E. Slaght, a professor of philosophy and psychology, made frequent visits to Curran's home and decided a "cosmic consciousness" was at work.

"My tentative conclusion...is we have here a manifestation of subconscious phenomena but in such unusual form...it has been able to reach out beyond the ordinary boundaries of knowledge and come in touch with the springs of some cosmic consciousness that gives deeper insight than any which comes through the ordinary channels of knowledge."

Others, such as the Reverend David C. Garrett, an Episcopalian clergyman, disagreed.

"I am convinced that it is just what it purports to be, the personality of Patience Worth," he said. "It is the simplest and most credible explanation for all who believe that the soul survives death and is immortal."

It's a puzzling question, noted Alexandra Usher.

"I think it had to have come from somewhere outside of Mrs. Curran, because she was uneducated," she said. "There was no way she could have done that, I don't think, without input from somewhere. It's very mystifying. I don't know what to make of it, really."

J. Richardson Usher said he will withhold final judgment on the question of whether Patience Worth was a spirit.

"I'm not prepared to dispute it—let's put it that way," he said. "I may not be able to say 'yes,' but I'm not able to say 'no.' As a historian I've learned to say, 'To the limit of my knowledge, it's good.' We have to wait and see what else shows up."

And what did Patience have to say? Was she part of the "cosmic flow," as one observer asked her?

"I be me," she responded. "Dusts o' me do spray 'pon airs, yet I be me."

25 [OUR OWN OTHERWORLDLY ODDITIES]

Our beloved Mound City, named for the Indian burial sites that once brightened its topography, still has treasure waiting to be unearthed.

Here may be found a wonderful sampling of oddities for those willing to invest a little effort finding them. There is a Lafayette Square townhouse that is said to have a portal to the Great Beyond; a home that still reverberates with the smells of Dad's aftershave and Mom's pumpkin pie, even though the parents are gone; and a 1920s home-brew operation thwarted by a recently deceased mother.

There's also a Florissant bathtub that somehow turned itself on and ran full force; a woman attending a conference who was literally "sat on" by a ghost; a little boy's vision of a witch; a ghost who brought baby shoes to the lucky residents of a Ferguson home; and a man who spent his boyhood in an Edward Scissorhands–style home, complete with quirks. Ralph Graczak would be proud!

Lafayette Square: Portal to the Great Beyond

Since 1974, Norman Sadler and his partner, Larry Keck, have lived in a brick townhome on Lafayette Square's Kennett Place that practically reverberates with unusual activity.

"It was built in 1878," said Sadler, a bartender. "We've got pictures from 1896, when the tornado came through St. Louis—we don't have a third story anymore. We've got records of the first few people that owned the house…it was a rooming house at one time, I know that. The way it was originally set up, it had the servants' quarters in the back hallway, and the basement was sectioned off into rooms.

"The house burned up in '83—it seems like that's when they [spirits] all started coming," he added. "It was completely gutted—you could stand in the basement and see the sky. People think I'm nuts when I talk about this kind of stuff, but it really does happen here."

Among the more frequent spirits are what Sadler believes is a former servant and a towboat captain.

"[The former servant] has been here since we bought the house in '74, and her job is to greet the guests as they come in," he said. "She still greets them—I guess that was her job when she was living. She's a tall, slender lady, and she's wearing a gray, Confederate-gray-type, wool straight dress and keeps her hair up in a bun on the back of her head.

"She's the only one who I see all the time," he added. "I've seen a little kid one time, and I've seen a towboat captain—I think it was a towboat captain, anyhow, the way he was dressed—a heavyset, older man with a beard and a mustache. I've seen him a couple of times."

The dining room and foyer boast a literal traffic jam of psychic impressions, Sadler noted.

"That's the reason I painted the foyer the pink color, because one night I saw a party going on in this house, and it was all in that hallway there," he said. "And the room was done up in the pink colors and stuff. They were all in the big ball gown dresses. That hallway was full of people. I think that I get little intuitions, whatever you call it, of things that actually happened throughout the house. It doesn't happen all the time."

When local mediums visited the home, they had a difficult time picking up any one impression in the dining room due to all the psychic activity, he said. Part of the reason may be because the Sadler-Keck home is connected to the other world.

"They pointed out I had a portal here in my back bedroom, upstairs, that they said the spirits come and go from," Sadler said. "I can't see it. I know what they're talking about, but I've never seen it. That really surprised me."

The portal must be working well, because Norman also has had visits at the home from his deceased father and, more recently, from his brother who supposedly committed suicide (see Chapter 26, Tragedies through Time).

"All these spirits we've had in the house, none of them are bad," he said and chuckled. "We have all good, positive spirits in this house. There's nothing there that can hurt you. I don't tell this kind of stuff to everybody, so when a friend comes in the house and they start talking about the same thing you know about, it kind of makes you feel a little eerie, you know."

I'll Have That Pie at the Computer, Mom!

In the late 1940s, Mary Westerhold's parents built a comfortable home in Edwardsville, Illinois. After they died in 1998, one of Mary's brothers purchased it to use as rental property.

"After a divorce, my daughter and I moved into the house in March 2000," recalled Westerhold, an historical and genealogical researcher who works part time at the Madison County Historical Museum. "Since then, I have occasionally noticed the smell of my dad's aftershave and a favorite perfume of my mom's. I do not keep either the aftershave or perfume in the house.

"On the day after Thanksgiving in November 2000, I was up at 5:00 A.M. to get some computer work done before my daughter woke up," she added. "I was working on the computer when I smelled the aroma of baking pumpkin pie. All of the windows were closed, and I knew I had not put a pumpkin pie in the oven. There was no source for the smell that I could find. I was definitely disappointed that it was not from a real pie!"

Mary's brother also has had a few strange experiences at the home while renovating it, including "misplacing" a padlock key that somehow moved from inside a kitchen cabinet to a nail outside the back door.

"My brother accused me of playing a joke on him, because I had teased him about 'disturbing the spirits of the house' during the renovation," she said. "It would have been a good joke, but it wasn't my doing."

So Much for the Home Brew

The sprawling frame two-story on Genevieve in the Walnut Park neighborhood of north St. Louis originally was the home of Betty Crossno's grandparents. And over the years this home had the reputation of being very haunted (see chapters 9, On the Road; 30, Someone to Watch Over Me; and 22, Happy at Home).

One of the first "haunts" was Crossno's great-grandmother Elizabeth, who died in 1921 but returned to scare the daylights out of Crossno's mother, Nellie.

"She had a little bell, and whenever she needed anything, she'd ring that bell, and my mother would have to get it for her," Crossno recalled. "About two weeks after she died, my mother started hearing this bell ringing upstairs…there'd be nobody there. One day she was sitting on the side of her bed getting ready for church, and she looked up and saw her grandmother walking toward her. She said it just scared the bejeezus out of her, you know, and she said, 'I did a backflip over the bed and into [my mother's] room.' Her mother, Cora, said, 'You should stop and ask her what she wants. She's trying to tell you something."

About a week later, two of Crossno's uncles were finishing up a batch of home brew.

"They were in the closet under the stairs, capping home brew—that's when they used to make home brew, you know," Crossno said. "The other uncle was in the living room, and he was painting the linoleum—that's when they used to paint the floor. It was before they had a basement, and as they were capping, they looked up and saw Grandma coming toward them into the closet. And of course they both panicked, just scared out of their wits, went running out of the closet and crossed the living room floor that had just been painted.

"The whole closet blew up," Crossno added and laughed. "And they never saw her again."

A Faucet Full of Mystery

Cheryl McKenzie's Florissant home is twenty-five years old and very normal—or, at least, it was until recently.

"My mom had that home built, and she was the only one who lived in it," noted McKenzie, a hairstylist. "She died in a nursing home in January 1990. The years I've lived in it, I've never seen or heard anything.

"It's kind of odd," she added. "My daughter got married last March, and they bought a home in September. It's in Florissant, too, just about five minutes from my house, and she told me her house was haunted. I said, 'Oh, yeah, right,' and she told me about all these little things she hears, like a glass dropping on the floor and breaking in the kitchen, and there's nothing there, and the sounds of cooking and frying and splattering grease, and there's no one cooking. She's never seen anything, but she hears things."

McKenzie began to wonder if something followed her home recently, after an incident in her home. It was about eight in the morning, and McKenzie was preparing for work.

"I was brushing my hair in the mirror, and the bathtub's right behind me," she said. "All of a sudden the water in the bathtub turned on while I was in front of the mirror, full-force like you're filling the bathtub. I've got a curtain over the bathtub, and I thought my [other] daughter got up and got in the bathtub, and I didn't see her.

"I said, 'Jessica? Are you going to take a bath right now?' because she normally sleeps until noon, and she didn't answer. I pushed the curtain over, and nothing was in there, but the water was running like crazy. I called my daughter and turned the water off, and it took three turns to turn the water off. When I told my daughter about it, she about freaked out."

Pardon Me, But You're on My Lap

A few years ago Nicole, of north St. Louis, attended a ghost-hunters convention hosted by Right Brain Activities and psychic Antoinette Eason. Nicole, who asked that her last name not be used, was listening to a presentation by author-storyteller Jim Longo on the second floor of the Piasa Masonic Lodge, in Alton. The building is reputed to be haunted (see *Spirits of St. Louis: A Ghostly Guide to the Mound City's Unearthly Activities*).

"All of a sudden I got this overwhelming feeling of this weight on my chest and on my stomach," said Nicole, who works for a computer software company. "Then I got really cold, and then I felt really nauseated. I thought, 'Is this indigestion?' because we had eaten not too long before. It was just gross.

"I didn't want to be rude," she added. "I sat there and took it as long as I could, then I got up and went into the bathroom because I thought I was going to be sick; it was that bad. When I got up to go to the bathroom, it subsided—not instantly, but it slowly started to go away."

Surprised, Nicole mentioned the incident to one of Antoinette's colleagues.

"He said it sounded to him as if an entity took up the same space I was sitting in; in other words, a ghost sat on me," Nicole said. "I was more annoyed by that than I was frightened. Maybe they thought it was funny to sit on a person—I have no idea. It was odd. And I've never experienced anything like that in my life."

The second-floor auditorium was bustling with activity, Nicole noted.

"One of those nights, we watched one of the seats flip down and flip up all by itself," she said. "All kinds of things go on in that room. I always get this little vibraty feeling when I walk in there.

"Many people feel different," she added. "Some people feel the hair on their arm stand up; some feel the hair on their neck stand up; I feel like a vibration on my skin. You know how, if someone takes a balloon and rubs it on the carpet and holds it next to you, you feel all tingly and stuff from the static electricity? I feel it all over, on my face, my neck, my arms. It just feels like the air is electrically charged. I get that in the Masonic temple a lot because that place is so incredibly active."

"Witch" in Woodson Terrace

After she moved out of her family's home in the Walnut Park neighborhood, Betty Crossno and her second husband purchased a home on Calvert, in Woodson Terrace, that seemed to be equally haunted. (Crossno is quick to note that her current home in Kirkwood is blessedly nonhaunted).

The nondescript figure of a tall man would appear frequently in the home and, on one occasion, walked through the bedroom wall. Crossno named him Tim so that her children wouldn't be frightened.

There was also another presence, but it was elusive and seemed to center around her daughter Rhonda's bedroom.

"I'd smooth the bed over the pillows when I was cleaning, and [I'd] come home, and there would be a headprint in the pillow," she recalled. "You'd try to open the door, and it wouldn't open—it was like a suction was in there. Finally, when it would open, you'd go in, and her dolls would be scattered here and there and everywhere. Only one night I can remember getting very, very scared—enough to petrify me [so] I couldn't move. But I couldn't tell you what it was—it was just overwhelming fear. Almost everybody who came to the house had some kind of experience there."

One afternoon Crossno's son Michael was playing in the kitchen, when he became very startled and came over and buried his head in her lap.

"He said, 'Mommy, there's a witch in the living room.' I said, 'Michael, there's no witch in the living room.' 'Yes, there is. She's right by the couch, Mom.' And I looked and said, 'Michael, there's no witch there.' And he looked up and said, 'Nope, she's gone' and started playing again like nothing had happened."

About a month later, she visited a friend of a friend who read a crystal ball. The woman did a reading for Betty and told her she had two ghosts at her house: a man and a woman. The woman, she said, cries all the time.

"So I got curious," Crossno recalled. "The lady across the street told me that [the former owner] was a very old lady and that she dyed her hair black, and she died in the bedroom where my daughter had hers—she had been bedridden and died in that room. I said, 'Well, there's your witch,' because, to a little kid, if she was old and bedridden, she was probably a very white-looking lady with black hair."

Baby Shoes from George

Etha Lutz grew up at the old Frost House on North Clay, in Ferguson. In the book *Ferguson: A City Remembered*, by the Ferguson Historical Society, Lutz recalled some strange incidents that took place at the home.

"We had a ghost called 'George,'" Lutz recalled. "He blew in my ear, closed doors and performed other unexplainable deeds. We had been in the house for some months when I came across a small child's button shoe on the basement floor. When I questioned my family, they knew nothing about it. Several weeks later the second shoe appeared. We never learned where they came from so we blamed it on George."

Hazelwood House: Edward Scissorhands Revisited

While growing up in Hazelwood, Randy Bibb lived in a little subdivision much like the one in the movie *Edward Scissorhands*. The subdivision was built on land that used to be part of a large farm, and Randy knew the owner, farmer Joe Knobbe.

"We used to play in his field, and he gave us a tree to build a tree house in—nice guy," said Bibb, a house cleaner and papier-maché artist who now lives in Belleville, Illinois. "Our little ranch house was built about 1959. I like to tell people I grew up in the Edward Scissorhands neighborhood."

He laughed. "On our street were something like twenty-two houses in four styles, and all the colors were real primary colors, blue, green, and yellow. There was an area in the house where the doors of the bedrooms and the bathroom all sort of came together—not really a hallway, but a little opening there where you could go in each of the rooms."

And in that opening one could, at times, sense a presence that traveled from the bathroom into the living room, always in the same direction, Bibb said.

"We all saw it; you could really only see it out of the corner of your eye," he said. "Over every doorway was a heat register, so the hallway was the warmest room in the house, but the temperature dropped in the hallway when the thing went by. There was a very slight, very faint sweet smell. My mother said it smelled like roses, but it didn't smell like flowers to me. Just sort of a sweet smell."

Randy's mother died in 1990, and the house was sold to an elderly woman.

"I'd love to ask her, 'Do you ever see anything go by in the hallway?'" Bibb said. "I don't want to spook her."

26 [Tragedies through Time]

In many instances, they never show up on the "cosmic radar." But emotionally charged events such as painful deaths and murders, in certain situations, leave ghostly impressions for years. Are these the spirits of those who have died? An electrically charged psychic imprint of sorts on the place where they died, destined to play over and over like an aging motion picture? A time warp of sorts? You be the judge.

Cozy Bedfellows in Kirkwood

"We had always talked about ghost stories, and I always thought they were fun to listen to," recalled Debbie Odle, of Jefferson County. "I never really thought they were true."

Odle, an operating room assistant/unit secretary for a local hospital, changed her mind when, in 1974, she stayed at her best friend Tracy's old wood-frame house on Kirkwood's Craig Road for several days.

"She asked me to spend the night on her porch because she said that there were ghosts in her room, and she didn't want to sleep there," said Odle, who was a seventh-grader at the time. "I said, 'I think we should just spend the night in your room. I don't know if I believe in what you're telling me, and I think we should just go up there and find out for sure what's going on.'"

One day everyone—including Tracy's mom and three brothers—left the house to go to the swimming pool.

"Tracy and I were the last ones in the house, up in her bedroom on the second floor," Odle said. "When we left, her room was spic-and-span clean, all the drawers were shut, everything was fine, and we locked the door at the very top—she had a lock on the outside. We were the last ones to leave,

196

and when we came back from swimming, we were the first ones to come back in. We unlocked the door and opened it, and her drawers were all pulled out, socks were all over, clothes that were in the drawer were all over—her room was just a disaster. The calendar had X's on it, and a couple of things on the calendar were just ripped off and thrown on the floor.

"I thought that was strange, but maybe somebody came in somehow," Odle added. "I didn't really have an explanation for it. She cleaned up the mess, and we stayed up there a couple more nights."

Then one night, Odle was awakened by the sound of footsteps.

"I thought, 'Maybe it's her dad.' Her mom and dad's room was down and across the hall, her brothers' room was across the hall, and then there was a bathroom. I thought maybe her dad or one of her brothers got up to go to the bathroom.

"It just kept coming, going back and forth up and down the hallway, heavier and heavier—it was more like army boots. It got louder and louder and louder. I laid there for a while, and I tried to nudge Tracy and say, 'So you think you're being funny with those footsteps, but that's not scaring me.' Well, for some reason I just laid there and couldn't move.

"Then I felt pressure, like someone was sitting on my legs," she said. "I was awake. I didn't see anything, but I could feel pressure on my legs, and I went to move and couldn't move."

Odle tried to talk to Tracy, but couldn't speak.

"I went to scream, and nothing would come out," she said. "I couldn't move even my arm or my leg. I guess I was just scared to death, because I never had that happen before or ever since. In the morning I told Tracy about it, and she said, 'I told you there was a ghost up here.' I called my mom: 'I think you need to come get me.'"

Odle was not the only one to witness strange occurrences in the house. Tracy and her mother saw an apparition, felt cold spots, and encountered other ghostly phenomena, Odle said.

"They did a history on the house and found out there was a slave who was chained up in the attic and had starved to death and died there," she said. "One year Tracy got into the attic, and they said that's what got it all started. The previous owners never did bother with the attic."

The family now lives in Florida, Odle said.

"They sold it to the neighbor, and he was rehabbing it, and I also heard that the foundation wasn't stable anymore on this house," she said. "I don't know if that played a part in it, too, but it's strange because they've been out of it for a long time, but nobody's moved in since they were there."

Haunted Hospital: Little Girl Lost

Back in the mid- to late-1960s, an employee at a well-known St. Louis hospital for children observed a strange turn of events: the appearance, at night, of a little girl believed to have died there several years earlier.

The employee, who is known to be a credible source, has asked to remain anonymous. Officials of the hospital report that if there was ever a ghost in the ward, there is nothing strange going on there now and have asked that the hospital not be identified.

This is the story:

"Haunted hospitals are unusual in this country," the employee noted. "They're all over the place in England. Florence Nightingale's old hospital has a couple of ghosts. And it's always nurses, never patients. It's interesting: the logic is that wherever this ghost nurse existed, the floors were lower than they are now, and that's why you can't see her feet. I'm convinced she just walked her feet off.

"The nurses' stations at this hospital are set up in a central area, and the kids' rooms are cubicles kind of in a circle around the nurses' station. So if you sit in the nurses' station on a swivel chair, without getting up you can crane your neck and see all the cubicles. It's basically a round nursing division. At one end is a hall that goes out to the rest of the hospital, and at the other end there are doors that go out to big, railed balconies used—at least at the time I was there—as big, open play areas. They could take the kids out and get them in the sun.

"But there was no [other] way to get up to the balconies because the nursing division was on the second floor, and these huge balconies were over first-floor areas that didn't have a floor above them. And it's not built on a hill.

"They would see shadows of the child on the frosted glass that led out to the balcony, and children would talk about the little girl who came in their room and was washing her hands at the sink. No one ever felt as though there was any malevolence in it; she was just kind of around. My supervisor, the head of medical records, said, 'Yeah, we think we know who it is. We had a little girl die here.'

"Basically, the girl had a back problem. She coded, went into cardiopulmonary arrest on the table, they got her back once, put her in the recovery room. She coded three more times there, and she finally died."

Among other things, patients' charts would fly off the desk, several at a time.

"There's a rack for charts, normally," the employee said. "They're all kept in one tidy place. If you have it out, you're going to put in the vital signs and nurses' notes from your shift. Sometimes you get a bunch out to work on, and you lay one down because you hear something or there's a call light.

"Those were the charts that were flying off the desk. There were, apparently, multiple 'chart flies.' Several people reported them, one of whom was the night-shift supervisor."

The girl was about thirteen, the employee said.

"Poltergeists tend to occur where there are adolescents, and they are usually emotionally disturbed adolescents," the employee said. "And there had been a psychologist brought in on the child because there were behavioral problems, and the notes never got to the chart. I've never seen a psych consult done before—that was very unusual."

Unhappy Forces on Utah Place

Doug Harding and his wife, Robin, had found a home along south St. Louis' historic Utah Place, but Harding worried about some settlement that had occurred in the basement and had been repaired. Would the basement leak or settle further?

"The neighborhoods down there have old clay mines, and they dug out the clay to make bricks," noted Harding, a park ranger for the National Park Service. "Most of the bricks made here in St. Louis came from, like, Morganford. Even the bricks that are in the alleys, they've got the name of the brick company on them: Hydraulic Brick Company. There is a street in the area called Hydraulic."

Hollow spaces make for foundation problems, and Harding noticed that a home two doors east of the one they were considering was for sale. He decided to check the basement of that home to see if the same settling was going on.

"The Realtor's sign and phone number was in the front-door window; it wasn't out in the yard," he said. "So I had to walk up on the porch to write the phone number down to contact the Realtor. When I stepped up on the porch, I got that same feeling that I had gotten when I stepped up on the porch of the tavern at the battlefield—an uneasy feeling, but I could sense there was something there (see Chapter 11, Civil War Chills).

"I met the Realtor, we went through the house, and it was an odd house—it had rooms added on to rooms," Harding noted. "I walked into the bathroom on the second floor and really got a strong, uneasy feeling in there. I checked out the basement, and it was fine, no signs of settling.

"So I went back to the Realtor and said, 'Okay, tell me the ghost story in the house.' Well, she got white and looked at me like, 'How do you know?' I said, 'Someone died here, and they died in that bathroom. What's the story?' I could feel something happened there.

"She told me that a maid had committed suicide by hanging herself in the bathroom of that house," he said. "A pair of guys bought that house right after I bought mine, they lived in it for a while, then they sold it and moved to another house. I told them what the Realtor told me, but they said they hadn't felt anything. So now it's changed hands twice since then."

Kidnapped by Indians in Manchester

A brand-new subdivision in Manchester has put an end to the 150-year vigil of a pioneer woman for her son, believed to have been captured by Indians.

"It hasn't happened since the subdivision went in less than five years ago, to my knowledge," noted Til Keil, historian and member of the board of directors of the Old Trails Historical Society.

"Peter and Elizabeth Breen were early settlers, and in about the 1850s they built a house on their property for their daughter," she said. "The daughter's son was about six years old when he disappeared. There were Indians in the area, and legend says that they may have kidnapped the boy. It's noted that the children of that area did occasionally play with Indians.

"Every August, the Breens' daughter would appear in 1850s costume on Carman Road," Keil said. "She's still looking for him, and neighborhood people have seen her. There's a high school out here, and one of the teachers was coming home, using Carman Road going toward Kirkwood, and he saw this lady in period costume on the road. He slammed on the brakes, and by the time he got himself together, she was gone."

Keil chuckled. "That's what made it so extra-special—he was not one of the neighborhood people; he just happened to be at the right place at the right time. So it's not just the neighbors here."

After the old house was demolished, the appearances stopped. However, off Weidman Road across the street from Queeny Park, residents have reported two little African-American girls, ten or twelve years old, at the edge of the woods, singing.

"Now this is still happening, they tell me," she said. "The people who saw the little girls live in the Dutch Mill area. That's the name of a road that goes west from Weidman. There used to be a lot of open space back there. One time there were some children playing in a backyard there, and it frightened them when they saw the ghosts. By the time the mother came out, the two singing girls were gone.

"There were many slave families living out here before the Civil War; in fact, the majority of the people living here before the Civil War were slave owners."

Keil's own house, built around 1895, also is said to have a ghost.

"We have one nephew that comes in here, and whenever he goes to the bathroom, which is in the old part of the house, he feels the presence," she said. "When we first moved here in 1997, our grandson wasn't comfortable going into that part of the house. This is before he knew all about [the presence].

"Now I don't feel a presence, but that's neither here nor there."

Death Fails to Stop Would-Be Suitor

He was a strange young man who had a crush on Shelley Romo, his classmate at McCluer High School in the early 1980s.

"Later that year his seat was moved behind mine, and he would tell me stories about how his father and brother committed suicide," Romo recalled. "He would somehow put flowers and gifts in my locker. Throughout high school, he would call me often and stop by my home. We never dated."

Then, a couple of years later, the troubled young man came by again, except this time his wrists were cut, and he was bleeding all over the porch, Romo said.

"He said he just wanted to tell me goodbye, and he left," she said. "I drove to the police station, and they said a car matching that description just hit a telephone pole. I never heard from him after that."

Soon after, Romo and her two-and-a-half-year-old son moved out of her parents' home and into the Brighton Apartments in North County.

"The carpet had spots on it from the bath into one bedroom and out the door," she said. "My son asked me, 'Who's that man?' as he looked down the hall, which was icy—the rest of the home was warm."

When she went to her new mailbox a couple of days later, Romo was in for a surprise.

There was a lot of mail, but it was all addressed to the boy from high school," she said. "I immediately went down to the office, told them I knew what happened in that apartment, and demanded they clean the carpets.

The next three years were very quiet and probably among the happiest of my life. Then I met my current husband in 1991."

When Romo's future husband began making frequent appearances at the apartment, strange things began happening.

"I would walk in from work, and the TV would be on and changing channels," she said. "We would both see shadows moving. My son said he remembers shadows of a man walking down the hallway as a child, but he just thought it was normal."

One of the creepiest phenomena was the hooded black figure that appeared on two occasions in the middle of the night, she said.

"On two occasions, my husband [then boyfriend] woke up with a hooded black figure standing above him," Romo said. "It was very tall and thin, and the head was normal sized and faceless. The body was limbless and thin as a broomstick. It was as if a black hooded cape was draped over a black bowling ball on a stick. Once we both saw that same figure come out of the bedroom closet and walk through a wall into the hall."

Another time, Romo was talking to her husband in the bathroom and heard the front door open, slam shut, and footsteps run down the hall. She assumed it was her son, who had been playing with a friend two buildings down, but there was no one in the house.

"One time my husband was sitting on the bed, and I was combing my hair in the mirror," she said. "He asked me what I thought about marriage, and a statue that I had received from my grandmother flew off the dresser and shattered.

"Thank goodness, my lease was up soon afterwards."

Unspeakable Acts: Wronged Brother Returns

Several years ago, Lafayette Square resident Norman Sadler was startled to see the apparition of his brother, Steven, who was believed to have committed suicide by fatally shooting himself in the head with a military rifle.

"He came back and told me that his wife and her boyfriend killed him. That really spooked me," recalled Sadler, a bartender. "He told me he came in from work that morning, went to sleep in the recliner like he always did, and when he woke up those two were doing what they were doing. That's the last he knows."

Steve's rifle seems to corroborate the story, Sadler said.

"I have the rifle here at home, and I'm a smaller person. I've tried to put the gun up to the side of my face, and it's hard for me to reach the trigger," he said. "And Steve was a really big man, like 350 pounds, with a lot shorter arms than me even, you now. So there's no way possible he could reach that."

Though he has no concrete evidence, Sadler said he told Steve's wife he knew she was responsible.

"She just looked at me, and I told her, 'You know, D——, when I do come up with the truth, you'd better hope that the cops get to you before I do," he said and laughed. "I've got her worried, anyhow. I would have thought her conscience would have gotten to her before now, but then again, you've got to have a conscience before it can get to you."

[WHO WERE THEY?]

The strange manifestations we call ghosts often appear without a clue as to their identity. And they seem to lurk everywhere—from historic Cupples House to the Ellsworth Apartments and Lafayette Square to DeSoto. You'll even find one evading the security guard in an office building on Washington Avenue, downtown.

People Support: "Oh, a Wise Guy, Eh?"

John Barr has a fascinating job in an even more fascinating building at 555 Washington Boulevard, downtown. He works for PeopleSupport, a high-tech company specializing in customer service for client companies that have included the U.S. Postal Service, World Book Encyclopedia, Universal Studios, Spencer Gifts, Captain Morgan Rum, Expedia, Armani Exchange, and more.

"I worked with World Book for a while," noted Barr, who also lives downtown. "See, if you had problems installing a World Book encyclopedia, you dialed a help line—that was us. The one that's fun is Universal Studios, or Spencer's Gifts:

'Oh, you want the vibrating pickle.'

'It's not for *me*.'

"It never is," he laughed. "Never is. So if you got to Spencer's gifts.com, 'Talk with a live chat person,' that's us. I do chat, too."

Barr has been "babysitting computers" for more than a year in the large building, which also houses several other companies. It was designed as separate buildings between 1875 and 1888, then converted first to Crawford's Dry Goods Company and, later, to the May Company Department Store, according to information from the Landmarks Association of

St. Louis.

A solid, handsome brick building with features of cast iron, terra cotta, brick, granite, sandstone, and limestone, 555 Washington, in later years, was home to the old "Dollar Store" and enjoyed a brief renaissance as an upscale office building. It was renovated in 1986 by Kimble Cohn & Associates.

"This whole building was totally done for the information age," he noted. "This was all going to be the technology corridor, all the way up to Tucker, and then technology went belly-up. We're one of the last surviving companies."

And that's where the ghost comes in. Is he a long-ago clerk from Crawford's Dry Goods, a customer of the May Company who overstayed his visit, or an unhappy manager of the Dollar Store? Whatever his reason for hanging around, he seems to be unhappy with all the recent changes.

"I guess he's upset," Barr said. "He slung a chair one night—it sounded like one of those big roller chairs—but there was nothing over there. It sounded like somebody just slung a chair from one end to the other side of the building.

"There were only four of us on that night, and we were all accounted for, with our headsets on, doing our thing," he added. "It was probably about one-thirty in the morning. We asked each other if we wanted to go over and check it out.

"'You guys want to go over and see what it is?' 'Nope.'"

Early one spring morning, at about 3:00 A.M., a security guard came rushing in, and he was angry.

"We were all sitting there doing our thing," Barr recalled, "and he came roaring in, 'Where's the man who was hiding from me in here? Huh? Somebody came in here.'"

"He got really, really mad. He thought we were hiding him. He kind of hooted and hollered a little bit. He's standing there glaring at us, and we're sitting there looking at him like, 'What, have you lost your mind?' By the time we sit down there and plug into the phones, we're [confined] pretty much, as far as the phone cord will reach. We couldn't have gotten over there to let anybody in. And, really, there's no place to hide in there."

But the guard was most disturbed and refused to leave until he searched the place thoroughly, Barr said.

"He started searching every little place, looking underneath desks, thinking we were hiding somebody," he said. "He turned the office apart and searched access areas even I can't get into."

The elusive gentleman, whoever he was, couldn't be found, and for good reason, Barr believes: whatever it was, it wasn't alive.

"Nobody came in here," Barr said. "We would have heard the door. And our area is secured by a pass-card reader."

Cupples House: Speak Up, Please

Edna Dieterle, of South County, enjoys volunteering at historic homes around the area when she's not hard at work as a registered nurse.

Edna's husband, Mark, also is an avid volunteer, and a few years ago the two were visiting Cupples House during the Victorian Society's annual meeting. Located on the St. Louis University campus, the beautiful forty-nine-room mansion was built in 1890, in the Richardsonian Romanesque style, and is particularly known for its fine woodwork and forty fireplaces.

"I think they had someone talking about Victorian jewelry and things, and everybody else had moved out of the dining room," she recalled. "I was in the hallway, and my husband was left in the dining room by himself. He calls me Eddie—all of a sudden he says, 'Eddie, come here.'

"I went into the dining room, and he said, 'The weirdest thing just happened.' He looked shook up about something. He was standing there, and he didn't realize I had walked out of the room, and right next to him he heard somebody go, 'Aaaahhhh,' as if they were drawing a breath to speak. He said it was so real, the sound of inspired air. He thought it was me, and he turned. As he turned, out of the corner of his eye, at about his level, there was a woman's face, very faint. It faded as soon as he saw it, and that was it—it was gone."

Though caretakers of the mansion say it isn't haunted, the old *St. Louis Globe-Democrat's* "Spirits of St. Louis" *Official Guide to Local Legendary Haunted Houses* suggests that the spirit of its builder, wood-products manufacturer Samuel Cupples, may still hang around the old homestead.

"We have some information from Cupples House, and I was looking through it and showing [my husband] pictures of different women such as Mrs. Cupples and their daughter," Edna said. "None of the faces looked familiar, but we were saying, 'Gosh, there's so many servants and people that were in and out of that house over the years.' Nobody looked familiar to him."

Mysterious Lady Walks DeSoto

In her book *Witchcraft, Wickedness, And Other Wacky Happenings In*

Jefferson County History, Jefferson County historian Della Lang tells the story of an elusive woman whose identity remains unknown after decades of speculation.

The "Lady in Black" was described in print by Eddie Miller, a columnist for the *DeSoto Press*, during the 1960s, Lang noted. Beginning about 1915, a mysterious lady dressed in black often appeared on the street corners of the small town, where everyone knew each other.

"She wore a long black silk dress, black gloves and a huge black hat with a dark veil covering her face," Lang wrote. "She often appeared—and disappeared—from the vicinity of Boyd Street anywhere between Main and Fifth Street for a period of six years or more."

Was she a woman in disguise spying on her unfaithful husband, as some amateur sleuths have concluded?

"Miller said the lady was never seen again after 1921," Lang noted. "But that gives us another mystery to solve. Did she divorce her husband or kill him that year? Or…was she killed?"

Lafayette Square Townhouse Holds Strange Secret

More than a dozen years ago, in the late 1980s, Mary Beth Ruby spent a few days at a good friend's home in the Lafayette Square neighborhood. The three-story townhouse was located on Hickory Street at Dolman Avenue.

"Her parents had gone out of town, and I had stayed there with Jamie for, like, a weekend," recalled Ruby, a St. Louis Hills resident and 911 operator for the St. Louis County Police Department. "She had gone off to work, and I was there during the day by myself and was in a second-floor bedroom. I kept hearing noises coming from upstairs, and I knew there was nobody up there. It was the very distinct sound of footsteps—not real heavy, but footsteps going back and forth. I was too afraid to go up there and look, but to this day I'm convinced there's something about that house.

"That was the only kind of experience like that I've ever had," she added. "It was just very bizarre. I didn't feel threatened at all, and I knew there wasn't a burglar in the house, and I had already heard the story that they thought there was a ghost in the house. But I didn't want to go up there!"

Ruby called Jamie at work about the strange noises.

"'Don't worry about it,' she said. 'They're not malevolent spirits, they're just there.' She acted very nonchalant about it."

Was the ghost that of a publishing magnate's son, who died under the wheels of a carriage, just shy of his upcoming wedding?

"The story that I was told from Jamie was that at one time Simon & Schuster, the publishing people, one of [the families] had lived there, and I don't know which one it was," Ruby said. "Their son was to be married, and before he got married he was killed in some kind of horse-and-buggy accident or something, and I think it was in the Lafayette Square area. Since then, strange things have been happening at the house, and they thought it was haunted."

The owners and Jamie regularly noted strange occurrences, she said. Jamie now lives in Louisiana, and her parents are in California.

"They kept the third floor closed, generally, throughout the year because it's such a big house, and they didn't want to heat it during the wintertime and have the a/c on up there in the summertime," she said. "Jamie and her parents had both told me of a couple instances where they had been out for walks in the evening: they'd be walking down the street looking at their house, they knew there was no one there, and up on the third floor they saw what appeared to be someone pulling back the curtain from the third-floor window looking out on Hickory Street.

"Of course, when they got home, they looked and there was nobody in the house. Her parents are very well-to-do, and they had an alarm system and everything in the house. It wasn't a burglar or something like that."

Since then, Ruby has been trying to learn more about the historic home and the accident that supposedly occurred so many years ago.

"I can't seem to find anything written about it anywhere, " she said. "I've dug and dug, and I just keep hitting dead ends."

Tonight's Entertainment: The Lady in White

Several people in the Ellsworth Apartments, 4405 West Pine Avenue, have seen the "Lady in White." And one night a decade ago, former resident Randy Bibb did, too.

Bibb was waiting for his ride one night to the Omni Hotel (now Hyatt Regency), in Union Station, where he worked night audit at the front desk.

"I was standing inside the lobby. Of course, there were lights inside the lobby, and it was dark outside, so I could see in the glass a reflection of the lobby behind me, because of the lights. And I wasn't looking at the door; I was looking out into the street, when all of a sudden my attention focused on the reflection, and there standing behind me was a woman in a long white nightgown, standing on the stairs.

"When I turned around, there was nobody there," noted Bibb, who now cleans houses and is a papier-maché artist living in Belleville. "And when I went back to the reflection, the reflection was gone, too.

"There was nothing frightening about her," he recalled. "The dress was real nondescript, but it was very clearly something to sleep in. She had long hair of a brownish-reddish chestnut color, not quite auburn. I would guess she was probably 5'4", 5'3". She wasn't looking at my reflection; she was looking out into the street. [The dress] wasn't as old as the turn of the century, but it could have been anywhere from the '20s through the '40s. She was just a complete human person standing on the steps, with one hand on the banister."

Several others at the apartments—other tenants, the manager, and the janitor—also were treated to appearances by the Lady in White, Bibb said.

"From what I saw, she was just as solid as you please," he said. "And when I turned around, there was nothing there."

[TRIUMVIRATE OF THRILLS]

Around greater St. Louis are three old homes with mysterious pasts: one on Lee Avenue, in Webster Groves; another on Wyoming Street, in the Benton Park West neighborhood of south St. Louis; and a farmhouse near Millstadt, Illinois, about twenty minutes from St. Louis.

As residents of these homes have learned, remnants of that strange past often weave into the present for an undeniably eerie experience.

Lee Avenue: Murder Site?

It was a dark and stormy evening when the stranger from the big city arrived in town by train. He was on his way to visit his sweetheart but he never reached her house. Three men conspired in the saloon near the station and, while one of them acted as his guide, the other two hid in ambush to rob him. He pulled out a gun. So did they. And the stranger was dead.

This melodramatic tale would seem to have little in common with Webster Groves and the image it has attained through the years. But it was because Bertram E. Atwater, of Chicago, was murdered on Lee avenue in January 1896 that the loosely knit together communities which made up Webster Groves took steps to incorporate and insure law and order.

It was also because Brennan's saloon had played a part in providing the setting for the plotters that the sale of liquor was prohibited for many years in Webster Groves and is still allowed only in eating places, causing detractors to say scornfully, "You can't even buy a drink in that town."

—from *Webster Groves*, by Clarissa Start (1975)

In 1973, Thomas and Georgia Harding and their children, Doug, Scott, Lori, and Chuck moved into a two-and-a-half-story, stucco-fronted house on Lee Avenue. The home was built around 1900 on the foundation of an

SP|R|TS

older house that had burned down.

"We were always curious about that: where was the house on Lee Avenue that caused Webster Groves to go dry?" recalled Doug Harding, now a park ranger with the National Park Service.

"Our water main coming into the house broke, and it turned out to be on our side of the meter, so we had to pay to have it fixed," he said. "So we had the front yard dug up—they repaired the pipe and put the dirt back in. Shortly after that, we had a couple rainy days. My little sister was out on the sidewalk where they'd been digging, and she found on the sidewalk a .44-caliber bullet, possibly from that same shoot-out. It kind of washed out of the mud after they'd been digging up the soil. It was from an old black powder gun, so it would fit about the time period. I was thinking maybe our house was the one, because there weren't many houses on Lee Avenue at the time that happened."

There was also something creepy about the old carriage-house-turned-garage in the rear of the property, he said.

"After I got out of high school and I had my own car, I would park down there in that garage instead of in front of the house because my mom had a car and my dad had a car," Harding said. "A lot of times when I would park my car there late at night, I had a very, very strong sense of uneasiness—sometimes it was so strong I would literally run into the house. The daytime never bothered me. Years later I discovered my dad admitted having the same feelings. We don't know what happened down there."

Things routinely disappeared at the old house, spurring arguments between family members. The Hardings' ancient French poodle, Feisty, had always slept on Doug's bed, until the family moved to Lee Avenue and Doug took a third-floor bedroom.

"He did not like, and would not stay up on, the third floor," he said. "If I did bring him up into that room at night, he would scratch on the door to be let out."

Then one night, Harding was babysitting his nine-year-old brother and seven-year-old sister when he realized they weren't alone in the house.

"My girlfriend was over, and we were in the living room, and there was a fire in the fireplace, and we had the stereo going, and they were in the TV room [a sunporch off the dining room] watching TV. My girlfriend says, 'Look,' and I looked up at the doorway going to the front hall, and I see this little face kind of poking around the corner of the door looking at us.

"My first thought was that it was my little brother, because it was about the right size and everything, and I hollered, 'What do you want?' and jumped up. And I walked to the door. There was nobody there. From there I could see through the dining room into the TV room, so if anybody had been there I would have seen them running or heard them running into the TV room. So I immediately went in there, and my brother and sister were in there watching TV.

"I remember it was a small boy with kind of long, blondish hair, maybe six years old, and I could see, like, a Little Lord Fauntleroy type of big white collar and little black jacket, but it wasn't clear enough in the couple seconds I saw him that I could make it all out in real detail.

"My girlfriend used to get headaches in the house—she didn't like it. She'd get real severe headaches until she left the house."

Another time Harding and a friend were in his room rolling blank rounds of ammunition for an upcoming Civil War reenactment, and Harding was called by his mother several times to help out downstairs. His friend later asked if the house was haunted.

"He said, 'Somebody's playing with the scissors,'" Harding recalled. "'I lay it down there, and when I go back to get it, it's not there, and I keep finding it under the couch. And one time I set 'em down, and I watched them scoot across the floor by themselves.'"

The family sold the home in 1979. Harding's parents retired to Arizona, and Harding himself prepared to move to an apartment because he was staying in town to study at the University of Missouri.

"That night I'm upstairs in bed—I had been watching a movie late," he said. "It was early summer, and I turn off the TV, turn off the light, lay down, and all of a sudden I can feel this weight on my legs on the bed. And I got such a deep sense of depression; I felt like I wanted to cry.

"You know how a little kid will grab you around the legs? That's what it kind of felt like. So I got up, turned on the light and looked around, and nothing's there. The cat wasn't anywhere on the third floor. When I went back to bed, got into bed, and turned off the light, that's when I felt the weight on my legs. It happened about three times that night. Finally I said, 'Okay, I'm going to sleep.'"

Harding laughed. "And I went to sleep."

Although they did some research on the house, family members never figured out who the child was.

"We did a lot of remodeling, stripping the paint off the woodwork, baseboards, and my dad was taking the baseboard off by one of the fireplaces," Harding recalled. "There was this little gap between the fireplace and the wall, and newspaper had been stuck down there...When he pulled out the newspapers he pulled out a shipping label for chickens with our address on it. They raised Rhode Island Reds. So at one time our house was a chicken farm.

"We also found a letter that had fallen down behind the baseboard by the stairs, talking about a wedding that had happened in the house, I think around the 1930s."

Bewildered in Benton Park West

In June 2001, Suzanne Schopflin and her boyfriend, Danny Lundry, purchased an old two-family brick flat in the 2700 block of Wyoming Street. They call it "Pigeon Central" because of the more than one hundred pigeons they later learned were roosting in the attic through holes in the side of the house.

"Danny thought it looked creepy immediately, and he really did not want to live here, but he followed me—my business is down here," said Schopflin, owner of Bark Avenue Pet Grooming, in Soulard. "We haven't even moved into this house—because of the pigeon problem, we're suing—we've got boxes everywhere."

But dying pigeons falling into the walls were nowhere near as creepy as the antics Schopflin and Lundry, a painter, would encounter over the next nine months. Many of the "weird vibes" were concentrated in the main hallway leading to the basement, Schopflin said.

"We started seeing these shadows of cats out of the corner of our eyes—you'd see a cat run by, but it wasn't one of our cats," she said. "I have a parrot, an African Grey, and he sits by the hallway leading to the bathroom in the downstairs family room. Parrots are really smart. If you bring a new person in the house, a new pet or a new object, he'll squawk at it, and he'll try to bite it, and he is obviously afraid of it. He does that at the corner of his cage, to 'nothing' in the hallway, all the time—it's like there's somebody there. He sits there and squawks and screams and pecks at nothing. The longest he's done it was forty-five minutes once."

The three cats and six dogs also refuse to enter certain rooms at times, and the cats swat at thin air in the hallway.

"I've had people come over who don't know about anything I've experienced in this house, and they even say to me, 'This hallway gives me the creeps,'" Schopflin said. "The basement itself I won't even go in: stone walls, dirt floor, particle board laid over the dirt—God only knows what's underneath that. A guy two houses over actually pulled up the wood flooring, and underneath the dirt were three caverns leading to other basements."

The house has been converted partly into a one-family, in that the stairs to the upstairs are indoors. However, there is a family room, kitchen, and bathroom on each of the two levels. Upstairs, the kitchen and bathroom are particularly spooky.

"This has happened to me, like, twenty times—I'll be facing away from the center of the room, toward the cabinets, or washing my hands in the sink, and I'll think I see Danny walking into the bedroom," she said. "We don't have a door to the bedroom, so we have a sheet to keep in the heat, and I'll follow him in there, and nobody will be there.

"Two or three times I felt Danny behind me, breathing down my neck, and he's not there. I've felt someone touch me on my back, and there's nobody there. And I was sitting in the kitchen in one of the chairs watching TV one night, and I literally felt him poke me in the side. And I turned around and went, 'You ass.' He wasn't there—he wasn't even upstairs."

Schopflin now refuses to take a shower in the house when nobody's home.

"You know the really old showers with the wraparound curtain? You get in there, and they stick to you sometimes, right? So you push them away. I was in there one night and it stuck to me, and I went to push it, and there was some resistance at first, like somebody was pushing back. I won't go in the bathroom and close the door if nobody's home."

Schopflin and Lundry, who aren't coffee drinkers and don't own a coffeemaker, regularly smell cooking odors such as coffee, baked goods, and pork products upstairs. The door leading into the family room from the hallway occasionally opens on its own, and in the upstairs kitchen, at times, the cats will arch their backs, hiss, and run for no apparent reason.

"That was the mild stuff, and that was okay," Schopflin said. "We were here for two or three months when Danny—he's a very rational man—came upstairs, woke me up, and said somebody pushed him down the stairs. He didn't slip or trip, and he wasn't drunk, and he knows what it feels like to be pushed. He was laid up for probably a week and a half.

"After that happened, I started seeing in our bedroom—he would put me to bed, and he would come downstairs and watch TV because he's a night owl—I'd be laying in bed, and seven or eight times I've seen a black man walk through the sheet on the bedroom doorway and look out the side window in my bedroom. I can describe what he's wearing: a dark blue suit with a white shirt and one of those old black Colonel Sanders bow ties. I never really could see his face."

She laughed. "Honestly, that's the last thing I wanted to see."

Schopflin told Lundry about seeing the man but never described what he was wearing. Lundry thought she was losing her marbles, and so did Schopflin, until Lundry came running up the stairs in terror late one night.

"I turn on the light, and he's as white as a ghost, and he's shaking," she said. "He couldn't talk, and I said, 'What's wrong? What's wrong?' He's going, 'Ohmygod, now I've seen it all. Ohmygod, ohmygod.' I'm like, 'Tell me what you saw.'

"We have two chairs in the kitchen and a coffee table that's separating them. He was sitting on the chair closest to the bedroom, and the cat was sitting in his lap, and he saw her looking at something, thought she was looking at a fly. 'Get it, girl,' he said, and she jumps over to the other chair, the one I got poked in, and he saw her look up toward the refrigerator."

Danny looked up, too, and saw a black man wearing a dark suit and a white shirt with the Colonel Sanders–style tie.

"Danny said he saw his face, and he was definitely an older man with gray hair, probably about 5'10"," Schopflin said. "He said this guy said to him, 'I know you can feel me. Now you can see me.' Danny said it's not really a voice that he could say came out of this thing's mouth—it wasn't a voice like we know it. But it was more like he heard it in his mind—he said he can't really describe it."

Now Schopflin and Lundry wonder if the man in the suit was responsible for the push down the stairs, and they're afraid. They've contacted Philip Goodwilling, president of the Haunt Hunters, for advice, and at press time for this book were considering leaving the house.

"Danny walked around the house for two hours after that with a knife, and I kept saying, 'What are you going to do? It's already dead!'" she recalled. "He's like, 'I don't know, but there's a man in our house. Somebody is looking at us in our house.' And if you think about it that way, it might just drive you batty. He didn't want to stay another night in the house. He won't go to the bathroom now without taking the cat with him. And that's not something that a rational man does.

"The fact [that this spirit] communicated with my boyfriend, that scares the hell out of me. To think that Danny might be hurt by this in some way scares me. Philip Goodwilling said there's no doubt in his mind that what we're experiencing here is very real, and it may be the beginning of a haunting, or it could be just a spirit that's here. It might not be that big of a deal. He said they feed off your energy and your mind a lot and said, 'Try not to think about it.'"

Easier said than done, noted Schopflin, who plans to research the home's history. According to neighbors, the house was vacant for a number of years.

"Now I know I'm not nuts," she said. "Now I know there is something there. I told Goodwilling that Danny has a bad feeling toward this house, and he said that might be some indication as to why this thing is talking to him and coming after him. I love the house; I had dreams for it. He said maybe I have a more positive influence, and I'm not a threat to whatever this is."

Mayhem Near Millstadt, Illinois

For twenty years Dan, his brother and mom, and for a time his stepfather, lived in an old frame farmhouse near Millstadt, Illinois. From an otherworldly "laundry service" to doorknobs turning and shadowy figures in the hallway, the house had plenty of chills to go around, recalls Dan, a customer service representative for a local company, who asked that his last name not be used.

"We just don't want to feel like freaks," he said. "It's a very interesting part of our lives, and people don't seem to believe us when we talk about it. We've all had experiences. My stepfather was abusive, and we kind of think that had something to do with it, because we never had anything happen until that point in our lives."

Family members had nearly an ever present sensation of being watched, and they would often hear footsteps walking in vacant rooms and see doorknobs turn for no reason, Dan said. And things would disappear from plain sight and, just as mysteriously, reappear days or even months later.

"My brother and our neighbor would play outside in an old barn we had in the back," he said. "They were two years younger than me and came running inside one day and said they were throwing apples at the barn, and an apple flew back out at them, and they actually saw these ghostly figures up in the barn—an older person in a rocking chair and an older gentleman standing behind him with a pitchfork and two people on the side of him. We never believed it, just because they were kids."

One day Dan's mom and his cousin were sitting at the kitchen table, peeling apples for a pie.

"At the kitchen table, you could see all the way down the hallway to the front door," he said. "They saw these shadows moving down the hallway, like someone was walking there. We've always had chihuahuas, and the one that we had there was a very good 'people-person' dog. She would go running down the hallway to see what it was and come back crying.

"Shortly after that, my cousin was doing dishes at the kitchen sink, and when she went to reach for one of the coffee cups, it actually started to spin on the counter."

Another time Dan's brother was alone in the house, placing laundry on hangers in the kitchen.

"He hung them up in the stairwell—because there was the banister, and you can just hang the clothes there before you take them up—because he was going to take a shower [downstairs]," Dan said. "He had all the clothes hanging there, including the shirt he was going to wear for that day. When he returned to get the clothes, the shirt that he wanted to wear was no longer there. He went upstairs, and it was laying on his bed, folded. He had hung it up."

But the scariest episode convinced even the stepfather that all was not right with the house, Dan said. One night Dan, his mom, and stepdad were in the living room, and the TV was blaring.

"Next thing you know, we hear this banging noise coming from above, which was my bedroom," Dan said. "The noise started getting louder and louder. At first I thought it was my brother, and I knew I had to stop him, or we would have gotten in trouble. So I ran into the kitchen and said, 'Jason, would you stop it?' He says, 'It's not me.' The noise kept getting louder and louder, and the windows started shaking. My stepdad got up and, just as he turned off the TV, there was a loud crash."

It was also dark upstairs.

"With a two-way switch, where there's a switch downstairs and a switch upstairs, if they're wired incorrectly the last place you turn it off is where it has to be turned back on, and the last place it was turned off was upstairs, so no one wanted to go upstairs," Dan said. "I ended up flying up the stairs and flipped on the light, and everyone came upstairs—my stepdad, my mom, my brother—and there was nothing. Nothing out of the ordinary, nothing laying on the floor."

And the family's chihuahua was nowhere to be found.

"I ended up looking underneath my bed, and she was there, shaking, and wouldn't come out," he said. "I had to pull her out from underneath the bed. We still don't know what happened."

After Dan's mother divorced his stepfather, much of the strange activity ended.

"You would still have the sensation that someone was there with you," he said. "Five years ago, my uncle bought the house and gutted it, and so far he hasn't had any problems. But he's one of those old-fashioned German men who doesn't discuss anything, you know."

[Spine-Tingling Stories]

Imagine working at a very old television station and hearing footsteps approach, even though you're alone at the time; or setting up shop in an old antique mall and battling with an unseen observer to keep the lights on; or feeling someone blowing on your neck when no one—no one *visible*, that is—is there; or waking to see a large, shadowy figure of a man beside your bed, reaching out for you.

For most red-blooded humans, just reading about those experiences is sure to make one's skin crawl. These and more spine-tingling encounters happened to a few unsuspecting St. Louisans not long ago.

KPLR-TV: Who Goes There?

Once upon a time, they were the Chase Apartments, until the late Harold Koplar purchased the 1920s building and made it home base for his new television station.

KPLR-TV's first broadcast was of a Cardinals baseball game, on April 28, 1959, at 7:00 P.M., noted feature-entertainment reporter Patrick Clark. The announcers were Jack Buck, Harry Caray, and Joe Garagiola.

"You used to be able to walk back and forth between the Chase Hotel and the station in the basement of this building," noted Clark, a Central West End resident and employee of WB 11 since 1995. "They would bring the stars over to the station and have them on the air here, and they'd never be seen."

During a renovation a few years ago, the tunnel opening was cinderblocked up, he said.

"The basement of our building is an interesting place because they used to do the *Bowling for Dollars* down there—they had a bowling alley in the basement. And they used to do *Wrestling At The Chase*, but what many people don't realize is when the Khorassan Ballroom would be booked, they would have it here in our studio, and they had a big black curtain that they put up around the edges—this was before we had news here. The viewers at home never knew.

"Another story that's interesting is...there was a tunnel in the subbasement of that building that led underneath Lindell, across the street, to our parking lot—at one point there was a hotel there—but then went up toward Forest Park. And there were tunnels that were offshoots that went to the really nice homes there along Forest Park."

Built around the turn of the century, the tunnels were used during Prohibition to transfer bootleg liquor from the hotel to the fine residences nearby and also so that the servants would not be seen, Clark said.

"My friend went down in the tunnel and said there were lights, and it was still lit. That was two years ago," he said. "He said these were from the 1920s, and they were just built to last."

Secret tunnels aside, the old KPLR-TV offices are creepy at night, Clark said.

"Many times I've been here late at night after everybody leaves, 10:30 at night," he said. "You'll be working on a script, and it feels like somebody's watching you. It might not sound like a lot, but it's the oddest sensation. Everybody's gone home from the station. It's happened numerous times. It's to the point, really, where people don't like to hang out around here by themselves at night. You just hear odd noises for whatever reason."

On the third floor was a conference room that was formerly the office of Ted Koplar, Harold's son.

"In one room they had a little lunchroom with tables, then off to the side is a room with a couch, and you could shut the doors like a little sunroom," Clark said. "And I went in and took a nap one afternoon, about one o'clock. There are wood floors in the lunchroom. I was laying on the couch, and I heard footsteps coming toward the door. And somebody tried the door—it was almost like they didn't really try to open it, but just jiggled the lock. So I got up to go see, and there was no one there. And it took all of a second to get up to the door from the couch, so there was no way anyone could have left that room.

"That lunchroom was notorious for always being cold," he added. "They always joke about it—'Oh, it's just the ghost of HK.' Or, if things go wrong, a light goes out unexpectedly for no reason. Ted's dad loved the station; it was his lifeblood. They always say entities always reside in the places that they were most happy or where they had the fondest memories."

Theresa Pauli-Ojeda, a videographer and ten-year employee of the station, also encountered the strange footsteps after ending a workout in the room early one morning.

"I had just finished my stretches and was starting to change, and I heard footsteps coming," recalled Ojeda, of Edwardsville. "I hurried and ran over to the door, put my shirt back on and opened the door, and there was nobody out there."

She chuckled. "I peeked out underneath the door, too, before I opened it, because I was already on the floor. And I didn't see anybody there, either."

Ojeda also checked with the assignment manager and other employees who had just come in the building. No one had been on the third floor.

Last spring the station moved to new digs out in Westport, and the station's old building was converted back into condos and apartments, Clark noted.

McPike: Creeps at No Additional Charge

Clark and Ojeda often work together on assignments and have been out to Alton's creepy McPike Mansion twice. The first time, while standing in the home's old wine cellar during the filming of a Halloween story in 1999, Clark felt an intense chill run up his back, as though something very cold had grabbed his spine. Investigators from the group Para-Vision were along and filmed the incident, in which an orb-like bubble appeared above Clark's head and followed him out the doorway.

"Then we got a call from Fox Family Channel in January 2001," Clark recalled, "and they said, 'We've talked to the ghostbuster guys...Would you be willing to go back in for this show we have?' I said, 'Sure, why not?'"

After they arrived, dozens of crows cawing outside competed with Clark and Ojeda during their interviews. Once inside, Ojeda busied herself shooting footage, when she heard footsteps and noticed a dark shadow move across the floorboards upstairs.

"I was looking in my viewfinder and shooting up, because you can see through the floorboards in that place—the ceilings are torn out," Ojeda said. "I heard something up there. And I said to Patrick, 'Now, who just walked by upstairs?' And he said, 'We're all right here.' I was a little creeped out, you know?"

Down in the wine cellar, there were no incidents this time, and Clark and the crew prepared to leave.

"About that time, we hear what sounded like somebody picked somebody up and just tossed them down the steps," he said. "It sounded like somebody just took a header off the first step and fell all the way down the steps to the basement. You could hear it on tape."

All nine crew members were safely in the basement, and there was nothing to explain the noise. The Fox Family crew posed one last question to Clark on the way out: "Well, is there something in the house?"

"I don't know," Clark answered. "I think so. Sometimes you can let your imagination get the best of you."

Just as he was saying that, Clark recalled, they heard a big POW! sound.

"Across the street, a transformer—I swear to God, I'm not making any of this up," he said. "A transformer on a power line blows just as I'm doing the interview, and power is knocked off to the entire block.

"That was enough for me. I've not been back since, and I won't go back in."

Big Chills at Big A's

Kelly Graettinger doesn't believe in ghosts. But she does believe men enjoy playing practical jokes.

So Graettinger, who has tended bar for five years at Big A's on the Riverfront, 308 North Main Street, in St. Charles, blamed the kitchen manager when she felt someone's heavy breath down the back of her neck.

"It was about nine-thirty in the morning," she recalled. "I was in the kitchen doing some work. The kitchen manager was back by the sink, and I felt this massive cold air on my back. I turned around, and I thought it was him blowing on my neck. I'm like, 'What did you do that for?'

"And he looked at me and said, 'I did not do anything.' He said, 'I was wondering why you had such a look on your face.'"

The two were the only ones in the building, which had yet to open for business.

"We were so creeped out he wouldn't even go downstairs by himself," Graettinger said. "I kept saying, 'Don't screw with me, because it was too much a blast of air'—I thought he had done it."

It wasn't the first time strange things happened at the bar, she noted.

"I've been down here opening, when I've been by myself, where it felt like somebody has pushed my back, nudged right by me. And it's always in the kitchen or when I'm down here by myself, because I live upstairs. And nothing ever happens upstairs.

"About three years ago, one of the servers here, we were just sitting at the bar, and we had an ashtray between us," she added. "It was just sitting there, and it cracked right through the middle and flew off the bar."

Older customers, including an eighty-seven-year-old regular who stops by for draft beer, have said that the upstairs portion of the old building used to serve as a brothel, and downstairs was a hardware store and a furniture store. During its brothel days, barges used to dock right behind the building, on the river.

"I do not believe in any of this," she said. "I think if I had proof, and I would see it, I would. But it's just weird I've had these three things happen."

Mineral Springs Hotel: Lights Off, Please!

A dozen years ago, Godfrey, Illinois, resident Melanie Luchtefeld was having much success on the craft show circuit and decided to rent a space at the Mineral Springs Antique Mall, in Alton.

"She did tole painting, basketweaving, woodworking, dried flowers and plants, other crafts, and had started collecting, trading, and selling antiques," recalled her husband, Steve. "The space that we had rented was in the back portion of the mall that was still being remodeled to make room for more shops. It was a large rectangular room, with one large picture window and one door, both of which faced the hall."

Melanie decided to divide the business, "Simply Country," into booths and rent out spaces to other antique dealers or craftspersons, to help pay the rent. So she and Steve purchased cedar boards and latticework and began putting the booths together, often working long after the mall closed, until nine or ten o'clock at night.

"At this time, we knew nothing of the ghosts that were supposed to be there," Steve noted. "One of us would pick up our children after they got out of grade school, and they would stay at the mall with us."

One night after the mall had closed, Melanie took the children and drove off to pick up wood screws and other materials for the booth work, as well as fast food for dinner.

"The locks on the mall entrance doors required a key to lock and unlock them," Steve said. "She had to lock the door behind her when she left because she only had the one key. That meant that I was locked in the mall. While we would work there, we would leave the lights off in the front area of the mall and only have on the lights in the hallway that her shop was on and, of course, in the shop where we were working."

That night Steve was cutting wood with a jigsaw and using a power drill to screw the pieces together, when he noticed that the light in the hall was off.

"I really didn't need it on, but figured I would turn it back on for when Melanie and the kids came back," he said and smiled. "Besides, it was kind of creepy being in there alone."

Steve turned on the light, returned to the shop area, and began measuring and marking more wood to cut. Then he heard what sounded like someone running down the steps at the beginning of the hallway. The steps went upstairs to the floor that the owners of the mall had turned into their home.

"Then the light went out, and I heard the footsteps running back up the stairs," Steve said. "I went out and turned the hall lights back on. This happened several times before I decided to leave them off."

After Melanie arrived and the family sat down to eat, Steve told her what happened.

"She said that the owners were out of town, so it couldn't be them, but [she] had no explanation for who would have been turning the lights out," Steve said. "While we were discussing this, our son asked who the man was looking in the window. We both looked at him and asked what man. He said the man who was in the hall looking in the window. We opened the door and looked down the hall, but did not see anyone. We then walked down the hall and around the rest of the mall area, but never did see another person. Our son told us what the man looked like, but Melanie didn't recognize the description as anyone she knew from the mall. We tried going up to the owner's apartment, but no one was there."

The next day, Melanie was talking to a couple of the other shop owners at the mall and described the man who had been looking in the window. They replied that the Luchtefelds had experienced two of the ghosts of Mineral Springs Mall.

"Supposedly there was a woman killed in the hotel by her husband for cheating on him," Steve said. "She was heard or seen by people running up and down the stairs. The man was usually seen in the front area of the mall, but showed up back in our area that night. There was a third one, too, but we don't remember what that story was."

During the time she owned her shop, Melanie would come in each morning to find items moved around and put in strange places. Other shop owners reported similar occurrences.

Melanie and Steve now live in Decatur, Alabama.

"I don't think I ever will forget finding out after the fact that the place was haunted, and I had been locked inside it while one of the ghosts kept turning out the lights," Steve chuckled.

The Drowned Man—He Was Murdered

Antoinette Eason, a psychic and former antique dealer who hosts Antoinette's Haunted History Tours, also used to have a space at the Mineral Springs Hotel (see *Spirits of St. Louis: A Ghostly Guide To The Mound City's Unearthly Activities*). In the 1980s, Antoinette and daughter Alixandria picked up on several ghosts at the hotel through psychometry, or the theory that objects absorb the emotions of their owners and those around them indefinitely.

"Originally, what Alix and I picked up was this couple coming into the swimming pool area from a party in the ballroom to get away from the crowd, got into an argument, and she got so angry that she slipped off her high-heeled shoe, hit him in the temple, knocked him in the pool, knocked him out, and he drowned," Antoinette said.

"Well, now it has become part of the legend of the building, which was fine. When we rented the pool area and were able to spend a lot of time in there recently, Alix and I got more to the story. We were down there one evening, and we were doing this psychometry again, and it was like, 'Oh, my God!' They were fighting over another woman—we've got names, we've got everything. The upshot is, they went in there because they were arguing over another woman. She hit him in the head, he fell in the pool, and then he swam over to the ladder and started to pull himself up. And she hit him repeatedly with that shoe—she killed him. She murdered him.

"I took twenty-five people from my metaphysical group down there the first part of September without telling them any of this ahead of time," Antoinette added. "So many people picked up the same information—it was just phenomenal."

Reach Out and Scare Someone

It wasn't your typical haunted house, just a small, forty-year-old cottage on Winkler Drive, in unincorporated St. Louis County. And Cheryl McKenzie, who lived there for twenty-five years, had just returned to bed about five in the morning after her husband, Bill, left for work.

"Sometimes he forgot his keys," noted McKenzie, a hairstylist who now lives in Florissant. "I had only laid down a couple minutes, and I heard walking in the house, and I said, 'Bill, is that you?' I thought he came back and left his keys. I kept saying, 'Bill, is that you?' I heard walking and movement, but didn't see it."

"There's a window to the right of the bed, maybe just two, three feet—just enough to walk between the window and the bed—and I looked to the right of me, and in front of the window there was this form standing between me and the window. You could see the outline of a man. It was like a dark outline all around the outside, but you could see through it. I said, 'Bill,' and the right arm reached out to me, toward the bed, and I took my arm and flung it—you know, like you're going to go through something? I flung it around, and there was nothing there—I just went through."

She laughed. "And I screamed, and I threw the cover over my head. Very brave! When I took the cover back down, it was gone."

The figure was about six feet tall, with a distinct form but no details such as a face or hair, McKenzie recalled.

"It's like somebody drew an outline with a pencil, you know. You could see the whole outline in dark, but then you could see through it. But you could tell, when his right arm reached to me, you could see the hand and the arm coming toward me. And that's what freaked me out—I thought, 'My God, I'm going to die! He's come to get me!' That's the first thing I thought."

DeMenil Mansion: A Tussle in Time

Officials of the historic DeMenil Mansion, in south St. Louis, have long maintained there are no ghosts in the landmark that narrowly avoided demolition when I-55 was built several decades ago.

But Randy Bibb, of Belleville, insists he witnessed a long-ago argument on the DeMenil's porch during a recent visit to the Lemp Mansion next door.

"When I went to see the [presentation] with the psychic Antoinette [Eason] at the Lemp Mansion a couple years ago, and for years and years when I have gone by the DeMenil, I have felt the reenactment of a scene," he said. "There are two men standing on a porch, and they are arguing at the top of their lungs. I can sense that there is a coffin in the living room with an older woman, possibly their mother, laying in state. I have felt this for years. I have never actually been in the home; when I go past it, you can feel it."

Antoinette noticed it, too, that day, Bibb recalled.

"Antoinette said, 'There's a couple of guys there.' I said, 'What's going on?' She said, 'They're arguing about something, and I think someone's died.' And somebody else in that same group said they heard somebody else say the same thing about that scene being reenacted, so several people have picked that up. During that same conversation, somebody said that they picked up that one of those two men pulls out a gun, but I've never sensed that there was a pistol or gun of any kind involved."

Ghosts? Not really, Bibb said.

"I think what we're picking up is a psychic vibration from another time," he said. "I don't think it's a haunting. Like a little time warp, and you just kind of zap through this little black hole, and you experience that scene again."

30 [Someone to Watch Over Me]

Contrary to popular belief, your garden-variety ghosts don't always hang around this plane of existence just to scare us. Sometimes, it would seem, they are concerned about our well-being and want to make certain our lives are copacetic before they depart for that great candy store in the sky.

Crown Candy: Shades of Uncle Pete

Offering delectable ice cream concoctions, sandwiches, and homemade candy in an old-fashioned confectionery setting, the Crown Candy Kitchen is a Mound City institution. And behind that institution is an inspiring tale of diligence, dedication, and the American Dream.

Pete Jugaloff was born in Greece in 1885 and immigrated to America as a young man with his friend Harry Karandzieff. When Karandzieff opened Crown Candy, 1401 St. Louis Avenue, on the near North Side, in 1913, Jugaloff owned a portion of the property and worked in the business. He lived in an adjacent apartment until his death in 1984.

"He didn't own part of the business, but he worked with my father. He was just always here," Harry's grandson Andy Karandzieff recalled. "We would call him Uncle Pete because he'd been around forever, and he was like my grandfather's brother. I was his favorite."

Karandzieff and his brothers grew up in the shop, spending time there on weekends and in the summer. He began working at Crown Candy at age thirteen, and now lives in Uncle Pete's former apartment above the store.

"When I was, like, six, seven, eight years old, I used to get to come down here on the weekend," noted Karandzieff, co-owner of the family business. "Under the soda fountain there's about a two-, three-inch gap, and change used to fall underneath there. It was my job to clean it out, and I'd get to keep all the change. So I'd get down there with my yardstick and my flashlight, start scraping all the money out. I always thought, 'Man, there's a lot of money underneath,' because I would walk away with twenty, thirty, forty dollars in change. That's a lot of money back then for a little kid."

He laughed. "It turns out what was going on is, when my uncle knew I was coming down, he was taking rolls of quarters and busting them open and throwing handfuls of quarters underneath. He always used to take care of me—I was always his favorite. I didn't find that out until years later, too—nobody ever told me. It kind of came as a surprise."

A lifelong bachelor, Uncle Pete had only one blood relative, a niece, in St. Louis. He didn't drive and lived upstairs over the store until he was too old to climb the steps, then opted for a ground-floor apartment in back.

"He was a very frugal man. He was a carpenter; he built a lot of things. The booths, he cut these booths down, made them shorter, built these booths and the cabinets and the counters around here—there's a lot of him still in this business. He used to work in the basement, do carpentry work."

In his later years, Pete concentrated his time in the back room adjacent to the kitchen.

"He spent a lot of time in the room over here," Karandzieff said. "He had a rocking chair, and he used to sit in the rocking chair and watch a little black-and-white TV. His favorite show was *Sanford and Son*—he used to call it 'The Junkman.' He'd get up and make peanut brittle or taffy and do stuff in the kitchen. He didn't really do a whole lot of traveling, pretty much from this room to that room."

When Uncle Pete died, Crown Candy wasn't nearly as crowded as it is now. It also had a door, since replaced, between the kitchen and the front area that contained a large window.

"Usually in the winter, when it was slow, there might only be me and one waitress, and we could handle the whole thing because it wouldn't be that busy," Karandzieff recalled. "I was out here by myself. She was at the end of the counter. It was one of those things where you're looking back there, and you're not looking back there, and I'd see something go past the window in the shape of a person. And I'd think, 'Wait a minute, everybody's out here.'

"The more I thought about it, the shape of the person was my uncle, who was a little bit shorter and a stocky man. It was a pretty distinct silhouette of him. It didn't click at first, but the more I thought about it, he probably spent the last ten, fifteen years of his life in those two rooms. He'd just go out the back door to his apartment and be back here the next morning to do it again. That was kind of his domain."

The waitresses noticed, too.

"They'd say, 'Did you just walk by the door?'" Karandzieff said. "I'd say, 'No, I was back in the candy room.' They said, 'Well, we thought we saw somebody go by the door.' Sometimes I wouldn't say about the time I saw it because I didn't want to spook these girls, because then you have employees who won't go in the back room because they're afraid of the ghost back there. So I'd just dummy up.

"I'd say I'd probably seen it happen twice—always in the wintertime, never in the summertime—and I'd probably say maybe four of the girls who worked here probably had an experience."

Karandzieff never had any strange encounters in the basement, but the waitresses did.

"Some of the girls swore they'd either seen and/or heard stuff down there," he said. "Directly below us is his woodshop, where he used to do all his carpentry work. Sometimes the girls would be so scared they wouldn't go in the basement. I'd say, 'Why?' 'I thought I saw something.' 'What'd you see?' 'I don't know, but I thought I saw something.' There's nothing down there but cups and lids and storage stuff and junk, but that was his domain, too, now that I think about it."

The activity was at its peak for about three or four years after Uncle Pete's death. Since then, it's been relatively quiet, Karandzieff said. On the other hand, the popular eatery is much busier than it ever was, so a shadowy figure could slip by unnoticed.

Perhaps Uncle Pete is satisfied now that his beloved confectionery is in the good hands of his favorite nephew. Or it could be that he still stops by occasionally just for old times' sake, very inconspicuously.

One More Time in Walnut Park

Betty Crossno lives in Kirkwood with her husband of twenty-six years, Gary. She has three grown children and five grandchildren.

Growing up, she spent much of her time in the big, asbestos-shingled home of her grandparents on Genevieve, in the Walnut Park neighborhood of north St. Louis. Crossno and her extended family lived in a close-knit neighborhood with a bakery at the corner; a local elementary school, Walbridge, a block away; and corner stores all around.

The neighborhood was nice, but the house was very haunted, she said.

The building has since been demolished.

"We had things happen all the time—footsteps on the stairs, footsteps overhead, you could hear somebody closing a door that wasn't closed, just strange stuff," Crossno said. "I was scared there. Everybody that lived there experienced one thing or another.

"People used to laugh at us all the time," she added. "They would just think we were crazy. Most people do, you know? But it all happened, and it's all true."

Who Was the Man in the Archway?

After she married her first husband and her daughter, Rhonda, was young, Crossno rented part of the old Walnut Park house where her uncle still lived. Her mother paid for the rent, and her father divided the large kitchen in half and made a small bedroom for Rhonda, adjacent to her parents' bedroom.

"She had a rollaway bed," Crossno recalled. "In the daytime, I'd put the rollaway bed up, and at night fold it down. The room was so small, when [the bed] came down the head of the bed was halfway through that arch. I could reach through and touch her. And our bed was right there on that side, next to that arch.

"One night I'd put her to bed. My husband was already asleep. All of a sudden she says, 'Mom, Mom, Mom, Mommy?' I said, 'What's wrong?' 'There's a man standing in the doorway.' I said, 'Oh, Rhonda, there's nothing there. Go on back to sleep, Sweetie.'

"And to tell you the truth, I was scared to death anyway, because you heard footsteps upstairs when no one was there, and a couple of times I heard somebody throwing things down in the basement, but when you'd go down and look, there wouldn't be anything out of place or anybody down there.

"She said, 'Mommy, he's really there—there's a man in my doorway.' I said, 'I tell you what—I'll put my hand around the corner, and you grab my hand and I'll pull you—you come on and get in bed with Mom.' And all the while I'm trying to wake my husband up and couldn't do it. He wasn't that heavy of a sleeper. I don't know; it was like being in the Twilight Zone, you know? She came on through the bedroom, and when I had put my hand through to hers, it was just like ice. And this was in the summer. I grabbed her real tight and didn't say anything more because she was just three years old, and I didn't want to scare her. But when I pulled her through that doorway, it was like something walked across the room and blotted out the light from the bathroom—see, the people next door had a yard light that came in through that bathroom window—and it blotted out that light."

The next day, Rhonda told Crossno's mom that the man had one hand against the side of the arch and the other on his hip, and he had red hair. When her mom grabbed her hand through the archway, she said, she looked up and walked right through him.

Several years later, Crossno was married to her second husband and living in a house on Calvert, in Woodson Terrace. Her second husband, like the first, was a heavy drinker and abusive.

"He drank, and he would come home and want to start a fight, and it didn't matter what it was about—you said 'yes' the wrong way or whatever," Crossno said. "One night [my son] Michael was crying, and I lay down and got in bed with him in hopes, really, that when [my husband] came home he wouldn't bother me, he wouldn't come in."

Earlier, a slat had fallen out of the couple's bed, and Crossno had stashed it in the closet, behind all the clothes.

"He was drunk, and he went in to go to bed, and—this is his story, not mine," she said. "We had a bookcase bed, and the closet was next to the bookcase. And he fell across the bed, and the slat came out of the closet, from behind all the clothes, and came all the way around to the other side of the bed and smacked him on the head. Now, he says it fell out of the closet, so he got back up, opened the door, and put it back. And the door opened again, and it came out and smacked him again.

"If it would have fallen out of the closet, it would have hit the bookcase and fallen on the floor," Crossno added. "But it didn't. It hit him. Of course, to this day, he'll swear it's not true. But it did happen, because he came in there and woke me up, and he was scared to death, and he was crying."

In hindsight, Crossno wonders if the man in the archway—her late grandfather, perhaps, or an uncle—had followed her to the Calvert home to protect her.

"Maybe I'm completely wrong, but what if it was the same man who was there on Genevieve, watching me?" she asked. "I always thought...because my grandfather was a big man, maybe it was him, and he just followed us.

"The first experience I ever had that was just mine, totally, I was in the back bathroom at our [Walnut Park] house, sitting on the toilet, and I must have been seven or eight years old, and a man said to me, 'Hey, Little Bit, what are you doing?' It startled me so bad, and I jumped off and went running in the kitchen and said, 'Mom, there's a man in the bathroom, and he's talking to me, and I can't see him.' I told her what he said, and she said, 'Oh, don't worry about it. That's just your grandfather. That's what he called you when you were little.'"

Nellie Keeps in Touch

After Crossno's mother, Nellie, died in 1967, she made her presence known to several people.

"My dad was an alcoholic, and he wasn't the nicest person on earth," she said. "And there were six of us. I had a brother, Larry, who had polio, but don't feel sorry for him, because he did everything that anybody else wanted to do. He was one of the gang. I imagine it bothered him inside, but he never showed it outside. He joked all the time.

"One night my dad and Larry had gotten into an argument, and my mom came and sat on the edge of my dad's bed and just stared at him. And he kept asking her to talk to him, but she didn't do it. She just stared at him."

Crossno's mother also appeared to her daughter's mother-in-law.

"My little sister, Barbara, hadn't been married too long, and she and her husband were going to move farther down in the city," Crossno recalled. "My mother was worried about that. Lorraine, who was [Barbara's] husband's mother, didn't believe in any of this [ghost] stuff, and when my mother would tell her what she'd seen, she would laugh at her, make a joke out of it.

"After my mother died, everybody had gone by the coffin, and I was the last to go by, and when my mother worked around the house, she had one curl that kind of fell down here on her forehead, so I just kind of pulled the curl back. A few weeks after she died, Lorraine was in her bedroom getting ready for bed, and she turned around, and my mother was standing at the end of the bed. She said, 'Lorraine, I just came to tell you to please take care of Barbara for me.'

"Lorraine said she was just dressed in a housedress and had her glasses on," Crossno said. "She didn't have her glasses when she was buried, but they disappeared several days after from a kitchen cabinet where my dad had put them. Never did find them. And she said it was the strangest thing—she had one curl going right down the middle of her forehead. And that's how I knew she really had seen her."

Another time, a learning-disabled uncle also claimed to see Nellie.

"Uncle Henry came over to the house, and he was real excited, and he said, 'Nellie came to see me, and she put her arm around me and told me I'd be with her soon.' And my dad said, 'Oh, he's just a retard—doesn't know what he's talking about.'

"Uncle Henry was dead three months later."

Grandma Elizabeth's Redemption

Years ago, Crossno's paternal grandmother, Elizabeth, had done something that bothered her so deeply that she worried whether she would ever get to heaven after her death. She read her Bible cover to cover and discussed her worries extensively with Nellie and Betty, becoming increasingly fretful as she aged. Finally, in 1970, she suffered a heart attack and died soon after.

"I went over there, and she was laying on the couch, and she said, 'I'm having a heart attack, Betty Jean, and I'm really scared.' They had called an ambulance, and they were waiting for it to come. She said, 'I'm scared God's not going to forgive me.' See, every time I would go over there, we would go over this. I said, 'Grandma, God forgives everybody. Anything that you're sorry for, He forgives, He understands, He knows."

Sometime earlier they had discussed their deaths.

"We had always talked before, because of everybody seeing my mom and all this, back and forth: if there was some way that either one of us [could], if something happened to us, we would come back and let the other know that there really is something on the other side."

Crossno laughed. "I said, 'Grandma, if you come, just sit down at the table, and let's have a cup of coffee. Don't come in the middle of the night and scare me.'"

Two nights after Grandma Elizabeth died, Crossno was getting ready for bed and heard music playing.

"I said to my husband, 'You hear that?' He said, 'No, I don't hear anything.' And I said, 'You don't hear that music? The radio's on.'

"And I got up to go to my daughter's room to see if she's got the radio on, and there was nothing on. Came back to bed, laid down, and I heard it again. Then he fell asleep, and I was sitting up in bed."

What Crossno glimpsed next still sends chills up her spine.

"There was my grandmother, and there was this man," she said. "She said something to him, and he said something to her, and I couldn't understand what they were saying, and all of a sudden he just waved his hand, waving her through, and she kind of walked away, and there was all this music and all these people singing. And then it just faded away.

I've never heard music like it before. It was like a chorus in the background—violins, a harp. It sounds corny, but it was like that, only a large orchestra."

The man was elusive.

"I just saw his back," Crossno said. "He had gray hair. It was long, and, to tell you the truth, I didn't pay attention to what he had on because I was looking more at her. His back was to me, and she was standing there, facing him. She was real short, only 4'8", 4'9", and she was looking up at him. And he's looking down, talking to her, kind of waved her through, and everything just disappeared except the music. You could hear that for several seconds.

"I just always thought that was her way of letting me know, because she was so worried about that. That was really the strangest experience—it wasn't so much because I'd seen her, but it was *all that music*. People say, 'You were asleep.' No, I wasn't asleep. It really happened. I know to this day what I saw, and I know there's something beyond here. This is just a stopping-off point, or whatever. There is something beyond here. And ever since that happened, I've just looked at death differently. It makes a difference in the way you look at things. That was, I guess, the best experience I think I've ever had, that night.

"I haven't had anything happen, I would say, in the last twenty years."

BIBLIOGRAPHY

"Alton Could Be Destination for the Goldenrod," Mark Schlinkmann, *St. Louis Post-Dispatch*, July 4, 2002.

"Bed and Breakfast Offers Deadly Fun," Tracey Bruce, *St. Louis Post-Dispatch*, Dec. 20, 1999.

The Case of Patience Worth, A Critical Study of Certain Unusual Phenomena, by Walter Franklin Pierce, Ph.D. Boston Society for Psychic Research, Boston, MA, 1927.

Conjuring Up Philip: An Adventure in Psychokinesis, by Iris M. Owen with Margaret Sparrow. Harper & Row, New York, NY, 1976.

"The Curse of Kaskaskia," by Jean Kueker of the Randolph County Genealogical Society (www.iltrails.org/kaskaskia/sub6.htm).

"DeSoto's Arlington Bed and Breakfast Has Quite a History," Chris Carroll, *St. Louis Post-Dispatch*, Dec. 20, 1999.

Encyclopedia of Ghosts and Spirits by Rosemary Ellen Guiley. Facts on File, New York, NY, 1992.

The Federal Writers' Project Guide to 1930s Illinois. Pantheon Books, New York, NY, 1939.

Ferguson: A City Remembered. Ferguson Historical Society, Ferguson, MO, 1994.

Article on 518 South Restaurant, *Ford Times Magazine*, 1980.

"518 South State Street," James R. Scheffel, Jerseyville High School (undated).

The Front Row: Missouri's Grand Theatres by Mary Bagley. Gateway Publishing, St. Louis, 1984.

The Gendarme, St. Louis Police Officers Association, Feb. 1990.

Ghosts of the Mississippi River, Keokuk to St. Louis, by Bruce Carlson. Quixote Press, Fort Madison, IA, 1988.

"The Goldenrod," part of a thesis by Walter James McCormick for Central Missouri State College, August 1965.

"Goldenrod May Rise Again," Mikal J. Harris and John McGuire, *St. Louis Post-Dispatch*, Feb. 21, 2002.

"Halloween Revives Gooseville Legend," Charles Burgess, *St. Louis Post-Dispatch*, Oct. 22, 2001.

Haunted Alton: History & Hauntings of the Riverbend Region, by Troy Taylor. Whitechapel Productions Press, Alton, IL, 1999.

Haunted Highway: The Spirits of Route US 66 by Ellen Robson and Dianne Halicki. Golden West Publishers Inc., Phoenix, AZ, 1999.

Haunted Places Web site, hosted by The Shadowlands Ghosts & Hauntings, Obiwan's UFO-Free Paranormal Page and GhostHound.com (http://sjgr.org/haunted-places/missouri.htm).

Hauntings and Poltergeists: Multidisciplinary Perspectives, edited by James Houran and Rense Lange. McFarland & Co., Inc., Jefferson, NC, 2001.

Heritage of the Bevo Area, Book Three. Betty Tighe and the Bevo Area Historical Society, Inc., St. Louis, MO, 1989.

"Indian Princess is Family Scapegoat," Cecil J. Smith, *Salem Leader*, Salem, IN, Jan. 14, 1993.

Jersey County website and history, (http://www.jerseycounty.org/history.htm).

Lemp: The Haunting History by Stephen P. Walker. The Lemp Preservation Society, Inc., St. Louis, MO, 1998.

Light From Beyond, Poems of Patience Worth, selected and compiled by Herman Behr. Patience Worth Publishing Co., New York, NY, 1923.

"Looking Back at Webster U.," Tammy Kranz, *Webster University Journal*, Feb. 1-7, 2001.

Missouri ghosts Web site, http://missourighosts.net/.

Missouri Ghosts: Second Edition With Ten New Chapters by Joan Gilbert. MoGho Books, Hallsville, MO, 2001.

More Missouri Ghosts by Joan Gilbert. MoGho Books, Hallsville, MO, 2000.

Museum of Talking Boards Web site, (http://www.museumoftalkingboards.com/ouistit.html).

National Register of Historic Places Registration Form, Greene County Almshouse, Carrollton, IL, Apr. 5, 1991.

Old St. Louis Homes, 1866-1916: The Golden Age, by Elinor Martineau Coyle. Folkestone Press, St. Louis, MO, 1971.

Ouija: The Most Dangerous Game by Stoker Hunt. Harper & Row, New York, NY, 1985.

Patience Worth, A Psychic Mystery, by Casper S. Yost. Henry Holt and Co., New York, NY, 1916.

"The Political Graveyard" Web site, http://politicalgraveyard.com/geo/MO/SL.html.

"Piping Hot: Stan Kann Plays Fox's Mighty Wurlitzer," Sarah Bryan Miller, *St. Louis Post-Dispatch* , May 20, 2001.

"Remembering the Mississippi's Smallpox Island," Tim O'Neil, *St. Louis Post-Dispatch*, April 26, 2002.

"Restored Brewery Attracts High-Tech Tenants," Charlene Prost, *St. Louis Post-Dispatch*, August 2001.

"Riddle of the Orbs," Phillip Carr, *Fortean Times Magazine*, March 2001.

"Rumors of Ghosts and Tunnels Persist About Old Pevely House," Tim

Rowden, *St. Louis Post-Dispatch*, Dec. 6, 1999.

St. Albans: History and Folklore of a Missouri River Town, by Lucie Furstenberg Huger. Fairfield Publishing Co., Kirkwood, MO, 2001.

St. Louis: An Informal History of the City and Its People, 1764-1865, by Charles van Ravenswaay. Missouri Historical Society Press, St. Louis, MO, 1991.

"St. Louis Globe-Democrat Presents the Spirits of St. Louis Official Guide to Local Legendary Haunted Houses," *St. Louis Globe-Democrat*, undated.

St. Louis Guidebook, Edna Carroll (contributor). St. Louis Guidebook Publishing Corp., St. Louis, MO, 1964.

St. Louis Union Station and Its Railroads, by Norbury Wayman. The Evelyn E. Newman Group, St. Louis, MO, 1987.

Selected poems by Patience Worth, private collection of J. Richardson and Alexandra Usher, Webster Groves, MO.

Shephard Family document by Jeanne Shortal, Jersey County Historical Society (undated).

Singer in the Shadows: The Strange Story of Patience Worth, by Irving Litvag. Macmillan Co., New York, NY, 1972.

Spirits of St. Louis: A Ghostly Guide to the Mound City's Unearthly Activities, by Robbi Courtaway. Virginia Publishing Co., St. Louis, MO, 1999.

The Survival of the French in the Old District of Sainte Genevieve, by Ward Allison Dorrance. University of Missouri Press, no location given, 1935.

"That Ain't No Way to Kill a Werewolf: The Modernization of an Old Legend," by Joel Bartow, *Missouri Folklore Society Journal*, Volume XI-XII, 1989-1990.

These Little Ones: The History of the Missouri Baptist Children's Home, by Jo Colay Ray. Missouri Baptist Children's Home, Inc., no location given, 1986.

The Vanishing Hitchhiker: American Urban Legends and Their Meanings, by Jan Harold Brunvand. W.W. Norton & Co., New York, N.Y., 1981.

Webster Groves by Clarissa Start. City of Webster Groves, Webster Groves, MO, 1975.

"What Are Buildings Made Of? A One-Hour Walking Tour Of Downtown Architecture," Landmarks Association of St. Louis, Inc., St. Louis, MO, 1993.

Wilson Price Hunt House documentation, Normandy Area Historical Association, Normandy, MO, undated.

Witchcraft, Wickedness, And Other Wacky Happenings In Jefferson County History, compiled by Della Lang. Della Lang, 1985, St. Louis.

INDEX

Joseph Immethun, founder of G.H.O.S.T.S., explores a local cemetery (photo courtesy Joseph Immethun). Chapter 1.

Spirit photographer E. Rick Dixon II (Robbi Courtaway photo). Chapter 1.

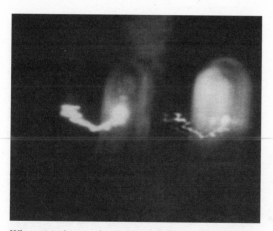

When spirit photographer E. Rick Dixon II developed this photo taken at the Godfrey, Illinois, City Cemetery in 1990, he found what he believes are white spirit energies. The gravestones are of Robert (left) and Nancy Smith, a retired sea captain and his wife, who died about 125 years ago. On the left, the wreath that adorns Robert's gravestone looks like a face in the photo, Dixon notes (photo courtesy E. Rick Dixon II). Chapter 2.

Parapsychologist James Houran at the entrance gate to Scotland's famed Edinburgh Castle during a recent study (photo courtesy James Houran). Chapter 1.

The Lemp Mansion (Robbi Courtaway photo). Chapter 4.

The Lemp Brewery (Robbi Courtaway photo). Chapter 4.

A two-minute time exposure taken at Lincoln-Shields netted Dixon an extra subject in his picture. Visible on the steps to the left of the two definitely live subjects is a misty figure Dixon believes is a Confederate soldier. The picture was taken with 400 speed film (photo courtesy Rick Dixon). Chapter 4.

The house in Otterville as it looked when Hotz and Schulte grew up there (Lori Pogue photo). Chapter 7.

An old photo of Debbie taken in the dining room of their haunted house in Otterville (Lori Pogue photo). Chapter 7.

Sisters Debbie Hotz, left, and Susie Schulte at Hotz's home in Jerseyville (Lori Pogue photo). Chapter 6.

S. Gene Prosser (Lori Pogue photo). Chapter 7.

A portrait of Miss Dorothy Hofsaes, whose spirit is believed to haunt the mansion (Lori Pogue photo). Chapter 7.

The 518 South at night (Lori Pogue photo). Chapter 7.

A portrait of Prentiss Dana Cheney (Lori Pogue photo). Chapter 7.

Miss Dorothy's old bedroom at the Cheney Mansion (Lori Pogue photo). Chapter 7.

Spirit photographer E. Rick Dixon II snapped this photograph at Alton City Cemetery in 1997. It is believed to be a family of four ghosts, with two other specters to the right. The four grouped ghosts are beleived to be Hilda, Julia, Emil and Artthur Floss. Emil and Julia, father and daughter, died within weeks of each other in 1900; son Arthur died at the age of one in 1895. Mother Hilda lived to 1938; now all are together, Dixon believes (photo courtesy E. Rick Dixon). Chapter 8.

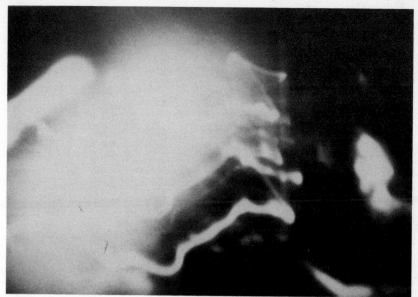

This infrared photograph was taken during parapsychologist James Houran's 1991 investigation of the Country House Restaurant in Clarendon Hills, IL. One of his investigative team members posed next to an area where specialized microphones detected brief but strong distortions out of the range of human hearing. When the photograph was developed, an intense burst of electromagnetic radiation was visible. Houran notes that a number of studies by Dr. Michael Persinger suggest that such effects result from natural and man-made sources of electromagnetism, which subsequently induce psychological and physical manifestations that seem "ghostly" (photo courtesy James Houran). Chapter 8.

The Dependahl farmhouse in Manchester, shortly after it was built in 1910 (photo courtesy Ken Aston). Chapter 8.

Louis and Louisa Dependahl, seated, with their children. From left, standing, are Lulu, Ervin, Arthur, Henry (Ken's grandfather), and Theresa Dependahl (photo courtesy Ken Aston). Chapter 8.

Ken Aston forgot to put on the flash when he took this routine shot of attic duct work (top). A second later, Ken realized his mistake and put on the flash, which resulted in the bottom photo (photo courtesy Ken Aston). Chapter 8.

The lobby of the recently renovated Chase-Park Plaza Hotel (Lori Pogue photo). Chapter 10.

Doug Harding (Robbi Courtaway photo). Chapter 11.

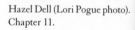

Hazel Dell (Lori Pogue photo). Chapter 11.

Famed organist Stan Kann demonstrates a diminutive version at his home in the Holly Hills neighborhood of south St. Louis (Robbi Courtaway photo). Chapter 12.

Gardenville Elementary School (Lori Pogue photo). Chapter 13.

The staff at Daruby Enterprises, from left, Lynda Anderson, Herb Crenshaw and Ruby Harriman (Robbi Courtaway photo). Chapter 13.

Writer Bob Schaper, shows a wooded area in Cool Valley where the ghost of a little girl is said to appear (Robbi Courtaway photo). Chapter 13.

Steve Powell (above), director of the Greater St. Charles Convention Center & Visitors Bureau, has caught a firsthand glimpse of Victoria (Robbi Courtaway photo). Chapter 15.

A page from the Menke family scrapbook hangs inside the Goldenrod Showboat. The presence of Capt. J.W. Menke also is believed to be on the boat (Robbi Courtaway photo). Chapter 15.

Radio personality, author and bon vivant Ron Elz, a.k.a. Johnny Rabbitt, pauses at one of his favorite stomping grounds: the Midtown area (Robbi Courtaway photo). Chapter 16.

The Federal Reserve Bank of St. Louis, 411 Locust St. (Robbi Courtaway photo). Chapter 17.

The main corridor of Edinburgh's underground South Bridge Vaults (photo courtesy James Houran). Chapter 18.

Vault 5 was one of 10 investigated by James Houran and Richard Wiseman in a recent study of paranormal activity (photo courtesy James Houran). Chapter 18.

Landmark House, located along Old State Road in Pevely (Robbi Courtaway photo). Chapter 19.

Chuck Banks, owner of Landmark House (Robbi Courtaway photo). Chapter 19.

The Greene County Almshouse, near Carrollton, Illinois (Lori Pogue photo). Chapter 21.

A view from inside the almshouse, showing an old silo in the rear of the property. Residents' duties here included growing crops and livestock for food (Lori Pogue photo). Chapter 21.

This burned-out house on Redwood Avenue in Cool Valley was supposedly so haunted, the final owner refused to go inside unless her husband was home. Chapter 22.

Alexandra and J. Richardson Usher in their Webster Groves home (Robbi Courtaway photo). Chapter 24.

A photograph of Pearl Curran taken from Walter Franklin Pierce's book *The Case of Patience Worth: A Critical Study of Certain Unusual Phenomena* (book courtesy of the Usher family). Chapter 24.

John Barr near his downtown home (Robbi Courtaway photo). Chapter 27.

Doug Harding, (above) a park ranger with the National Park Service, on the job at the Old Courthouse. Tour guide duties are among his responsibilities, so Harding often wears period attire to work (Robbi Courtaway photo). Chapter 28.

The Wyoming Street home (left) of Suzanne Schopflin and Danny Lundry (Lori Pogue photo. Chapter 28.

Andy Karandzieff takes a break from his usual hectic pace at Crown Candy Kitchen, 1401 St. Louis Ave. (Lori Pogue photo). Chapter 30.

The old Lindell Boulevard offices of KPLR-TV, WB 11, formerly the Chase Apartments (Lori Pogue photo). Chapter 29.

About the Author

A mildly eccentric community journalist for nearly two decades, Robbi Courtaway shares her home in Webster Groves with a menagerie that includes two potbellied pigs and two Scottish terriers. She enjoys reading books on St. Louis area history and is an ardent fan of garage sales, vintage horror movies, old cop shows, and swimming pools with twisty slides—not necessarily in that order. She may be reached at stlspirits@excite.com.